Planned Giving in a Nutshell

Fifth Edition

Craig C. Wruck

Craig C. Wruck

Craig Wruck's experience in charitable giving spans 40 years in both nonprofit and for-profit organizations. He currently serves as Vice President for University Advancement at Humboldt State University in California and has served as Director of Gift Planning for the University of Minnesota and Vice President of Development for The Saint Paul Community Foundation. In addition he has worked as Vice President at U.S. Trust Company, National Manager of Charitable and Nonprofit Services for U.S. Bank, and Director of Client Development for Kaspick & Company a provider of planned giving services to charitable organizations nationwide.

He is past president of the National Committee on Planned Giving (now the Partnership for Philanthropic Planning) and has served as chair of its Government Relations Committee and was chair of the Sixth National Conference on Planned Giving. A founding member of the Editorial Advisory Board of the newsletter Planned Giving Today, he has also served on the Editorial Review Committee of The Journal of Gift Planning.

Wruck earned his MBA from the University of St. Thomas and his bachelor's degree in journalism from the University of Utah.

Craig C. Wruck
craig@plannedgifts.com
http://plannedgifts.com

Table of Contents

3

Planned Giving in a Nutshell

Preface

POSTMODERN PLANNED GIVING

As I put the finishing touches on this edition of *Planned Giving in a Nutshell*, I've been thinking about the grove of redwood trees outside my window. As redwoods go, these are infants. They were mere seedlings when President Richard M. Nixon signed the 1969 Tax Reform Act which launched the modern world of planned giving. Even though these trees stand well over 100 feet tall today, they are not much more than knee high to their elders who can live for a thousand years and grow as tall as a 35 story building.

These past few years have been tumultuous for planned giving. There have been tectonic shifts. Today's prospective donors are likely to have an in-depth understanding of their options before you or I get our first chance to talk to them. We used to call ourselves planned giving officers but now we prefer "gift planners" or "philanthropic advisors." More and more charitable organizations are merging their stand-alone planned giving programs—as well as their planned giving officers—into their major gift efforts. And the drip-drip-drip of tax legislation continues to undermine the advantages and even some of the fundamental reasons for charitable gift planning.

It seems to me that planned giving has entered a new age, the postmodern age of planned giving. Like other historical epochs, it is difficult to pinpoint a precise starting point for this new era in planned giving and many aspects of the previous ages overlap and continue today even as the change progresses. Nevertheless, planned giving today is practiced in new and distinctly different ways than it was just a few years ago.

CLASSIC PLANNED GIVING

The first epoch of planned giving was classic era. Classic planned giving started a long time ago and, in some organizations, continues even today. The key activity in classic planned giving was the cultivation of individual prospects. Prospects were usually elderly individuals. And there was not much emphasis on qualification or ranking prospects. Classic planned giving was highly inclusive and had a "come one, come all" appeal.

In classic planned giving the primary objective was to encourage individuals to include our organization in their estate plans, usually via a simple charitable bequest provision. Once donors informed us of their decisions, we recognized and stewarded their commitment and interest. We continued to cultivate them for the rest of their lives until, one day, they died and we found out how successful we had been.

Complex gifts such as split interest trusts occasionally arose in classic planned giving, but usually only if the prospect expressed interest first. The primary emphasis was on understanding and fulfilling the charitable interests of the donor, on what the donor wanted to achieve with his or her charitable gifts. Classic planned giving was a highly personal approach, one which was carried out politely and in a low-key way.

MODERN PLANNED GIVING

The second era of planned giving was the modern age of planned giving. Although the modern age nominally began with the Tax Reform Act of 1969 which authorized the creation of charitable remainder trusts, it did not start in earnest until later in the 1970s. It took a few years to complete the Treasury Regulations governing the new planned gift vehicles. And then it took a few years more for charitable organizations to recognize the potential of modern planned giving.

Modern planned giving brought a major shift in emphasis toward the technical aspects of charitable giving. Unlike classic planned giving, the focus was broadened to include donors' financial and economic interests as well as their charitable impulses.

Modern planned giving also brought an influx of "professional advisors"—sometimes much to the chagrin of classic planned giving officers who worried about the onslaught of the barbarians invading the quiet and formal party that had been classic planned giving. However, professional advisors were quick to recognize the potential of planned giving and the value of adding this service for their clients.

Planned giving officers began to embrace collaboration with their donors' advisors … though many still complained about the emissaries from "dark side" and their impure influence on charitable giving. Modern planned giving led to the creation of the National Committee on Planned Giving in 1988, which was formed, in large part, to provide a common ground where non-profit and for-profit gift planners could meet and share interests.

Fueled by the broad acceptance of donor advised funds and other vehicles that allow a separation between the tax effect of a charitable gift and the final selection of the ultimate charitable recipient, modern planned giving also led to a loss of emphasis on the charitable purpose. In some cases the charitable beneficiary of the planned gift became fungible and the gift vehicle, the "deal," became paramount.

POSTMODERN PLANNED GIVING

Many planned giving programs today are still trying to work within the modern planned giving paradigm, but fewer and fewer charitable organizations find value in employing a planned giving specialist. Meanwhile, for-profit planners have realized that, while gift planning is an honorable and a valuable client service, just encouraging their clients to give away assets is not a lucrative practice.

Finally, there has been an enormous growth of popular interest in planned giving and a parallel explosion in the availability of detailed information about planned giving. A Google search for the unique term "planned giving" will yield well over a million hits. Your potential donors can select from among a couple of hundred thousand on-line planned gift calculators to explore the mysteries of life income gifts before they ever get in touch with you.

More than anything else, it is this quick and easy access to information—some of it good information and some of it not—that has led us to the third age of planned giving, the postmodern age of planned giving. And, like other postmodernist movements, the postmodern world of planned giving seems to be odd combination of the classical and modern planned giving eras.

In addition, the financial services sector has incorporated extensive charitable gift planning into their client services, especially for clients who qualify for the "wealth services" segments (generally a family net worth of $10 million or more). In the postmodern planned giving world, charitable gift planning is often seamlessly integrated into the entire financial planning process.

One unfortunate consequence is a tendency for the charitable organization to be excluded from the gift planning discussion. Clients believe that their financial service provider is more likely to take a team approach and to cover all aspects of the client's plan. Clients see their financial service provider as more technically proficient than most non-profit planned giving officers. As a result the charitable organization is "at the table" less and less often.

In this postmodern planned giving world, as clients see less need for input from charities and come to rely on their financial service provider to carry out their charitable wishes, the professional advisor carries an increasing obligation to urge clients to contact the charitable organizations in which they are interested—or, if necessary, to work with directly with the organizations on behalf of their clients—in order to ensure that the client's charitable wishes are fulfilled.

Finally, the postmodern world of planned giving is changing the nature of the conversations we have with our donors and clients. The ready availability of detailed information about planned giving makes it much more difficult for the development officer to control the order in which facts are revealed to prospective donors. This is important because a persuasive presentation rests, in large measure, upon managing how and when details are provided to the prospective donor. For example, it would be discouraging to open a discussion of charitable gift annuities with a full explanation of the complexities of capital gains taxation that can arise when funding a joint annuity with solely owned appreciated property. Of course this key information must be fully explained to the prospective donor before the gift is made, but it is much more persuasive to first discuss the advantages of a charitable gift annuity.

Paradoxically, in this postmodern world of planned giving charities benefit less from emphasizing the techniques of planned giving—those topics are being covered quite well by the financial services sector—and instead by redoubling an emphasis on persuasively explaining to prospective donors how their charitable objectives can meld with their financial circumstances. *Planned Giving in a Nutshell* is dedicated to providing you with a pathway to confidently engage your donors in those exciting conversations.

Over time the redwood trees outside my window will endure forest fires and wind storms, droughts and floods, insect infestations and all manner of challenges. But the California redwood is extraordinarily adaptable and versatile and through it all the best will continue to grow and one day become the giants of the forest. Metaphors are fragile things, but at the risk of stretching this one to the breaking point, I think my donors' planned gifts are like that.

Craig C. Wruck
Arcata, California
July, 2016

Planned Giving in a Nutshell

Introduction

"Planned Giving" "Gift Planning" "Deferred Giving" They all mean the same thing, right? No, not really. While "gift planning" has become the favored terminology, replacing "planned giving" and the antiquated "deferred gifts," this change is more than mere style. The practice of gift planning is a significant expansion of planned giving or deferred gifts. Planned giving is often thought of as a distinct fundraising strategy and deferred gifts usually refers to a set of specific types of charitable gifts. Gift planning, on the other hand, is a process that helps the donor and the charitable organization jointly determine which techniques will provide the greatest charitable potential for both the donor and the organization. The purpose of gift planning is to simultaneously help donors achieve their philanthropic and financial goals while helping charitable organizations fulfill their charitable missions.

Throughout this text our emphasis will be on the broader methodology of gift planning. While we will cover specific types of deferred gifts and the strategies of planned giving, our primary focus will be on how these can be used to unlock charitable potential for donors and the charitable organizations they choose to support.

KNOWLEDGE OF THE SUBJECT

A development officer—a generalist fundraiser in her organization—was asked by a generous donor to explain how a charitable gift annuity might work. The development officer was stumped. Until then her primary concern had been to secure outright gifts, and she was good at it. She had never bothered with planned gifts. And she was a bit embarrassed to admit that she didn't know enough about the charitable gift annuity to answer the question. A week later, following some quick study, the development officer sent the donor a letter that she hoped would help. However, neither the letter nor subsequent visits could ever revive the donor's interest in a charitable gift annuity.

Perhaps you have had that experience: a prospective donor loses confidence when you seem unprepared. If you lack at least a conversational knowledge about the tools of charitable gift planning not only do you close the door to gift opportunities, but you can cause donors to lose confidence in you as a fundraiser. A requirement of our profession is that we know our subject. This includes not only a deep familiarity with the mission of our organization—the reasons to give—but also a working knowledge of the many different ways in which a charitable contribution can be made.

This is not to suggest that you need to become expert on all the details and fine points of charitable gift planning. You do not. However, you ought to have a good working knowledge of the fundamentals of gift planning. You should be able to explain the tax treatment of contributions, such as the amount deductible, 50% and 30% limitations, carry forward provisions, and the taxation of income. You should know what you are talking about when you discuss holding period, cost basis, capital gain, bargain sales, and property valuation. You should know the differences among gift annuities, annuity trusts, and the varieties of unitrusts.

In short, you should have enough knowledge about charitable gift planning so that you can confidently converse with your donors and their advisors to help them plan their charitable contributions. *Planned Giving in a Nutshell* is dedicated to providing development officers with a working understanding of the basic concepts involved in charitable gift planning. The emphasis is on "plain English" explanations with examples and illustrations to help equip you to carry on a conversation about charitable gift planning with a prospective donor.

How to Use this Book

Planned Giving in a Nutshell began as a compendium of materials that had been developed for a variety of planned giving seminars in response to requests for a collection of reference materials that would be useful after the seminar presentation was over. The book is divided into six chapters and an appendix providing reference material:

Tax Fundamentals – We begin here because a grasp of the basics of income and estate taxes as they apply to charitable giving is fundamental to being able to understand the charitable giving vehicles and how they can benefit the donor. The emphasis is on the donor's "after tax cost of a gift" and the ways in which careful planning can encourage donors to make larger gifts than they may have thought possible.

Integrating Planned Giving into Fundraising – In this chapter we discuss several strategies for fundraising from individuals and make the case that planned giving should be viewed as one step in a continuum of life-long giving and that charitable gift planning can play an integrated role in each effort to negotiate contributions with individual donors.

Assets Used for Charitable Giving – Far too often we focus only on the amount of cash a donor can afford to contribute. That's too bad, because cash is often the smallest part of a donor's financial wealth. This chapter introduces some of the many assets other than cash that donors can contribute, and provides an overview of the rules and considerations for each.

Basic Planned Giving Methods – This simplest, and by far the most numerous planned gifts are charitable bequests. In this chapter we review testamentary gifts (those made at the end of the donor's lifetime), as well as life insurance and gifts from qualified retirement plans.

Advanced Planned Giving Methods – In this chapter we explore the possibilities afforded via life income gifts which allow the donor to retain an income as a result of a charitable contribution as well as a number of more sophisticated planned gift vehicles.

Organizational Considerations – Sophisticated planned gifts can involve financial relationships and fiduciary obligations that last one or more lifetimes. In the final chapter we highlight some of the issues a prudent organization ought to consider when launching a planned giving program.

Although there is a logical order to the chapters, each can stand on its own. You can either work through the book in order or consult chapters as your interest or needs dictate.

In addition, an extensive appendix includes several sample documents, detailed illustrations of some of the more complex planned gift vehicles, a selection of IRS publications, and a resource list.

Finally, American tax laws are ever changing. Income tax brackets change annually, tax rates are likely to change from time to time, and major revisions to tax law seem inevitable every few years. *Planned Giving in a Nutshell* is focused on the concepts of gift planning, which remain relatively consistent over time. Of necessity, the examples and illustrations this book were created using tax rates and brackets in effect when the text was written. However, in order to ensure that this book remains useful to you for as long as possible, where applicable worksheets, templates, or formulae are provided so that you can calculate your own illustrations even as tax rates and brackets change over time.

INSTITUTIONAL COMMITMENT AND SUPPORT

In addition to staff knowledgeable in the fundamentals of charitable gift planning the charitable organization ought to make a serious commitment if the gift planning program is to be successful. Institutional support should include:

- Formal action by the governing board authorizing the program, together with written policies and procedural guidelines.

- An adequate budget which includes educational opportunities for the staff, resource materials, access to professional help, and a marketing program.

- Administrative support to handle investments, record keeping, make payments to income beneficiaries, prepare tax returns, manage property and ultimately ensure that gift proceeds are used for appropriate charitable purposes.

Throughout this book we will discuss essential elements of a successful planned giving program, but the bottom line is this: charitable gift planning is a team effort, and all members of the team must work together with mutual trust and respect. The development staff is responsible for marketing and securing charitable gifts, and, in most organizations, the business office is responsible for administering the gifts once they are secured. The strength of the "team" is much greater than these parts alone.

ACRONYMS AND ABBREVIATIONS ENCOUNTERED IN GIFT PLANNING

Like other technical fields, charitable gift planning has developed its own extensive set of shorthand acronyms and abbreviations commonly used to refer to various terms. Here are a few of the more common acronyms and abbreviations you may encounter:

ACGA	-	American Council on Gift Annuities
AFR	-	Applicable Federal Rate
AMT	-	Alternative Minimum Tax
CGA	-	Charitable Gift Annuity
CLAT	-	Charitable Lead Annuity Trust
CLT	-	Charitable Lead Trust
CLUT	-	Charitable Lead Unitrust
CMFR	-	Charitable Mid-Term Federal Rate
CRAT	-	Charitable Remainder Annuity Trust
CRT	-	Charitable Remainder Trust
CRUT	-	Charitable Remainder Unitrust
FMV	-	Fair Market Value
IRC	-	Internal Revenue Code
IRS	-	Internal Revenue Service
LTCG	-	Long-Term Capital Gain
NICRUT	-	Net Income Charitable Remainder Unitrust
NIMCRUT	-	Net Income with Makeup Charitable Remainder Unitrust
PIF	-	Pooled Life Income Fund
PLR	-	Private Letter Ruling
SCRUT	-	Standard Charitable Remainder Unitrust
STCG	-	Short Term Capital Gain
UBI	-	Unrelated Business Income
UBIT	-	Unrelated Business Income Tax
UBTI	-	Unrelated Business Taxable Income

A Brief Gift Planning Glossary

Annuity	A contract or legal obligation to pay specified amounts over a specified period of time to specified individual(s) in exchange for cash, securities, or other tangible property.
Beneficiary	One named in a Will, trust or other legal document to receive an interest in an estate. One named in a trust to receive either income or the remainder of the trust. The income recipient or "annuitant" of a charitable gift annuity. The one who receives the death benefit paid by a life insurance policy.
Bequest	A direction in a Will to distribute property or money, a "legacy."
Estate Tax	A tax on the transfer at death of property or money.
Charitable Gift Annuity	A contract to pay a fixed dollar amount annually to one or two beneficiaries for life issued by a charitable organization in exchange for a contribution.
Charitable Lead Trust	An irrevocable trust that pays income to charity for a number of years and then distributes its remainder to one or more individuals.
Charitable Remainder Trust	An irrevocable trust that pays income to one or more individuals either for life or for a number of years and then distributes its remainder to one or more charitable organizations.
Gift Tax	A tax on the transfer made during lifetime of property or money.
Grantor	The creator of a trust.
Gross Estate	Everything in which the deceased person owned or had an interest in at the time of death.
Inter vivos	Latin for "among the living." An inter vivos trust is one created during lifetime while a testamentary trust is created through a Will.
Irrevocable Trust	A trust that cannot be changed or dissolved.

Legacy	A direction in a Will to distribute property or money, a "bequest."
Life Estate	A gift of property in which the donor retains the right to use the property for life.
Life Income Gift	A charitable gift plan allowing a donor to make a contribution and, as a result, receive an income for one or more individuals.
Personal Property	• Tangible: physical objects such as jewelry, artwork, antiques, automobiles, and clothing. • Intangible: items the value of which is not tied to their physical form such as royalties or patents.
Probate	The legal process of proving the validity of a Will, used loosely to mean the administration of an estate.
Real Property	Land and the buildings, fixtures, and other items that are attached to it in a relatively permanent manner.
Remainder	The amount remaining in a trust after income payments have ended.
Remainderman	The beneficiary who receives the remainder of a trust.
Revocable Trust	A trust that can be changed or dissolved by the grantor or others.
Testamentary Trust	A trust established through the Will of a grantor.
Trust	An arrangement whereby property is held and managed for the benefit of others.
Trustee	Party legally responsible for carrying out the terms of a trust.
Will	A legal instrument disposing of a person's property at the time of his or her death.

MODEL STANDARDS OF PRACTICE FOR THE CHARITABLE GIFT PLANNER

Gift planning often involves collaboration among a number of different professional advisors. More than 20 years ago the National Committee on Planned Giving (now the Partnership for Philanthropic Planning) developed a set of guidelines setting forth ethical practices for charitable gift planners whether they are nonprofit fundraisers or for-profit advisors. These "Model Standards of Practice for the Charitable Gift Planner" are the best practices for all who are involved in helping donors and clients plan charitable contributions.

MODEL STANDARDS OF PRACTICE FOR THE CHARITABLE GIFT PLANNER

PREAMBLE

The purpose of this statement is to encourage responsible gift planning by urging the adoption of the following Standards of Practice by all individuals who work in the charitable gift planning process, gift planning officers, fund raising consultants, attorneys, accountants, financial planners, life insurance agents and other financial services professionals (collectively referred to hereafter as "Gift Planners"), and by the institutions that these persons represent.

This statement recognizes that the solicitation, planning and administration of a charitable gift is a complex process involving philanthropic, personal, financial, and tax considerations, and as such often involves professionals from various disciplines whose goals should include working together to structure a gift that achieves a fair and proper balance between the interests of the donor and the purposes of the charitable institution.

I. PRIMACY OF PHILANTHROPIC MOTIVATION

The principal basis for making a charitable gift should be a desire on the part of the donor to support the work of charitable institutions.

II. EXPLANATION OF TAX IMPLICATIONS

Congress has provided tax incentives for charitable giving, and the emphasis in this statement on philanthropic motivation in no way minimizes the necessity and appropriateness of a full and accurate explanation by the Gift Planner of those incentives and their implications.

III. FULL DISCLOSURE

It is essential to the gift planning process that the role and relationships of all parties involved, including how and by whom each is compensated, be fully disclosed to the donor. A Gift Planner shall not act or purport to act as a representative of any charity without the express knowledge and approval of the charity, and shall not, while employed by the charity, act or purport to act as a representative of the donor, without the express

---

15

consent of both the charity and the donor.

IV. COMPENSATION

Compensation paid to Gift Planners shall be reasonable and proportionate to the services provided. Payment of finder's fees, commissions or other fees by a donee organization to an independent Gift Planner as a condition for the delivery of a gift are never appropriate. Such payments lead to abusive practices and may violate certain state and federal regulations. Likewise, commission-based compensation for Gift Planners who are employed by a charitable institution is never appropriate.

V. COMPETENCE AND PROFESSIONALISM

The Gift Planner should strive to achieve and maintain a high degree of competence in his or her chosen area, and shall advise donors only in areas in which he or she is professionally qualified. It is a hallmark of professionalism for Gift Planners that they realize when they have reached the limits of their knowledge and expertise, and as a result, should include other professionals in the process. Such relationships should be characterized by courtesy, tact and mutual respect.

VI. CONSULTATION WITH INDEPENDENT ADVISORS

A Gift Planner acting on behalf of a charity shall in all cases strongly encourage the donor to discuss the proposed gift with competent independent legal and tax advisors of the donor's choice.

VII. CONSULTATION WITH CHARITIES

Although Gift Planners frequently and properly counsel donors concerning specific charitable gifts without the prior knowledge or approval of the donee organization, the Gift Planners, in order to insure that the gift will accomplish the donor's objectives, should encourage the donor, early in the gift planning process, to discuss the proposed gift with the charity to whom the gift is to be made. In cases where the donor desires anonymity, the Gift Planners shall endeavor, on behalf of the undisclosed donor, to obtain the charity's input in the gift planning process.

VIII. DESCRIPTION AND REPRESENTATION OF GIFT

The Gift Planner shall make every effort to assure that the donor receives a full description and an accurate representation of all aspects of any proposed charitable gift plan. The consequences for the charity, the donor and, where applicable, the donor's family, should be apparent, and the assumptions underlying any financial illustrations should be realistic.

IX. FULL COMPLIANCE

A Gift Planner shall fully comply with and shall encourage other parties in the gift planning process to fully comply with both the letter and spirit of all applicable federal and state laws and regulations.

X. PUBLIC TRUST

Gift Planners shall, in all dealings with donors, institutions and other professionals, act with fairness, honesty, integrity and openness. Except for compensation received for services, the terms of which have been disclosed to the donor, they shall have no vested interest that could result in personal gain.

Planned Giving in a Nutshell

Tax Fundamentals

For many of us, the U.S. Federal Tax Code seems like the most complex set of laws and regulations ever written. What is more, Congress is forever adjusting, changing, and tinkering with the tax laws. Fortunately, in order to be successful a charitable gift planner need be conversant with only a few key concepts in the Federal tax law. It's true that many gift planners pursue a much broader knowledge and deeper understanding of tax law—and that can be a definite advantage. However, a confident understanding of the basic concepts is sufficient for most gift planners.

The point is this: a gift planner need not become an expert in all of the subtleties and nuances of tax law. The job of the non-profit gift planner in particular is to suggest creative solutions to prospective donors. Donors should always consult their own advisors in order to ensure that a contemplated gift will produce the results they anticipate. In any case, gift planners, particularly those employed by charitable organizations, should never exceed the limits of their expertise and knowledge.

We begin with the following tax fundamentals because a grasp of the basics of income and estate taxes applied to charitable giving is essential to understanding the charitable giving vehicles and how they can benefit the donor. Throughout, our emphasis is on the donor's "after-tax cost of a gift" and the ways in which careful planning can encourage donors to make larger gifts than they thought possible.

THE FEDERAL TAX SYSTEM

There are two Federal tax systems that are of particular interest in charitable gift planning:

- Income tax system – including income taxes and capital gains taxes
- Transfer tax system – including estate taxes and gift taxes

Tax incentives to encourage charitable giving are included in both the income and transfer tax systems. However, the impact of these incentives on an individual donor varies depending upon the donor's personal circumstances. While the income tax system itself generally applies to all taxpayers, the greatest income tax incentives for charitable giving are

19

available only to the approximately one-quarter of taxpayers who itemize their deductions. On the other hand, the transfer tax affects only a very small percentage of all taxpayers—estimates are that the Federal Estate Tax[1] applies to fewer than 1% of estates—but in many cases the value of estate tax incentives is greater than the value of income tax savings.

A key concept for charitable gift planners is the "after tax cost of the gift." The after tax cost of a gift is, simply, the out-of-pocket cost of the gift minus the amount by which the contribution reduces the donor's tax bill:

$$\text{Amount Contributed}$$
$$\text{minus} \quad \underline{\text{Amount of Tax Reduction}}$$
$$\text{equals} \quad \text{After Tax Cost of Gift}$$

These tax savings are real. Even though the donor may not receive the savings until the following April 15 when he or she files a tax return, the tax reduction reduces the donor's cost of making a charitable contribution. And, since most tax rates are progressive—that is the rate rises as the taxable amount increases—the amount of tax savings can be relatively greater for donors in higher tax brackets. This means that the after tax cost of making a gift can be lower for higher bracket taxpayers.

---

[1] Under the American Taxpayer Relief Act of 2012, the Federal Estate Tax applies to estates with a taxable value of $5.45 million or more for those dying in 2016. This threshold is adjusted for inflation each year. According to the Urban-Brookings Tax Policy Center, fewer than 1% of all estates are subject to the Federal Estate Tax.

THE FEDERAL INCOME TAX

ORDINARY INCOME TAX

The Federal income tax generally applies to all "income" from whatever source. However, not all income is taxed because a number of exclusions and deductions reduce the amount of income that is ultimately taxable. Most taxpayers file some variant of the Form 1040 (which is reproduced for your reference at the end of this chapter). "Taxable income" is calculated as follows:

Gross Income	everything earned or received as income during the year
minus adjustments	certain items (e.g., casualty losses, alimony payments, IRA contributions) are subtracted from gross income
Adjusted Gross Income	"AGI" is a key figure that determines the maximum amount of charitable deduction that can be taken in any one year
minus personal exemptions	a flat amount is subtracted for the taxpayer and each dependent claimed on the return (the exemption amount is $4,050 in 2016 and is adjusted for inflation each year)[2]
minus deductions	certain items—including charitable contributions—are deducted from income, however, deductions are itemized deductions only if they exceed the "standard deduction" amount ($6,300 for single filers and $12,600 for joint filers in 2016, adjusted each year for inflation)[3]
Taxable Income	the amount subject to Federal Income tax

Key Point →   **The charitable deduction reduces taxable income, and therefore reduces the amount of income tax due.**

Federal Income Tax rates are "progressive" so that a higher percentage rate applies to larger amounts of taxable income. They are also "graduated" so that everyone pays the

---

[2] The value of the personal exemption is phased out for high income taxpayers. In 2016 individuals with adjusted gross income over $259,400 (or married couples filing jointly with adjusted gross income over $311,300) must reduce the amount of their personal exemptions by 2% for each $2,500 (or portion of $2,500) that their adjusted gross income exceeds the threshold. As a result, in 2016 the personal exemption phases out completely at $381,900 in adjusted gross income for individuals (and $433,800 for married couples filing jointly). These thresholds are adjusted for inflation each year.

[3] The value of the itemized deduction is reduced for high income taxpayers. In 2016 individuals with adjusted gross income over $259,400 (or married couples filing jointly with adjusted gross income over $311,300) must reduce the total of their itemized deductions by 3% of the amount that their adjusted gross income exceeds the threshold, however the reduction cannot be more than 80% of the total itemized deductions (i.e., even the wealthiest taxpayers will retain at least 20% of their itemized deductions). These thresholds are adjusted for inflation each year.

21

lowest rate on the first dollar of taxable income and only those who have larger amounts of taxable income are subject to the higher rates. The tax "brackets" (dollar ranges at which each rate is effective) are adjusted each year. Below are the income tax rates for 2016:

Tax Rate	Single	Married Filing Jointly	Head of Household
10%	$0 – $9,275	$0 – $18,550	$0 – $13,250
15%	$9,276 – $37,650	$18,551 – $75,300	$13,251 – $50,400
25%	$37,651– $91,150	$75,301 – $151,900	$50,401 – $130,150
28%	$91,151 – $190,150	$151,901 – $231,450	$130,151 – $210,800
33%	$190,151 – $413,350	$231,451 – $413,350	$210,801 - $413,350
35%	$413,351 – $415,050	$413,351 -- $466,950	$413,351 -- $441,000
39.6%	$415,050 and over	$466,951 over	$441,001 and over

Note:	Different tax rate tables are used depending upon the filing status of the taxpayer (e.g., single, joint, etc.).

One of the implications of the graduated tax rate system is that the "marginal tax rate"—the top tax rate which is applied to the last dollar of taxable income—is usually much higher than the "effective tax rate"—the overall tax rate paid. For example, a taxpayer filing jointly in 2016 with a taxable income of $175,000 will pay a total tax of $35,989, as follows:

	Taxable Income	Tax Rate	Tax Due
	the first $18,550	10%	$1,855
	the next $56,720	15%	$8,508
	the next $76,600	25%	$19,150
	the last $23,130	28%	$6,476
TOTALS	$175,000		$35,989

A total tax of $35,989 on a taxable income of $175,000 is an "effective rate" of 20% even though the "marginal rate" paid on the last taxable dollar earned is 28%.

CAPITAL GAINS TAX

For our purposes, "capital gain income" is the "profit" when an investment is sold for more than it cost. It is "long term capital gain income" if the investment was owned for more than twelve months before being sold and is "short term capital gain income" if held for a year or less. Short term capital gain income is taxed at ordinary income tax rates. However, long term capital gain is taxed at lower rates: a maximum rate of 15% for most taxpayers and 20% for those in the top income tax bracket[4]. For example, if a taxpayer in

---

[4] There is a 0% long term capital gains rate for taxpayers whose taxable income is less than the top of the 15% marginal tax bracket ($75,300 for joint filers in 2016 and $37,650 for singles – the brackets are adjusted for inflation each year). The 20% long-term capital gains rate applies to taxpayers in the 39.6% income tax bracket: a taxable income over $466,950 if married and filing jointly, over $415,050 if single in 2016. While the general long term capital gains tax concepts outlined here apply to most gift planning circumstances, as always you should encourage prospective donors to consult a qualified tax advisor for advice on their specific circumstances and to review the latest revisions to tax law.

the 28% bracket sells for $10,000 an investment that cost $2,000 some years ago, he or she will owe a tax of $1,200—15% of the $8,000 long term capital gain.

NET INVESTMENT INCOME TAX (THE "MEDICARE SURTAX")

Since 2013 taxpayers with Modified Adjusted Gross Income above a certain threshold pay a 3.8% surtax called the Net Investment Income Tax, commonly called the "Medicare surtax." This tax is imposed on top of the taxpayer's regular income tax.

The Net Investment Income Tax is applied to the lesser of net investment income or the amount by which Modified Adjusted Gross Income exceeds the threshold. Modified Adjusted Gross Income is the total household Adjusted Gross Income plus any tax-exempt interest income.

The Net Investment Income Tax threshold depends upon filing status. For those married filing jointly it is $250,000 and for singles or heads of households it is $200,000. The threshold amounts are not indexed for inflation, so they will remain the same each year unless Congress modifies them with new legislation.

Note that the Net Investment Income Tax can increase a taxpayer's marginal tax bracket. For example, a married couple filing jointly with $100,000 in wage income and $200,000 of long-term capital gain will be in the 25% income tax bracket with capital gains taxed at a rate of 15%. However, since their Modified Adjusted Gross Income is $300,000, they would be subject to the Net Investment Income Tax on $50,000 ($300,000 Modified Adjusted Gross Income minus $250,000 Net Investment Income Tax threshold equals $50,000), which effectively increases their capital gains tax rate from 15% to 18.8%. This makes charitable gifts of appreciated property all the more attractive (see "After Tax Cost of Gift of Appreciated Property, below).

AFTER TAX COST OF A GIFT

A charitable contribution is deductible from taxable income, therefore reducing the amount of income tax due. This tax savings effectively reduces the cost of making a contribution.

Example: After Tax Cost of a Gift of Cash
Assume a donor who is in the 28% marginal tax bracket contributes $10,000 in cash:

$10,000	:	Cash contributed
-2,800	:	income taxes saved
$7,200	:	after tax cost of the contribution

Key Point → **The charitable deduction reduces taxable income at the margin (the last dollar of income) and therefore produces tax savings at the taxpayer's highest marginal tax rate.**

The example reflects Federal income tax savings only. The after tax cost of the gift may be even less when the donor's income taxes and the potential Medicare surtax saving are considered.

> A worksheet to calculate the after tax cost of a gift is in Appendix A on page A-1.

AMOUNT OF THE DEDUCTION: FAIR MARKET VALUE

In general, a donor is entitled to a charitable deduction for the "fair market value" of the contribution. The fair market value is defined as the price that would be reached between a willing buyer and a willing seller, both having equivalent knowledge of the facts and neither being under any compulsion to complete the transaction.

Determining the fair market value is straightforward for most contributions:

- **cash** – total of the cash contributed

- **publicly traded securities** – the mean (average) between the high and low prices for the securities on the date of the contribution

However, the rules become more complicated for harder to value items such as property, collections, and personal items. In general, the donor must make a reasonable estimate of the fair market value and must obtain a "qualified appraisal" if the deduction is $5,000 or more.

Notes: Valuation of "non-cash" contributions has been the subject of scrutiny by the Internal Revenue Service and Congress over the years. The rules have been changing and deductions for non-cash contributions are being examined more carefully. IRS Publication 526, *Charitable Contributions*, and Publication 561, *Determining the Value of Donated Property*, provide useful guides. Both are reproduced in the Appendix on pages A-39 and A-61.

Substantiating the value of a charitable deduction is a matter between the donor/taxpayer and the Internal Revenue Service. Although charities should, of course, be helpful to their donors, it is best to leave the specific valuation of non-cash contributions to the donor.

Donors should be fully informed that the amount of their charitable deduction may be significantly different than the amount eventually received by the charity. For example, while the deduction for a contribution of appreciated securities will be based upon the average between the high and low prices on the date of the gift, the amount received by the charity will depend upon the actual sales price (minus commissions and other costs of sale).

More detailed information about gift valuation can be found in IRS Publication 561, Determining the Value of Donated Property, included in Appendix H, page A-61.

AFTER TAX COST OF GIFT OF APPRECIATED PROPERTY

A donor may contribute long term capital gain property to charity, receive an income tax deduction for the full fair market value of the property, and pay no capital gains tax which would have been due if the property had been sold.

Example: After Tax Cost of a Gift of Appreciated Securities

Assume a donor who is in the 28% marginal tax bracket contributes securities now worth $10,000 that cost $2,000 more than a year ago:

$10,000	:	value of securities contributed
-2,800	:	income taxes saved
-1,200	:	capital gains tax avoided
$6,000	:	after tax cost of the contribution

Key Point →   **A donor can receive a charitable deduction and avoid capital gains taxes by contributing long term capital gain property to charity.**

Notes: In order to avoid the capital gains tax on a contribution of appreciated property, it is extremely important that the donor contribute the appreciated property itself, not the proceeds from the sale of the appreciated property. In short, if the sale of the property is arranged before the contribution, then the donor may be deemed to have sold the property and contributed the proceeds from the sale, in which case the donor would be liable for capital gains tax on the sale.

          Securities are the most common contribution of appreciated property. In the case of a contribution of securities, it is critical that the donor's stockbroker understand that they are to transfer the securities themselves to the charity, and that they should not sell the securities except at the direction of the charity after it has become the owner.

In other cases, for example real estate, it is critically important that there be no pre-arranged agreement to sell or buy the property prior to the contribution to charity.

> A worksheet to calculate the after tax cost of a gift is provided in Appendix A, page A-1.

DEDUCTION LIMITATIONS

Although charitable contributions are 100% deductible, the maximum amount a donor can claim in any one year is limited to 50% of Adjusted Gross Income (AGI) for contributions of cash and 30% for contributions of appreciated property.[5] However, charitable deductions that exceed the limit in one year may be carried forward for up to five additional years.

For example, assume a generous donor has Adjusted Gross Income of $160,000 and makes cash contributions totaling $100,000 during the year. Her or his charitable deduction for the year would be limited to $80,000 (50% of Adjusted Gross Income) leaving $20,000 in unused deduction which the donor can use to reduce taxable income in the following year. (Note that taxpayers are required to use as much of their charitable deductions as they can each year. They cannot save or time the use of their charitable deductions.)

There are special rules that apply when a donor has contributed both cash and appreciated property. In addition, a donor may elect to have 30% contributions (gifts of appreciated property) treated as 50%

> The charitable deduction rules are detailed in IRS Publication 526, Charitable Contributions, included in Appendix G, page A-39.

contributions, however the deduction will be limited to the cost basis of the appreciated property and the election will apply to all appreciated property contributions. Although, under certain circumstances, this may be advantageous, this is a complex matter and the donor should be urged to consult his or her tax advisor.

QUID PRO QUO REDUCTION

The amount of the deduction must be reduced by the value of goods or services the charity makes available to the donor as a result of the contribution. This arises most often when the charity offers a premium or other reward in exchange for the contribution or in cases of benefit-type events. A key point is that the deduction is reduced by the *value* of the goods or services, not the cost of these items to the charity. In addition, note that it is the

---

[5] The 50%/30% AGI limits generally apply to contributions to "public charities." Contribution to other charities (e.g., private foundations), while still deductible for income tax purposes, are subject to lower AGI limitations: 30% for contributions of cash and 20% for contributions of appreciated property.

availability of goods or services that reduces the deduction, whether or not the donor actually receives or takes advantage of them.

This information must be completely disclosed to the donor at the time of the contribution. Phrases such as "deductible to the extent allowed" should be avoided. If the solicitation indicates that a contribution is tax deductible, then it should also provide the details of how much will be deductible.

Finally, where nothing of value has been made available to the donor, the contribution receipt should include a statement that no goods or services were made available as a result of the contribution.

DATE OF GIFT

The charitable deduction becomes available on the date the gift is completed. The date of gift is a key concern for contributions made toward year end because in order to be claimed as a contribution deduction a gift must be completed by December 31 of the year in which the donor wishes to claim the deduction. The general rule is that the date of gift is the day on which the donor has irrevocably and unconditionally surrendered control of the gift. Determination of the date of gift is straightforward for most contributions:

Mode of Contribution	Date of Gift
by mail	postmark date (see note)
physical delivery	date delivered
credit card	date authorized by donor (see note)
electronic/telephone transfer	date completed by bank
stock/security certificates	date delivered in negotiable form
stock/security in brokerage account	date transferred to charity's account

> The rules applicable to other situations and circumstances can be found in IRS Publication 526, Charitable Contributions, included in Appendix G, page A-39.

Notes: Donors can create unanticipated complexity if they procrastinate at year end. For example, while a contribution dropped in the mailbox at the post office minutes before midnight on December 31 is no longer under control of the donor and ought to be considered complete, the proof of date will be the postmark which is likely to be January 2 of the next tax year. Similarly, credit card contributions are often processed in batches (either by the charitable organization or an intermediary) with the result that the transaction will appear on the donor's credit card statement at a later date than the donor intended. The best advice as year-end approaches? "Don't delay, give today."

As a general rule, the donor must surrender control over the gift in order for the contribution to be complete. While in most cases this is not an issue, gift planners should be careful to avoid inadvertently creating circumstances under which a gift is not complete because of commitments made to the donor. For example, if a contribution is made subject to a promise that unused funds will be returned to the donor, then the gift will not be completed until the funds are actually used by the charity.

SUBSTANTIATION REQUIREMENTS

As noted above, it is the donor's responsibility to substantiate the fact and amount of their charitable deduction. Nevertheless, charities usually make efforts to be of assistance to their donors. In general:

- Taxpayers must obtain a written acknowledgement from the charity for any deductible contribution of $250 or more, although the donor need not submit this acknowledgement with his or her tax return.

- If a donor claims more than $500 in deductions for non-cash contributions, he or she must complete Form 8283 (a copy is included in Appendix F, page A-25) which provides a description of the item(s) contributed and explains how the fair market value was determined. While the donor must have a reasonable basis for the claimed fair market value, an appraisal is not required (except for contributions of clothing and household goods valued at more than $500).

- If the deduction amount is more than $5,000 ($500 for contributions of clothing and household goods), then the donor must also secure a qualified appraisal to determine the fair market value. In addition, the charity must also sign the Form 8283. Note that by signing the Form 8283 the charity is *not* vouching for the value of the item(s), only acknowledging that it has received the contribution.

- Contributions of vehicles are subject to special rules. A donor who claims a deduction of more than $500 for a contribution of a qualified vehicle must attach to his or her tax return a copy of a written acknowledgement. The deduction is limited to the lesser of the fair market value of the vehicle or the gross proceeds from the sale of the vehicle unless the charity makes use of the vehicle for its charitable purposes.

Notes: If the charity signs a Form 8283, then it is required to file a Form 8282 if it sells or disposes of the contributed property within three years of the contribution. The Form 8282 requires the charity to report the amount that it received from the sale.

In general, the charity should avoid listing a dollar value on the receipt or acknowledgement for a non-cash gift. A statement describing the property in sufficient detail to identify it is usually enough.

> More detailed information can be found in the instructions to Form 8283 which are included in Appendix F, page A-27 along with samples of Form 8283 and Form 8282.

GIFTS OF PERSONAL PROPERTY

The term "tangible personal property" includes all of the "things" that a donor might wish to contribute, for example: equipment, tools, furniture, antiques, collections, or libraries. In general, a donor is entitled to an income tax deduction for a contribution of tangible personal property, but subject to certain rules regarding the use of the item:

"related use" items – If the item can be put to a use that is related to the tax-exempt purpose of the charitable organization, then the donor may take a deduction for the full fair market value of the item. For example, a contribution of specialized tools might be a related use contribution if given to a vocational school, but might not be if contributed to a hospice.

"unrelated use" items – If the use of the item is unrelated to the tax exempt purpose of the charitable organization, then the deduction is limited to the *lesser of* the donor's cost basis in the item or its current fair market value.

Note: There is an exception which applies to taxpayers who are "dealers" in certain items of personal property. Contributions of personal property made by a dealer may be a gift of ordinary income property (see below) which generally limits the charitable deduction to cost basis. Donors should be urged to consult their tax advisors regarding the rules that apply in these circumstances.

GIFTS OF ORDINARY INCOME PROPERTY

"Ordinary income property" is any item which, if the donor were to sell it, would result in taxable income. The determination of ordinary income property can be very specific to the individual. For example, a casual collector of dolls is different than one who is a dealer in the same items. For the dealer the dolls are ordinary income property, for the collector they are not.

The income tax deduction for a contribution of ordinary income property is its fair market value less any appreciation in value. Generally, this limits the charitable deduction to cost basis. These rules can be especially challenging for artists who wish to contribute their own works. In most cases an artist who contributes her or his own work will find that the charitable deduction is limited to the cost of materials.

***Example:* Contribution of ordinary income property**

Assume an artist contributes a painting he has created to an art museum and that the fair market value of the painting on the day he donated it is $1 million. Further assume that the donor spent $100 to produce the painting (the cost of paint, brushes, and canvas), and therefore the appreciation in value is $999,900.

The donor's deduction is limited to $100.

DEDUCTIBILITY OF SHORT-TERM CAPITAL GAIN PROPERTY

Similar to contributions of ordinary income property, the amount deductible for a gift of short-term capital gain property is its fair market value less the amount that would be taxable as short-term capital gain if the property had been sold, which will generally be the cost basis.

CONTRIBUTIONS OF CAPITAL LOSS PROPERTY

Of course investments do not always increase in value. Sometimes donors hold capital loss or "depreciated" property—investments that are now worth less than the donor paid for them. Contributions of capital loss property are usually unwise. The charitable deduction for a contribution of capital loss property will be for the current fair market value of the property, which is less than he or she paid for it.

Donors with depreciated or capital loss property should consult with their advisors about the advisability of selling capital loss property and using the loss to offset other capital gains. They will forfeit the possibility of using this loss offset if they give the capital loss property to charity instead.

ALTERNATIVE MINIMUM TAX

The alternative minimum tax, or "AMT," is designed to ensure that everyone pays at least some income tax. It was enacted out of a concern that some taxpayers might be able to accumulate large deductions and credits and avoid paying their fair share of income taxes. The AMT is a separate calculation that is similar to the regular income tax but that disallows certain deductions and exemptions (e.g., certain depreciation deductions, some mortgage interest expenses, excess long-term capital gains). Although the AMT rates are different than ordinary income tax rates, the taxable income under AMT is usually higher.

Taxpayers affected by the AMT must first calculate their ordinary income tax and then complete the AMT return. They then must pay the *higher* of the two.

The AMT was designed to apply primarily to high bracket taxpayers who were able to take advantage of certain tax breaks in order to reduce or eliminate income taxes. Over the years the AMT applied to more taxpayers because many of the thresholds in the AMT were not adjusted for inflation. From 2013 onward, the AMT thresholds have been adjusted for inflation each year.

TRANSFER TAXES, THE "ESTATE TAX"

A complete discussion of transfer taxes (estate, gift and generation-skipping taxes) is well beyond the scope of this text. For the past two decades Federal transfer taxes have been the subject of on-going debate. They were temporarily modified from time to time and, for one year, the Federal Estate Tax was eliminated entirely. In 2013 the American Taxpayer Relief Act brought more or less permanent rates and rules to the transfer tax system.

The Federal Estate Tax affects less than 1% of Americans. For these reasons, the following discussion is limited to providing a familiarity with the key points regarding transfer taxes and to highlight those areas where caution should be exercised when making statements to donors about these taxes.

The estate tax, gift tax, and generation skipping transfer tax are taxes on the transfer of money, property, or other items of value *from one individual to someone else.* Essentially, any transfer of value from one person to another is potentially subject to a Federal transfer tax. However, most people are not affected by these taxes because of generous exclusions and exemptions that effectively eliminate these taxes under most ordinary circumstances:

Annual exclusion – $14,000 per year ($28,000 for a married couple) can be given to an individual without a gift tax. In addition, payments of medical expenses on behalf of an individual are excluded from the gift tax. The $14,000 annual exclusion amount is adjusted periodically (but not necessarily annually) for inflation.

Lifetime exclusion – In addition to the annual exclusion amount, an individual can transfer a cumulative total of $5.25 million either as gifts during lifetime or at death without either gift or estate taxes. The $5.25 million exclusion amount is for 2013 and is adjusted for inflation each year.

Spousal exclusion – An unlimited amount can be contributed to a spouse without a gift tax.

Charitable deduction – There is an unlimited deduction for charitable contributions.

UNIFIED GIFT AND ESTATE TAX RATE

Beginning in 2013 all taxable transfers are taxed at 40%. The flat 40% rate replaces the old "Unified Gift and Estate Tax Rate Schedule" which was a progressive rate system beginning at 18% and ranging as high as 55%.

GIFT AND ESTATE TAX SUMMARY

Up to $14,000 per year -	Can be given to each of an unlimited number of individuals (a married couple can give $28,000 per individual)
More than $14,000 per year -	File a Federal Gift Tax Return and pay 40% tax when cumulative lifetime gifts exceed $5,450,000*
Up to $5,450,000* in total lifetime and estate giving -	No Federal Gift or Estate Tax
More than $5,450,000* -	Total value of combined taxable lifetime and estate giving in excess of this amount is taxed at 40%
* Note that the $5,450,000 exclusion is the threshold for 2016 and is adjusted for inflation each year. The $14,000 annual exclusion is the threshold for 2016 and is adjusted from time to time (but not necessarily annually).	

STEPPED-UP BASIS VERSUS CARRY-OVER BASIS

There is an important difference in the way capital gains are treated under the gift tax and the estate tax. When a taxpayer sells appreciated property that was received as a gift from a living individual, he or she will pay capital gains tax based upon the appreciation in value from the donor's cost basis. However, if a taxpayer sells appreciated property that was received from an estate, capital gains tax will be due only on the appreciation since the date of death.

For example, if, during their lifetimes, parents give their children appreciated property, then the children will be liable for capital gains tax on all of the appreciation that occurred during the parents' ownership as well as after the date of the gift. If the parents instead leave that same property to their children in their Will, then the children will be liable only for the appreciation occurring since the date of death.

GENERATION-SKIPPING TRANSFER (GST) TAX

The Generation-Skipping Transfer Tax is designed to prevent wealthy individuals from avoiding one or more levels of taxation by leaving substantial amounts of money or property to grandchildren instead of children, thus skipping the tax that would have been due if they had left it to their children who then left it to the younger generation. In general, the GST taxes generation skipping transfers as though the transfer had first gone to the intervening generation. For example, if a grandparent transfers to a grandchild, the Generation Skipping Transfer Tax would essentially double the tax as though the transfer had been made from grandparent to parent to grandchild.

SPLIT-INTEREST CHARITABLE GIFTS

Certain charitable gift plans allow the donor or others to retain a financial interest while making an irrevocable charitable gift. For example, charitable gift annuities allow the donor or others to receive payments for life and charitable remainder trusts allow the donor or others to retain income. Another type of gift, the retained life estate, allows the donor to continue to live in a residence after it has been irrevocably contributed to charity.

Such gifts are called "split interest gifts" because the donor has, essentially, split the ownership interests in the item and contributed the right to hold and own it from the right to either collect payments or, in the case of a retained life estate, live in it. The donor is entitled to a charitable deduction for a split interest gift, but the amount of the deduction is only for the value of the portion contributed, not for the entire value of the item contributed.

The value of the deduction is calculated using formulae, life expectancies, and interest assumptions set forth in U.S. Treasury Regulations. In general, the calculations take into account the amount of time before the charity will receive full ownership of the gift (usually one or more life expectancies) and the amount of the payment (or income) retained and then apply a discount to arrive at the value of the gift to charity.

As a rule of thumb for life income gifts:
- the older the beneficiary (and the smaller the number of beneficiaries) the larger the deduction will be since the charity is likely to receive full use of the gift sooner

- similarly, the younger the beneficiary (and the greater the number of beneficiaries) the smaller the deduction since the charity is likely to have to wait longer

- the larger the amount of the beneficiary payout the smaller the deduction because the value retained by the donor is larger

- and the smaller the payout the larger the deduction because the value retained by the donor is smaller

CHARITABLE MID-TERM FEDERAL RATE

One of the key variables in the calculation of the deduction for a split interest gift is the interest (or discount) rate used to arrive at the present value. Regulations call this the "Charitable Midterm Federal Rate" (or "CMFR"), which is defined as 120% of the "Applicable Federal Mid-term Rate" (or "AFR") for the month in which the gift is made, *or for one of the two months prior to the date of the gift.*

The CMFR changes each month. The IRS announces the new rate each month on or about the 20th of the previous month. Typically, the rate is published the next business day in the Wall Street Journal and other financial journals.

The CMFR has an impact on the amount of the charitable deduction. Since the regulations allow any one of three different rates (*the month of the gift or either of the previous two months*) to be used, donors should be careful to select the rate which produces the most advantageous result for their circumstances. In fact, with a little careful planning a donor can actually choose from among four rates by waiting until the next month's CMFR is announced before deciding in which month to make the gift. Usually a donor will choose the rate that yields the largest deduction. Gift annuity donors, however, should consider the impact of the CMFR on the tax-free portion of their annuity payment.

The following general rules can help a donor select the best CMFR:

- the highest of the three allowable CMFRs will produce the best deduction for:

  - charitable gift annuities, but also the lowest tax-free portion of the annuity payment

  - charitable remainder trusts

- the lowest of the three allowable CMFRs will produce the best deduction for:

  - charitable lead trusts

  - retained life estate agreements

- a change in the CMFR will have a much greater impact on the charitable deduction for annuity type arrangements and retained life estate agreements than it will on unitrust arrangements

CALCULATING THE DEDUCTION

The amount of the charitable deduction for a split interest gift can be calculated manually using table and forms available from the IRS. However, most organizations rely on specialized software to perform these calculations. In addition, there are many Web sites that offer free calculation services.

SUBSTANTIATING THE DEDUCTION

The donor is required to include the following information with the tax return on which a charitable deduction is claimed for a split interest gift:

- A description of the contribution, including a copy of the instrument (e.g., trust agreement, gift annuity contract) of transfer

- The valuation date of the transfer

- The names, birthdates, and Social Security numbers of the beneficiaries

- A summary of the calculation of the deduction amount showing the CMFR used to value the transferred interest and, if applicable, an explanation that a rate from a previous month has been elected

Form 1040
Department of the Treasury—Internal Revenue Service (99)
U.S. Individual Income Tax Return 2015 OMB No. 1545-0074 IRS Use Only—Do not write or staple in this space.

For the year Jan. 1–Dec. 31, 2015, or other tax year beginning _____, 2015, ending _____, 20 ___ | See separate instructions.

Your first name and initial	Last name	Your social security number

If a joint return, spouse's first name and initial	Last name	Spouse's social security number

Home address (number and street). If you have a P.O. box, see instructions. | Apt. no.

▲ Make sure the SSN(s) above and on line 6c are correct.

City, town or post office, state, and ZIP code. If you have a foreign address, also complete spaces below (see instructions).

Presidential Election Campaign
Check here if you, or your spouse if filing jointly, want $3 to go to this fund. Checking a box below will not change your tax or refund. ☐ You ☐ Spouse

Foreign country name | Foreign province/state/county | Foreign postal code

Filing Status

Check only one box.

1 ☐ Single
2 ☐ Married filing jointly (even if only one had income)
3 ☐ Married filing separately. Enter spouse's SSN above and full name here. ▶
4 ☐ Head of household (with qualifying person). (See instructions.) If the qualifying person is a child but not your dependent, enter this child's name here. ▶
5 ☐ Qualifying widow(er) with dependent child

Exemptions

6a ☐ Yourself. If someone can claim you as a dependent, do not check box 6a . . . . .
b ☐ Spouse . . . .

c Dependents:		(2) Dependent's social security number	(3) Dependent's relationship to you	(4) ✓ if child under age 17 qualifying for child tax credit (see instructions)
(1) First name	Last name			

If more than four dependents, see instructions and check here ▶ ☐

d Total number of exemptions claimed . . . .

Boxes checked on 6a and 6b ____
No. of children on 6c who:
• lived with you ____
• did not live with you due to divorce or separation (see instructions) ____
Dependents on 6c not entered above ____
Add numbers on lines above ▶ ____

Income

Attach Form(s) W-2 here. Also attach Forms W-2G and 1099-R if tax was withheld.

If you did not get a W-2, see instructions.

7 Wages, salaries, tips, etc. Attach Form(s) W-2 . . . . | 7
8a Taxable interest. Attach Schedule B if required . . . . | 8a
b Tax-exempt interest. Do not include on line 8a . . . | 8b |
9a Ordinary dividends. Attach Schedule B if required . . . . | 9a
b Qualified dividends . . . . | 9b |
10 Taxable refunds, credits, or offsets of state and local income taxes . . . . | 10
11 Alimony received . . . . | 11
12 Business income or (loss). Attach Schedule C or C-EZ . . . . | 12
13 Capital gain or (loss). Attach Schedule D if required. If not required, check here ▶ ☐ | 13
14 Other gains or (losses). Attach Form 4797 . . . . | 14
15a IRA distributions . | 15a | b Taxable amount . . . . | 15b
16a Pensions and annuities | 16a | b Taxable amount . . . | 16b
17 Rental real estate, royalties, partnerships, S corporations, trusts, etc. Attach Schedule E | 17
18 Farm income or (loss). Attach Schedule F . . . . | 18
19 Unemployment compensation . . . . | 19
20a Social security benefits | 20a | b Taxable amount . . . | 20b
21 Other income. List type and amount _____ | 21
22 Combine the amounts in the far right column for lines 7 through 21. This is your total income ▶ | 22

Adjusted Gross Income

23 Educator expenses . . . . | 23 |
24 Certain business expenses of reservists, performing artists, and fee-basis government officials. Attach Form 2106 or 2106-EZ | 24 |
25 Health savings account deduction. Attach Form 8889 . | 25 |
26 Moving expenses. Attach Form 3903 . . . . . | 26 |
27 Deductible part of self-employment tax. Attach Schedule SE . | 27 |
28 Self-employed SEP, SIMPLE, and qualified plans . . | 28 |
29 Self-employed health insurance deduction . . . . | 29 |
30 Penalty on early withdrawal of savings . . . . . | 30 |
31a Alimony paid b Recipient's SSN ▶ _____ | 31a |
32 IRA deduction . . . . | 32 |
33 Student loan interest deduction . . . . | 33 |
34 Tuition and fees. Attach Form 8917 . . . . . . | 34 |
35 Domestic production activities deduction. Attach Form 8903 | 35 |
36 Add lines 23 through 35 . . . . | 36
37 Subtract line 36 from line 22. This is your adjusted gross income . . . ▶ | 37

For Disclosure, Privacy Act, and Paperwork Reduction Act Notice, see separate instructions. Cat. No. 11320B Form **1040** (2015)

	38	Amount from line 37 (adjusted gross income)		38	
Tax and Credits	39a	Check if: ☐ **You were born before January 2, 1951,** ☐ Blind. ☐ **Spouse was born before January 2, 1951,** ☐ Blind. } Total boxes checked ▶ 39a			
	b	If your spouse itemizes on a separate return or you were a dual-status alien, check here ▶ 39b ☐			
Standard Deduction for— • People who check any box on line 39a or 39b or who can be claimed as a dependent, see instructions. • All others: Single or Married filing separately, $6,300 Married filing jointly or Qualifying widow(er), $12,600 Head of household, $9,250	40	Itemized deductions (from Schedule A) or your **standard deduction** (see left margin)		40	
	41	Subtract line 40 from line 38		41	
	42	Exemptions. If line 38 is $154,950 or less, multiply $4,000 by the number on line 6d. Otherwise, see instructions		42	
	43	Taxable income. Subtract line 42 from line 41. If line 42 is more than line 41, enter -0-		43	
	44	Tax (see instructions). Check if any from: a ☐ Form(s) 8814 b ☐ Form 4972 c ☐		44	
	45	Alternative minimum tax (see instructions). Attach Form 6251		45	
	46	Excess advance premium tax credit repayment. Attach Form 8962		46	
	47	Add lines 44, 45, and 46 ▶		47	
	48	Foreign tax credit. Attach Form 1116 if required	48		
	49	Credit for child and dependent care expenses. Attach Form 2441	49		
	50	Education credits from Form 8863, line 19	50		
	51	Retirement savings contributions credit. Attach Form 8880	51		
	52	Child tax credit. Attach Schedule 8812, if required	52		
	53	Residential energy credits. Attach Form 5695	53		
	54	Other credits from Form: a ☐ 3800 b ☐ 8801 c ☐	54		
	55	Add lines 48 through 54. These are your **total credits**		55	
	56	Subtract line 55 from line 47. If line 55 is more than line 47, enter -0- ▶		56	
Other Taxes	57	Self-employment tax. Attach Schedule SE		57	
	58	Unreported social security and Medicare tax from Form: a ☐ 4137 b ☐ 8919		58	
	59	Additional tax on IRAs, other qualified retirement plans, etc. Attach Form 5329 if required		59	
	60a	Household employment taxes from Schedule H		60a	
	b	First-time homebuyer credit repayment. Attach Form 5405 if required		60b	
	61	Health care: individual responsibility (see instructions) Full-year coverage ☐		61	
	62	Taxes from: a ☐ Form 8959 b ☐ Form 8960 c ☐ Instructions; enter code(s)		62	
	63	Add lines 56 through 62. This is your **total tax** ▶		63	
Payments If you have a qualifying child, attach Schedule EIC.	64	Federal income tax withheld from Forms W-2 and 1099	64		
	65	2015 estimated tax payments and amount applied from 2014 return	65		
	66a	**Earned income credit (EIC)**	66a		
	b	Nontaxable combat pay election 66b			
	67	Additional child tax credit. Attach Schedule 8812	67		
	68	American opportunity credit from Form 8863, line 8	68		
	69	Net premium tax credit. Attach Form 8962	69		
	70	Amount paid with request for extension to file	70		
	71	Excess social security and tier 1 RRTA tax withheld	71		
	72	Credit for federal tax on fuels. Attach Form 4136	72		
	73	Credits from Form: a ☐ 2439 b ☐ Reserved c ☐ 8885 d ☐	73		
	74	Add lines 64, 65, 66a, and 67 through 73. These are your **total payments** ▶		74	
Refund Direct deposit? See instructions.	75	If line 74 is more than line 63, subtract line 63 from line 74. This is the amount you **overpaid**		75	
	76a	Amount of line 75 you want **refunded to you.** If Form 8888 is attached, check here ▶ ☐		76a	
	b	Routing number ▶ c Type: ☐ Checking ☐ Savings			
	d	Account number			
	77	Amount of line 75 you want **applied to your 2016 estimated tax** ▶ 77			
Amount You Owe	78	**Amount you owe.** Subtract line 74 from line 63. For details on how to pay, see instructions ▶		78	
	79	Estimated tax penalty (see instructions) 79			

Third Party Designee
Do you want to allow another person to discuss this return with the IRS (see instructions)?   ☐ **Yes. Complete below.**   ☐ No

| Designee's name ▶ | Phone no. ▶ | Personal identification number (PIN) ▶ | | | | | |

Sign Here
Joint return? See instructions.
Keep a copy for your records.

Under penalties of perjury, I declare that I have examined this return and accompanying schedules and statements, and to the best of my knowledge and belief, they are true, correct, and complete. Declaration of preparer (other than taxpayer) is based on all information of which preparer has any knowledge.

Your signature	Date	Your occupation	Daytime phone number
Spouse's signature. If a joint return, **both** must sign.	Date	Spouse's occupation	If the IRS sent you an Identity Protection PIN, enter it here (see inst.)

Paid Preparer Use Only

Print/Type preparer's name	Preparer's signature	Date	Check ☐ if self-employed PTIN
Firm's name ▶			Firm's EIN ▶
Firm's address ▶			Phone no.

www.irs.gov/form1040　　　　　　　　　　　　　　　　　　　　　　Form **1040** (2015)

Integrating Planned Giving into Fundraising

All too often, "planned giving" is treated as a special domain within the realm of fundraising and a "planned gift" is thought of as one of a number of highly technical types of gifts—a charitable bequest, a gift annuity contract, a charitable trust—which provide benefit to the charity only in the distant future and are esoteric and somehow less valuable than "real" gifts.

That's too bad. It's much more efficient for the charitable organization when planned giving is viewed as an integrated part of the whole approach to fundraising ... and it is much better for donors when gift planning is a process offered to help them achieve their charitable goals.

THREE FUNDRAISING STRATEGIES

Successful development programs employ three distinct strategies for fundraising from individual donors:

- Annual Giving / Event Fundraising
  - Donors typically make contributions from their discretionary income
  - Contributed funds are used by the organization primarily for current operations
  - Contributions are solicited each year for immediate use
  - Contributions are typically of modest size
  - The objectives are higher rates of participation and increased contributions
- Major Giving / Capital Campaigns
  - Donors typically make contributions from their assets or in the form of payments pledged over a number of years
  - Contributed funds are used for capital need and special projects

- Gifts are solicited on an opportunistic basis or as a part of a focused campaign
- Contributions are typically of significant size
- Planned Giving
  - Donors typically make contributions from their estate wealth
  - Planned gifts are often used for endowment and/or designated purposes
  - Gifts are cultivated and solicited over time via education, on-going discussions, and sometimes protracted negotiations
  - Typically, among the largest contributions a donor makes

	Annual Gifts	**Major Gifts**	**Planned Gifts**
Uses of gift	Operating needs	Capital projects and special needs	Endowment and/or designated funds
Gift size	Modest	Significant	Largest
Timing	Annual	Opportunistic	Life-long
Prospects	Current constituents	Active and interested donors	Everyone
Fundraising Process	Annual solicitation	Opportunistic or focused campaign	On-going education and solicitation

BASIC PRINCIPLES OF EFFECTIVE FUNDRAISING

Whether it is an annual giving program, a major capital campaign, or a planned giving program, an effective development effort will include these basic principles:

- Develop a genuine and sound case, a compelling reason to contribute to the cause.
- Gain the unqualified commitment and the full participation of the board members and other volunteer leaders.
- Plan for an effective marketing program to convey the case to potential donors.
- Identify, prioritize, and cultivate prospective donors.
- Strategically build the involvement and commitment of the donor.
- Ask for contributions in specific amounts.

- Recognize donors and volunteers.

CHARACTERISTICS OF PROSPECTIVE DONORS

As difficult as it may be, consider the fact that not everyone is a prospective donor for your organization. The mere fact that an individual possesses wealth and is active in the community does not automatically make her or him a qualified prospect. There are three characteristics of a well qualified prospective donor: affinity, ability, and access.

Affinity – The prospective donor must have an interest in the work of your organization. The strength of this interest can be cultivated and may grow over time. Beginning with curiosity about the organization and its mission, we can turn mere awareness into interest and then into a passion for the mission of the organization.

Ability – The financial wherewithal to make a contribution is an essential element. There is no reason to seek a contribution that is truly beyond the prospect's financial means. However, the tools and techniques of charitable gift planning can increase a donor's ability to make a contribution that is larger than they may have initially thought possible.

Access – If the prospective donor will agree to meet on a favorable basis to have a conversation about his or her charitable contribution, then we have achieved access. To be clear, access is not simply the opportunity to meet with the prospect, it is the prospect's willingness to discuss his or her charitable contribution. Sometimes the development officer can gain direct access, but often a trusted friend or colleague will be a better point of access to the prospective donor.

THE DEVELOPMENT PROCESS

The process of cultivating and soliciting a charitable gift is remarkably similar whether the objective is an annual gift, major gift, or planned gift:

The Donor Development Process

Step 1 – Identification Stage

- Potential prospects come from many sources: prospect research, volunteer involvement, past giving history, responses to marketing including Web page inquiries, referrals from various sources

- Relatively little may be known about the individual's qualifications as a prospect at this point:

  - affinity for our programs and needs

  - ability to make a major contribution at or above the level sought

  - access on a favorable basis by staff or volunteers

Step 2 – Qualification and Assessment Stage

- Assess the level of affinity, ability, access and the:

- likelihood of addressing deficits in affinity and access

- potential to address deficits in ability through charitable gift planning

- Assessment usually involves one or more face-to-face meetings to determine the level of qualification of the prospect

Step 3 – Decision Point: Is the prospect qualified?

- Does the qualification assessment justify creating a specific strategy to develop this prospect at the current time?

  - If yes, move to Step 4

  - If no, return to Step 1

Step 4 – Strategy Stage

- Design a specific step-by-step strategy to:

  - develop the prospect's affinity for a specific program or need

  - gain or strengthen access to the prospect

  - identify gift planning opportunities to expand ability to give at the desired level

Step 5 – Cultivation Stage

- Cultivation steps are carried out according to the strategy with a decision point after each step to determine if the prospect if ready for a proposal or, if not, whether the prospect remains qualified

Step 6 – Proposal Development Stage

- A specific proposal and supporting materials are developed and an appropriate strategy for optimum proposal delivery is developed

Step 7 – Negotiation and Closing Stage

- The proposal is delivered by the most appropriate people and under most favorable circumstances

- Questions are answered and objections are overcome

- Details of the contribution are negotiated (which may involve several iterations)

Step 9 – Decision Point: Was the gift made?

- If yes, move to step 10

- If no, move back to Step 3

41

Step 10 – Stewardship Stage

- A specific stewardship plan is developed for each donor

SPENDING TIME WHERE IT COUNTS

One of the most difficult areas for development officers is to know when to "disqualify" a prospective donor. Our natural inclination is to look for an additional cultivation step that will bring the prospect closer to becoming a donor. Nevertheless, the fact is some individuals are unlikely to become donors no matter how much effort we lend to them. In order to be as productive as possible for our organizations, we need to work efficiently, and we need to find ways to graciously but effectively set aside those who are not qualified prospects.

This classification grid can help sort prospects.

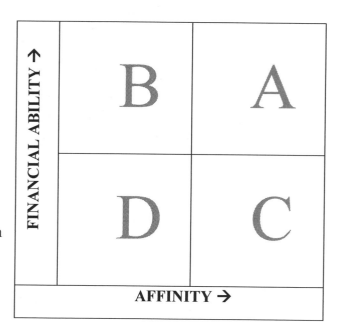

A. Successful development officers will spend as much time as possible working with prospective donors in quadrant A, those who have great affinity for the organization and the financial capacity to make significant contributions.

B. They will spend some time working with prospective donors in quadrant B, seeking opportunities to identify and build relationships with those who might have some interest and affinity for the organization.

C. Those who are in quadrant C, while they may be loyal and valuable volunteers for the organization, should not occupy much of the development officer's time.

D. Finally, respectful ways should be found to avoid devoting much time or effort to individuals in quadrant D who lack either the interest or the financial ability to become major donors.

CHARITABLE ENDOWMENT FUNDS

Many donors, especially when considering a planned gift, are interested in making a permanent contribution to an organization. An endowment fund attracts and preserves financial reserves for the organization and provides stability and consistency for the organization's financial planning. In addition to stability, a strong endowment fund can allow the organization to take advantage of special opportunities and to meet special needs as they arise.

An endowment fund is often described as "a savings account from which only the interest is spent." Although appealingly simple, unfortunately this explanation is inaccurate and fails to explain the robust power of a gift to an endowment fund. The objective of an endowment fund is to provide a consistent distribution over time while guarding the purchasing power of the distribution over time. In other words, an endowment fund is meant to provide a consistent amount of charitable service, year in and year out, forever. If an endowment really were simply "a savings account from which only the interest is spent," over time it would provide less and less charitable work by the organization due to the ravages of inflation.

TOTAL RETURN

Most endowments are not kept in savings accounts, but rather invested in a diverse portfolio with the objective of producing "total return." To understand total return, consider that there are essentially two ways to make money on an investment: you can collect the dividends and interest paid by the investment (the "income"), and the value of the investment can increase over time. The total of the two, income (dividends and interest) plus changes in market value (appreciation *or depreciation*[6]) equals total return.

Over the long term, investment managers will be more likely to produce the best results if they are free to invest for total return rather than focusing strictly on producing income (dividends and interest).

Since total return investing does not emphasize the production of "income" (dividends and interest), it is meaningless to call on an endowment to distribute its "income" each year. Instead, endowments invested for total return usually adopt a "payout policy" which sets a percentage of the endowment fund to be distributed each year. If income (dividends and interest) are less than the payout percentage, then net accumulated investment return (appreciation) may be distributed.

A carefully crafted payout policy will begin with the rate of net total return expected from investments and then subtract the expected rate of inflation with the remainder being the payout percentage made available for distribution. In many cases, the payout percentage is applied to an average of the value of the endowment fund at the end of a number of quarters in order to smooth out extreme year-to-year variations in market value.

---

[6] As experience in the investment markets reminds us, investment return can be negative from year to year as well as positive and, therefore, total return can be a negative number in down years.

A powerful case can be made for an endowment. Even a relatively modest contribution, when invested to provide for consistent distributions over a long period of time, can produce significant results. Following is a simple example:

***Example:* The Case for Endowment**

Assume an endowment fund earns a net total return averaging 7% per year. Further assume that this endowment fund has a payout policy allowing a 4½% distribution.

A contribution of $10,000 to this endowment fund 100 years ago would:

- distribute $5,187 this year

- have a value of $118,137 this year

- have distributed $194,647 over the years

The case for endowment is not the value of the $10,000 initial contribution, but rather the charitable work that $194,647 has provided, and the ability to continue to provide that level of charitable activity forever.

Key Point →   **The case for endowment is not the value of the initial contribution, but rather the value of the charitable work that the endowment will provide year-in and year-out forever.**

PERMANENT ENDOWMENTS AND QUASI-ENDOWMENTS

If a charity accepts a contribution that a donor has restricted to "endowment," it is a "true" or "permanent" endowment, which means that the charity must preserve the initial value—the principal—of the endowment fund. If, on the other hand, the charity chooses to restrict funds to endowment, it is a "quasi" endowment, in which case the charity may decide to spend the endowment principal at some future point.

Endowment funds are governed by state law, usually an adaptation of the Uniform Prudent Management of Institutional Funds Act (UPMIFA). Although a complete discussion of the intricacies of UPMIF is beyond the scope of this text—and not critical to the conversation with a prospective donor—the essential point is that when a charity accepts a contribution that the donor has restricted to endowment, the charity is obligated to protect the ability of the endowment to provide a certain level of charitable work by the organization in perpetuity.

Key Point →   **When a donor restricts his or her gift to endowment, the charity is obliged to manage the endowment so that the value of the charitable work by the organization supported by the endowment is not diminished over time. On the other hand, if the charity chooses to use its own funds as**

endowment, the charity may later decide to spend principal or even deplete the fund entirely.

ECONOMIC VALUE OF PLANNED GIFTS

Determining the real value of a specific planned gift in terms of its ability to support the delivery of charitable work by the organization can be quite difficult. Significantly different values can be calculated for the same planned gift depending upon the variables and methodologies used and the purposes for which the calculations are made.

There are at least four different systems commonly used to calculate the "value" of a planned gift, each designed for a specific application, and each capable of producing a different value for the very same charitable gift.

Tax Deduction – When determining the value of the charitable tax deduction the donor *must* use the formulae and factors set forth in U.S. Treasury Regulations. The deduction calculation is an estimate at a specific point in time (the date of gift) of the present value of the gift which, while irrevocable, is not fully usable by the organization until some time in the future. This point estimate methodology does not take into account changes in value that may occur between the date of gift and the time when the funds become available to the charitable organization, nor does it take into account how the gift may be invested over its lifetime.

Accounting Standards – The accounting rules based on FASB or GASB standards are designed to provide comparability for financial statement purposes in the estimation of payment liabilities, asset values, and contribution income among multiple charitable organizations. Unlike the tax deduction calculation, accounting valuations are typically re-calculated annually.

Counting and Recognition – Various standards may be used to determine the value of planned gifts for the purposes of donor recognition or reporting fund raising campaign totals. The primary purpose of counting and recognition valuations is the promotional value gained through the public recognition of contributions. While these standards should be sensible and consistent, the charitable organization has considerable leeway in designing and choosing standards for counting purposes.

Economic Valuation – A rigorous economic valuation of a planned gift during the gift negotiation and acceptance process and periodically throughout its life can help ensure that the amount of the gift is sufficient to eventually fund a chosen charitable purpose. Economic valuation should accommodate changes over time in order to accurately project the ultimate economic value to the charitable organization. The eventual economic value of a planned gift is determined in significant part by the way in which the gift is invested and managed.

The Partnership for Philanthropic Planning (formerly National Committee on Planned Giving—NCPG) has created standards for determining the economic value of planned gifts. The *Valuation Standards for Charitable Planned Gifts* are available from the Partnership's Web site, which is listed in the Appendix, A-77. The Partnership's objective in developing the Valuation Standards was to help charitable organizations estimate, in current dollars, what a specific planned gift would accomplish when it is eventually received and used for its intended charitable purpose. Unlike the accounting and charitable deduction calculations, the Partnership's Valuation Standards compute the present value by considering real-world data, including the long-term expected returns based on how the gift is invested, long-term inflation, and the costs of management. The Partnership's Valuation Standards are designed to help charitable organizations and donors understand the value of a planned gift in terms of its present purchasing power and to allow charitable organizations to:

- evaluate costs and benefits of planned gift fundraising and determine financial effectiveness of an organization's investment in planned giving

- allocate appropriate resources to a gift planning program and set planned gift fundraising expectations within a comprehensive fundraising program or campaign

- assess the effect of certain variables (e.g., term of the gift, investment strategy) on the ultimate value of the gift to the organization

Assets Used for Charitable Contributions

INTRODUCTION

In a perfect world, all of our donors would contribute cash—which would certainly make the tax ramifications easier to explain. But that's not reality. In fact, donors have many options for giving. Whether it's 100 shares of IBM stock, that rickety old cabin, or grandma's beloved china, sooner or later a generous donor is likely to offer it up as a charitable gift. For the most part, tax law allows taxpayers to deduct these gifts as charitable contributions ... with some exceptions.

TYPES OF NON-CASH GIFTS

In addition to cash, a wide variety of other items of value can be donated to charitable organizations. In general, these are referred to as "non-cash gifts," and can be divided into four broad categories:

Securities – including stocks, bonds, and mutual funds

Real property – including personal residences, farms, or other real estate

Tangible and intangible personal property – including art objects, rare books, coin collections and other items

Gifts-in-kind – such as equipment or other items which can be used in the ordinary course of the charity's operations

SECURITIES

Donors and prospects are likely to own securities as a part of their personal investments. Securities come in a wide variety of forms. Some are more advantageous as charitable gifts than others. Broadly, the most common types of securities used as charitable gifts are:

Stocks – proportionate share of ownership in a company, often referred to as "equities"

Bonds – essentially a loan to the company that issues the bond

Mutual funds – pools money from a number of individuals and invests it; may be highly specialized investing only in certain types of stocks, bonds, or other assets, or may invest in broadly diversified portfolios or index funds that mirror certain stock market indexes

TYPES OF STOCK

Common stock is the most frequently contributed asset. However, there are many specific types of stock and different varieties of corporate organizations. Some key types are:

Common stock shareholders may participate in the profits of the corporation in the form of dividends which can be distributed from the profit earned by the corporation. The amount and timing of common stock dividends are determined by the corporation and are neither fixed nor guaranteed. Some corporations elect to pay no dividends to their common stock holders at all, instead relying on increases in the value of the stock to provide investment return for the shareholders.

Preferred stock usually pays dividends that are pre-determined as to amount and timing regardless of how well (or poorly) the company performs. In addition, preferred stock shareholders often have a claim on corporate property if company assets are liquidated.

Closely-held stock is an equity security that is not publicly traded. Like common stock, these shares represent ownership and may pay dividends, but they are not generally bought and sold among the public. Depending upon the specific restrictions of the corporation, it can be difficult to sell shares of closely-held stock.

C-corp refers to the legal form under which most large publicly traded corporations are organized. In general, a C-corp must pay corporate income tax on its profits. C-corp stock presents no unusual challenges when contributed as a charitable gift.

S-corp refers to a special form of corporate organization which allows only a limited number of shareholders. For tax purposes, an S-corp is treated much like a partnership in that there is no corporate income tax, but rather the corporate profits are taxed as ordinary income to its shareholders. A charitable remainder trust *may not* own S-corp stock. If a charity accepts a contribution of S-corp stock it will have to pay Unrelated Business Income Tax on any distributions (dividends) received from the stock and on any appreciation in value when the stock is sold.

LLP, LLC, PLC, PA, PA are among the initials that refer to specialized forms of corporate organization that may be authorized by state law. Great care should be exercised when considering acceptance of a contribution of any of these forms. Significant restrictions may preclude the contribution of these interests. For example, a medical practice may be organized as one of these specialized types, but state law may restrict ownership to licensed physicians.

CONTRIBUTING STOCK

A contribution of stock is straightforward. The donor transfers ownership of the shares to the charity and is allowed an income tax charitable deduction for the fair market value of the stock on the date the transfer is completed. For publicly traded stocks, the deduction is based upon the average between the high and low prices on the date the stock is transferred.

Note that in order to maximize the tax advantages, it is critically important that *the securities themselves be transferred* to the charitable organization. If the donor sells the shares and gives the proceeds to charity, the donor will be liable for capital gains tax on the sale.

TRANSFERRING PUBLICLY HELD STOCK

Making a contribution of appreciated securities need not be complicated. These days most investors use a stock brokerage to manage their securities rather than holding physical certificates themselves. Securities held by a broker are relatively easy to transfer. The specific details of the transfer of securities depends upon how the donor holds the securities:

"DTC" or "book entry" – Most people no longer hold physical stock certificates. Instead their securities are held in "custody" accounts provided by an investment firm or bank. Many such brokerage accounts are serviced by the Depository Trust Company (DTC), which holds custody of securities in the form of electronic files. The donor simply instructs the broker to transfer shares to the charity's account and then DTC makes the appropriate entries to transfer ownership to the charity. The date of the gift for a DTC transfer is the date when the shares actually enter the charity's account. Most DTC transfers are made in 72 hours or less.

certificates – If a donor holds physical stock certificates, he or she should sign a stock power (a legal form authorizing the transfer of ownership) for each certificate contributed and deliver the stock power and the *unendorsed*[7] certificates to the charity. A stock power form can be obtained from most brokers or financial institutions. Care should be exercised to make certain that the signature on the stock power is properly certified. Usually the signature on either a stock certificate or a stock power will need to be guaranteed (sometimes called a "medallion signature") which is a service provided by either the donor's broker or bank. The date of gift for a contribution of securities is the date the charity receives physical custody of the documents or, if mailed, the mailing date.

transfer agent – Occasionally the owner of the securities will direct the company's transfer agent to reissue shares in the name of the charity. This method offers the least certainty regarding the date of transfer because the timing relies upon the internal processes of the corporation and its transfer.

---

[7] Although the donor may simply endorse the stock certificates themselves, for security reasons, it is preferable to use a stock power separate from the certificate because an endorsed certificate can be negotiated by anyone who is in possession of it. For this reason, if a donor wants to mail a gift of stock certificates, he or she should send two separate envelopes, the un-endorsed certificates in one and the signed stock powers in a separate envelope.

The transfer and valuation of closely held and restricted stock is complex and depends upon the specific conditions and requirements of the security. Often, the only purchasers for this stock are people involved with the company who may fully expect to buy the stock back from the charity. Care should be exercised in these cases to avoid a pre-arranged agreement to sell the stock.

STOCK OPTIONS

Sometimes donors will offer "stock options" as a contribution. A stock option is simply an agreement that gives the holder of the option the right to buy a certain number of shares in a corporation at a fixed price during a certain period of time. There are two types of stock options which are most likely to be encountered as a proposed charitable gift:

"Non-qualified" stock options – may be transferred to a charity if the company's stock option plan permits it to do so. These option contracts can be very complex. Donors should be urged to consult their own advisors to determine the suitability of non-qualified options as a charitable contribution.

"Incentive" stock options – are, by law, not transferable.

Although contributions of stock options may have only limited value to the charity, a donor who exercises stock options often encounters significant tax liabilities as a result in addition to receiving a sometimes significant increase in income or net worth. These circumstances can provide an opportunity for other creative charitable gift planning.

BONDS

The owner of a bond is a lender or creditor who is owed money by the corporation (or other entity) that issued the bond. Unlike shareholders, bondholders do not own "a piece of the corporation." Like other loans, bonds pay interest to the owner for a specified period of time, after which the principal is repaid. Bond holders are usually entitled to a priority claim on company's assets—that is, bond holders would be paid before stockholders in the event of a bankruptcy or liquidation of the corporation.

There are many types of bonds:

Corporate bonds are a major source of corporate borrowing. Sometimes called "debentures," corporate bonds are usually backed by the general credit of the corporation. Specialized bond issues can be backed by certain specific corporate assets.

Municipal bonds (or "munis") are issued by state and local governments. General obligation bonds are backed by the general funds of the issuer; revenue bonds are backed by revenues from the particular project being financed. In general, the interest paid by municipal bonds receives favorable income tax treatment, often tax-free.

U.S. Treasury Notes and Bonds are issued by the Federal government and pay the holder a fixed interest payment. Although treasury bonds are no longer issued, many are still unredeemed and earning interest.

50

U.S. Treasury Bills (T-bills) are backed by the Federal government. As such they are considered a "zero risk" investment and therefore are often used by investors for cash reserves. T-bills are a large component of the "money market."

Zero coupon bonds do not pay interest at all, but rather are sold at deep discount from their redemption value. Investors in zero coupon bonds do not collect interest, instead they rely on the increasing value of the bond for their investment return. The advantage is that these bonds do not produce taxable income while held but rather capital gain income when sold.

Savings Bonds are in a class by themselves when it comes to charitable giving. According to the U.S. Treasury, millions of Americans own U.S. Savings Bonds. One of the reasons they are attractive to investors is that the interest paid on these bonds is usually exempt from state and local income taxes. U.S. Savings Bonds are problematic as a charitable gift during lifetime because the bond cannot be transferred but must be sold first, which triggers all of the accumulated income tax liability. However, Savings Bonds can be left to charity through a bequest and avoid the income tax entirely.

CONTRIBUTING BONDS

A contribution of a bond is similar to a contribution of stock. The donor transfers ownership of the bond to the charity and is allowed an income tax charitable deduction for the fair market value of the bond on the date the transfer is completed.

It is critically important that *the bond itself be transferred* to the charitable organization. If the donor sells the bond and gives the proceeds to charity, the donor will be liable for capital gains tax on the sale.

MUTUAL FUNDS

Mutual funds are very popular investment vehicles for both individuals and institutions. Most American investors now own mutual funds—either individually or through a retirement plan—for some or all of their portfolio.

The transfer of mutual funds as a charitable gift must be completed by the mutual fund company at the direction of the donor. Since each mutual fund company has established its own forms and procedures, the process of making a charitable gift of mutual funds can be time consuming. In addition, the recipient charity may be required to open an account with the mutual fund company, a process which is likely to require formal action or signatures.

Notes: | The date of gift for a mutual fund contribution is the date on which the shares are transferred to the account of the charity. Since the donor may have little control over the timing of this transfer, special care should be exercised if a donor wishes to make a year end mutual fund gift.

Special care should be taken to ensure that the mutual fund company transfers the shares themselves to the charity and does not sell the shares and forward the proceeds to charity.

51

CONTRIBUTING MUTUAL FUNDS

Like contributions of stocks or bonds, the donor transfers ownership of the mutual fund to the charity and is allowed an income tax charitable deduction for the fair market value of the mutual fund on the date the transfer is completed.

Note: Determining the cost basis and holding period for mutual fund investments can be complicated if fund dividends are reinvested automatically. Dividend reinvestment is a common practice in which dividends are used to purchase additional shares of the mutual fund instead of being paid to the owner. However, dividend reinvestment can make it difficult to determine the cost basis and holding period because each dividend reinvestment purchase has its own acquisition date and cost basis.

If a donor is considering a gift of mutual fund shares, ask if the donor has fund dividends reinvested automatically. If yes, the donor should be encouraged to consult with his or her advisors to determine the cost basis and holding period.

As with stocks and bonds, it is critically important that *the mutual fund itself be transferred* to the charitable organization. If the donor sells the mutual fund and gives the proceeds to charity, the donor will be liable for capital gains tax on the sale.

SPECIAL NOTE REGARDING DEPRECIATED SECURITIES

Although we generally assume donors will contribute securities that have appreciated in value (are worth more than the donor paid for them), sometimes donors hold depreciated securities (those that have lost value and are now worth less than the donor paid for them). Usually donors should not contribute depreciated securities. The charitable deduction will be for the fair market value on the date of the gift. In the case of a contribution of a depreciated security, this means that the donor's income tax deduction will be less than the donor paid for the security.

Donors who own securities that have depreciated in value should consult with their own tax and financial advisors on the advisability of giving them to charity.

REAL PROPERTY

Real property, more commonly called "real estate," is generally defined as land and the structures and fixtures that are relatively permanently affixed to it. Examples of real property include:

- Undeveloped land

- Residential property

- Property held for investment such as apartments, office buildings, and malls

- Commercial property used in the taxpayer's business

- Agricultural property used for the production of crops or livestock

When contemplating contributions of real property, a charity will find it advantageous to have in place a set of ground rules:
- Don't be pressured to accept a gift of real property. The decision to accept real estate must be a careful and reasoned one. Even under the best of circumstances, this is a process that will take time.

- Develop gift acceptance policies that clearly define what will and will not be accepted, what the charity will and will not pay for, and a requirement for an environmental audit.

- Establish an objective process for reviewing proposed gifts of real property so that quick action can be taken when an opportunity arises.

Beyond the apparent economic value of the contribution, there are several other important questions a charity should consider before accepting a contribution of real estate:
- What is the property's marketability? How quickly can it be sold for a fair price?

- If the property is to be retained—either by choice or by unintended circumstances—what are the expenses required to hold the property?

- Are there restrictions, reservations, easements or other limitations that might affect the marketability of the property?

- Is the property environmentally clean? Will the cost of the environmental audit and possible remediation override the value of the gift?

- What are the motivations behind the offer? Is there real donative intent or is it a self-serving offer?

- Is the offer acceptable according to the policies of your organization?

CONTRIBUTIONS OF REAL PROPERTY

In order to contribute real property, a donor transfers ownership of the property to the charity, usually with the assistance of a real estate attorney, Realtor, or other professional. The donor is allowed an income tax charitable deduction for the fair market value of the real estate on the date the transfer of ownership is completed.

As with other gifts of appreciated assets, it is important that *the real property itself be transferred* to the charitable organization. If the donor sells the real property and gives the proceeds to charity, the donor will be liable for capital gains tax on the sale.

"ORDINARY INCOME" REAL PROPERTY

If the real property is considered ordinary "income property," then the donor's charitable deduction is limited to the fair market value less appreciation—generally the cost basis minus any costs already deducted. Real property may be considered ordinary income property if it is:

- Property that has been held less than one year by the donor

- Property held by the donor as a real estate dealer (owners may be considered dealers if they hold and develop property as inventory for sale to customers or if the owner is engaged in the frequent purchase and sale of real property)

- Property that is subject to depreciation recapture (depreciation recapture can occur when the owner has claimed depreciation deductions on prior tax returns)

The determination of real property as ordinary income property is a complex matter. Donors should be urged to consult their own tax advisors if this is in question.

PARTIAL INTERESTS

Partial interests occur when a property owner shares the ownership of property with another person or entity, or ownership is limited in some other way. In order to be deductible as a charitable contribution, the transfer to charity must be an undivided partial interest. This means, for example, that a donor could transfer a 20 percent interest in land and claim a charitable deduction for the contribution. The charitable organization would then join the donor in the subsequent sale of the land.

Notes: When a donor contributes a fractional interest in property, even if it is his or her entire share, the valuation for charitable deduction purposes must reflect that the gift is either a minority or majority interest, which may affect the marketability of the parcel.

Before accepting a partial interest in real estate, the charity should consider the potential for environmental liability (see below) since it will become a part owner of the property.

DEBT ENCUMBRANCE

A mortgage reduces the amount of the charitable deduction for a gift of real property. The deduction will be the fair market value minus the amount of debt outstanding. The transfer of debt encumbered property is usually considered to be a bargain sale (since the donor is relieved of the debt obligation he or she is deemed to have been "paid" that amount), which means that a portion of the capital gain will be taxable to the donor. In addition, the donor may incur income taxes as a result of having been relieved of the debt obligation.

The tax implications of contributions of encumbered property are complex. Donors should be urged to consult their own tax advisors in these situations.

TIMESHARES

Timeshares generally don't make good charitable gifts—at least not from the charity's point-of-view. They are usually difficult to sell, and the resale value can be significantly less than what the donor originally paid for the timeshare. In addition, the charity may find itself responsible for maintenance and other fees until the interest is sold.

CROPS AND TIMBER

Occasionally your organization may be asked to consider a gift of land that comes with crops. "Un-harvested" crops sold with the land on which the crops are located (and which has been owned by the seller for more than one year) are considered long-term capital gain property.

If harvested crops are contributed to charity, they are usually considered tangible personal property. However, if the donor regularly produces crops for sale to customers in a trade or business, they may be ordinary income property.

Contributions of timber represent one of the most complex of all property gifts. Factors that determine the tax treatment of charitable contributions of timber include whether the:

- Timber is standing and being contributed with the land

- Timber has been cut and is being contributed separately

- Donor holds the timberland primarily for investment

- The donor sells timber to customers is in the ordinary course of business

MINERAL INTERESTS

A mineral interest (sometimes a "mining interest" or an "oil and gas interest") is the legal right to exploit or produce minerals that lie below the surface of the land. In most cases the mineral interest is included in the ownership of the property. This combined ownership is referred to as a "fee interest" in the property. However, mineral interests can be separated from the surface rights to the land and the mineral interest can then be sold or contributed separate from the land itself. The separation of mineral interests is complex. Before accepting a contribution of real property the charity should be certain that it understands exactly what rights it will own. For example, in some states the owner of a mineral interest is given a right to use the surface land in order to access the mineral interest. In addition, the management and administration of mineral interests is a highly technical area requiring special expertise.

ENVIRONMENTAL AUDITS

Under Federal law, the owner of a polluted property can be held financially responsible for the clean-up of the pollution. This includes a charity that becomes owner of a polluted property as a result of a contribution.

In light of the potentially enormous costs of environmental remediation, it is prudent for the charitable organization to conduct a careful environmental review of the property before

55

agreeing to accept it. Professional environmental audits are conducted by specialists in environmental remediation and usually proceed in three phases:

Phase I – a physical inspection of the property and review of the title history of the property to identify potential environmental hazards (e.g., Is there an un-capped well on the property? Was the property ever used for industrial purposes?)

Phase II – a more in-depth review including some sampling of soils and materials from the property (e.g., Is there asbestos insulation in place? Are there abandoned buried oil tanks on the property?)

Phase III – usually involves extensive on-site investigation possibly including drilling test wells and examination of soil samples

Of course, the costs of environmental audits increase at each stage. The good news is that the environmental review can be conducted in steps. For example, if a Phase I audit shows little cause for concern, the organization may decide that there is no need to proceed with further in-depth work.

It is prudent to conduct an environmental review even on seemingly mundane properties. For example, a personal home may have been built on the site of a former gas station where leaking storage tanks polluted the subsoil years before with no visible evidence.

Finally, note that even if an environmental issue is identified, the property may still be acceptable provided that the costs of remediation are reasonable and that the charitable organization is aware of these issues before accepting the gift.

Note → | The purpose of the environmental review is to identify potential environmental liabilities and remediation needs. Even the most careful environmental review cannot guarantee a perfectly clean property. Once the charity has accepted ownership of the real property, it will be liable for all environmental issues, even those that were not identified by the environmental audit.

TANGIBLE AND INTANGIBLE PERSONAL PROPERTY

Tangible personal property is property that can be held physically while intangible personal property has no inherent physical characteristics that lend value.

Examples of tangible personal property include:

furniture	store fixtures	old musty books
production machinery	storage equipment	mobile homes
office equipment	grandma's china	portable buildings
appliances	a doll collection	motor vehicles

Examples of intangible personal property include:

copyrights	installment obligations	partnership interests
royalties	life insurance contracts	securities
patents	annuity contracts	service contracts

As with real property, there are a number of questions the charity should consider before accepting a contribution of personal property:

- What is the property's marketability? How quickly can it be sold for a fair price?

- If the property is to be retained—either by choice or by unintended circumstances—what are the expenses required to hold the property?

- Are there restrictions, reservations or other limitations that might affect the marketability of the property?

- What are the motivations behind the offer? Is there real donative intent or is it a self-serving offer?

- Is the offer acceptable according to the policies of your organization?

DEDUCTIBILITY OF TANGIBLE PROPERTY CONTRIBUTIONS

Contributions of tangible personal property present several special issues for income tax charitable deduction purposes.

Related Use Rule – The donor is allowed a deduction for the full fair market value of the tangible personal property only if the use of the item is related to the tax-exempt purposes of the charity. Otherwise, the amount of the deduction is limited to the *lesser of* the donor's cost basis or the fair market value.

***Example:* Related Use Rule**

If an individual donates a painting to a museum and it is of the type normally retained by the museum, the painting is a related use item and the contribution deduction will be for the full fair market value of the painting.

If the person donates the same painting to a food bank to be sold at a charity auction, the charitable deduction will be limited to the lesser of the cost basis or fair market value because the use of the item is unrelated to the exempt purposes of the charity.

Ordinary Income Property Rule – Another reason the charitable deduction might be reduced is because the asset is "ordinary income property," i.e., the individual would realize ordinary income if he or she sold the item. Ordinary income property, in this context, includes items created by the donor (such as artwork, music, or a manuscript), items of inventory held for sale to customers in the course of business, and items held for one year or less. When ordinary income property is transferred to a charity, the charitable deduction is the *lesser of* the fair market value of the item or its cost basis.

Long Term Capital Gain Rule – Tangible personal property that is acquired as an investment may be considered a long term capital gain asset (assuming it is held for more than one year). For example, a person who collects paintings by Monet as a passion, but then holds and trades them as investments, may be considered to hold long term capital gain assets because he or she trades them as investments.

DEDUCTIBILITY OF INTANGIBLE PROPERTY CONTRIBUTIONS

The deduction for donations of a patent or other intellectual property such as copyrights or software, is limited to the lesser of the fair market value or the donor's cost basis.

GIFTS-IN-KIND

Gifts-in-kind are non-monetary items that the charity is able to put directly to use for its charitable purposes. Examples include cribs donated to a crisis nursery, blankets to a homeless shelter, or computers donated to a school.

Generally, the rules for tangible personal property apply in regard to the charitable deduction for gifts-in-kind. Note that in some instances, the fair market value of the tangible personal property is less than the donor's cost basis. This is often the case, for example, with donated computers and other equipment that has been surpassed and made obsolete by later technology.

It is important to note that there is no deduction for contributions of services. For example, the attorney who provides free services to a charitable organization may not claim an income tax deduction for the value of those services. These rules can be especially challenging for artists who wish to contribute their own works. In most cases an artist who contributes her or his own work will find that the charitable deduction is limited to the cost of materials.

Notes: From time to time tax laws have been enacted to encourage certain types of gifts-in-kind. For example, the American Taxpayer Relief Act of 2012 included a temporary extension of an expanded deduction for contributions of food inventory. Similarly, temporary special provisions have been enacted from time to time to encourage gifts of computers and other hardware.

Charities should check with their own advisors to determine the current availability of special incentives for gifts-in-kind.

Planned Giving in a Nutshell

Basic Planned Giving Methods

INTRODUCTION

No doubt the simplest and most straightforward gift is an outright contribution for the unrestricted use of the charitable organization ... preferably in cash. However, there are a great number of other ways in which a contribution can be made. Some charitable gift plans can provide an income or stream of payments to the donor or others. Some allow significantly greater tax advantages than a simple outright contribution. Others can allow a donor to meld complex financial and estate planning goals with charitable objectives.

Why pursue these alternatives, especially given all their added complexity? First, the charity will provide a valuable service to its most loyal donors by working with them to create charitable gift plans that meet donors' needs as well as those of the organization. In addition, by offering the full range of charitable giving opportunities the organization will appeal to a much wider audience. Finally, other charitable organizations will offer alternatives and so, if only as a matter of keeping current, your charitable organization should be familiar with these more sophisticated methods of charitable giving.

TESTAMENTARY GIFTS

A testamentary charitable gift is simply a formal direction or instruction to transfer money, property, or other assets to a charity at death. The testamentary gift is usually made by executing a formal legal instrument during lifetime. Typical tools for making testamentary gifts include charitable bequest provisions in Wills and trusts as well as beneficiary designations on all manner of financial instruments and accounts.

What is the appeal of testamentary charitable giving?

For the donor there is an intuitive appeal. A testamentary contribution is a logical extension of one's lifetime accomplishments and ambitions. It is a way to make a final statement about one's visions and beliefs. Testamentary giving also provides the donor with an opportunity to accommodate various contingencies and conditions specific to his or her circumstances. Finally, a testamentary gift, unlike other kinds of charitable gifts, preserves flexibility for the donor in that it can be changed, modified, or deleted completely if the need arises.

Testamentary gifts appeal to charitable organizations because they provide an opportunity to seek support for long-term needs without disrupting fundraising for current needs. In addition, testamentary gifts provide an opportunity to identify and address entirely new groups of constituents. Even those who are either maximizing their current giving or who are unable or unwilling to give currently can be asked to consider a testamentary gift. Indeed, testamentary gifts can be a key prospecting and cultivation step in pursuit of further gifts of all kinds.

Finally, there is a large and potential audience for testamentary giving. According to research conducted by the Partnership for Philanthropic Planning (formerly National Committee on Planned Giving) less than 8% of the population has included a charitable bequest in their estate plans. And, of those who have, only one in four has notified the charity of their plans.

THE PROBATE PROCESS

Prior to considering specific types of testamentary contributions, we will first briefly review "probate," the process by which an estate is administered and settled. Although the term "probate" has specific legal meaning, it is frequently used by non-lawyers to describe all of the steps and processes involved in gathering, administering, and distributing an estate following the death of an individual.

The rules governing estate administration vary from state to state, and the process is usually carried out under some level of court supervision. In broad strokes, these are the steps that must be taken to settle and distribute an estate:

1. The estate administrator—the one responsible for managing and administering the estate, sometimes referred to as the "Executor" or "Personal Representative" in state laws—must locate the Will (or other testamentary documents) and submit it to the Court for certification and appointment as Estate administrator. An opportunity is provided for others to object to the appointment of the Estate administrator or question validity of the Will.

2. Once appointed, the Estate administrator has legal authority over the estate and its assets and is responsible for locating, preserving, and maintaining property and assets of the estate.

3. The Estate administrator must take an inventory and value all of the assets and property in the estate, and must account for all expenditures and income during administration of the estate.

4. The Estate administrator must attempt to identify all creditors or others who may have a claim against the estate. This usually includes advertising to notify those who believe they may have a claim so that they have an opportunity to come forward and seek payment.

5. Then the Estate administrator pays the valid claims and denies others. At this point a court hearing may be held to allow those who have not been paid to have an opportunity to object.

6. The final income tax return and estate tax return are prepared and filed.

7. In most cases the Estate administrator must provide the court with a final accounting and inventory and seek permission to make distributions according to the Will.

8. Finally, distributions are made.

The entire process can easily take a year or more following the death of the donor. Charities should monitor the process and, while exercising patience, be vigilant to make certain that the process is moving along and to ensure that the donor's charitable wishes are carried out.

CHARITABLE BEQUESTS

The most straightforward way to make a testamentary gift is by a charitable bequest—a provision included in a Will or trust directing a gift to charity upon the death of the donor. There is an almost endless variety of ways in which a charitable bequest can be structured. Some of the most common forms are:

Specific bequest – an exact amount, or a specific item, is left to charity

- "I bequeath the sum of $100,000 to…"

- "I direct my Executor to distribute my collection of barbed wire to…"

Percentage bequest – a percentage or fraction of the estate is left to charity, often used with a remainder or residue provision

- "I bequeath 50% of my estate to …"

- "I direct my Executor to distribute one-half of the remainder to…"

Bequest of remainder or residue – directs that what is left (if anything) after other distributions should be given to charity, often expressed as a percentage

- "I bequeath all of the rest remainder and residue of my estate to…"

- "I direct my Executor to distribute one-third of the remainder to…"

Contingency bequest – a contribution is to be made only if certain other things happen first (e.g., my spouse dies before I do)

- "If I am trampled to death by a herd of buffalo in the starboard isle of a west-bound Boeing 747, then I bequeath..."

RESTRICTIONS

Donors often wish to provide instructions or restrictions as to how their charitable bequest should be used. These restrictions can become problematic if the direction is unclear, or if it is impractical. Ultimately, the charity may be forced to decline the bequest if the restriction is unacceptable.

In order to avoid these complications, charities often suggest that the donor set forth the restrictions in a memorandum or other written document negotiated with the charity. Then, the provision in the Will can direct that the bequest "...be used in accordance with the most recent memorandum that I have placed on file with Charity." Of course, the donor should seek the advice of his or her legal counsel as to what details should be included in the Will.

> A sample "gift instrument" is in Appendix B on page A-3.

In addition, it is prudent to ask donors to include "safety valve" language, such as:

> "If the Board of Directors determines that it has become unwise or unnecessary to use this gift for the purposes I have specified, then I direct that this gift be used for other purposes the Board of Directors may designate, bearing in mind my original intention."

QUALIFIED RETIREMENT PLANS

There are a number of retirement plans under current tax law. "IRA," "Keogh," "401(k)," "403(b)," are just a few of the "qualified retirement plans." Qualified retirement plans are designed to encourage individuals to save money to be used to provide income in their retirement years.

In general, qualified retirement plans offer the opportunity to set aside pre-tax income and invest that money on an income tax deferred basis. Since no taxes are paid on the money as it is earned, nor as it is invested and grows, withdrawals from qualified retirement plan are subject to income tax.

In addition, since these programs are designed specifically to provide retirement income, they are subject to a number of rules that make it unattractive to use them for other purposes. There is a minimum age (generally 59½) before which withdrawals are subject to a penalty which serves to discourage use as a savings account. In addition, there are requirements mandating minimum annual withdrawals generally beginning at age 70½. This so-called "Required Minimum Distribution" is designed to prevent the accumulation of estate wealth.

In general, qualified retirement plans are *not* a good source of funds for lifetime charitable gifts because the donor will have to recognize as taxable income any amounts withdrawn from the account. Even though the charitable deduction can offset the additional taxable income, the complexities involved—including the likelihood that the administrator will be required to deduct standby withholding— make lifetime gifts from qualified plans unattractive to donors. However, a new law enacted in 2015 simplifies certain lifetime contributions of IRA assets for donors age 70½ or older (see "Charitable IRA Rollover" below).

In any case, qualified retirement plan assets make an *excellent* testamentary gift. The reason is very simple:

- Any amount left in a qualified retirement plan at death is treated as though it was withdrawn by the estate. The effect is that the total amount left in a qualified retirement plan at death is subject to income tax. What is worse, the taxable income on an individual's final income tax return is often higher than in prior years resulting in a higher marginal income tax rate and perhaps triggering the Medicare surtax.

- However, transfers at death from a qualified retirement plan directly to charity escape the income tax completely!

Example: **Testamentary Contribution of IRA versus Charitable Bequest**

A donor has a modest sized estate worth $500,000 including a home, life insurance policies, other assets, and an IRA worth $100.000. The donor has decided to make a charitable bequest of $100,000 and wants the rest of the estate to go to heirs. The donor has written a Will directing $100,000 to charity and the rest of the estate to heirs. Here are the effects of a gift of the IRA to charity versus the simple charitable bequest:

	charitable bequest	IRA to charity
Total value of estate including IRA	$500,000	$500,000
IRA transferred to charity	n/a	$100,000
Income tax on IRA (assume 36%)	- $36,000	-0-
charitable bequest	- $100,000	n/a
remainder to heir	$364,000	$400,000

By naming the charity as the remainder beneficiary of his IRA the donor could save $36,000 in income taxes (or $39,800 if the 3.8% Medicare surtax is triggered) that will be due on the IRA as it passes into the estate—money that will reduce the amount for heirs.

Note that this example illustrates income tax savings only. For larger estates there are potential estate tax savings too.

Remember that in order to avoid the income tax the qualified plan must be directed to charity upon death. The donor must work with the administrator of the qualified plan to name the charity as the remainder beneficiary of the qualified plan. If the donor simply provides a direction in her or his Will to use qualified plan assets, the IRS will conclude that the qualified plan first distributed to the estate and then to the charity, and the distribution to the estate will be subject to income tax.

Similar to a bequest provision, the donor can direct the plan administrator to distribute all or part of the qualified plan or make the contribution contingent upon other circumstances, for example only if the donor's spouse is no longer living. Since it is impossible to know exactly how much the qualified plan will be worth at the moment of the donor's death, the donor may consider including a coordinating provision in her or his Will to make up the difference should the balance available in the qualified plan fall short of the amount the donor wants to give to charity.

Finally, the rules surrounding IRAs and other qualified retirement plans are complex. Donors should work with their retirement plan administrators and other advisors in order to ensure that their charitable plans do not produce other unintended consequences for their heirs.

"CHARITABLE IRA ROLLOVER"

A special rule made permanent by Congress in 2015 allows certain donors to use their IRA assets to make a "Qualified Charitable Distribution" without incurring income tax on the withdrawal from the IRA. The Qualified Charitable Distribution is subject to several limitations:

- The donor must be age 70½ or older at the time the gift is made

- The account must be a traditional Individual Retirement Account (IRA) or Roth IRA

- The contribution must be outright (no contributions in exchange for charitable gift annuities nor contributions to charitable remainder trusts or pooled income funds)

- Total IRA charitable rollover contributions cannot exceed $100,000 for the year

- The transfer must be from the IRA administrator directly to the charity (the donor cannot withdraw the money and then make a contribution to the charity)

- Contributions must be to a public charity and cannot be to a donor advised fund, supporting organization, or private foundation

Note that the donor does not receive an income tax deduction for a qualified charitable distribution, but does not pay income taxes on the withdrawal as would be the case otherwise.

The charitable IRA rollover appeals to donors for reasons that include:

- It is relatively simple to complete

- It does not increase the donor's taxes, even if the donor's charitable deductions are limited in some way or the donor does not itemize deductions

- The charitable contribution counts toward the donor's Required Minimum Distribution which can be especially appealing to donors who are forced to withdraw and pay taxes on income they may not need in the current year

GIFTS OF LIFE INSURANCE

Life insurance is a powerful and flexible financial and estate planning tool. For charitable giving purposes, the value for the charity lies in receiving the "death benefit" which is paid upon the death of the insured. However, policy loans, withdrawals, and other obligations can reduce the dollar amount coming to the charity.

At its core, a life insurance policy is simply a contract that promises to pay a specific amount of money (the death benefit) upon the occurrence of a specific event (the death of the insured during a specific time period). There are four parties to the life insurance contract, each with its own interests and obligations under the policy:

Owner	Insurer	Insured	Beneficiary
Buys and pays for the policy; has the right to change the beneficiary and to give away ownership	Promises to pay an amount of money (the death benefit) upon the death of the insured	The one upon whose death the insurer will pay the death benefit	The one to whom the death benefit will be paid

The contractual promise to pay the death benefit is usually good for one year and is renewable each year. The insurer charges a fee (often referred to as the "mortality charge") in exchange for the promise to pay the death benefit. The older the insured the higher the fee since the likelihood of paying out the death benefit increases as the insured grow older.

Most modern policies include provisions that allow the owner to pay either a fixed or variable amount each year (the premium) which is projected to accumulate sufficient value to pay for the cost of insurance each year. The accumulated payments which have not yet been used to pay for the cost of insurance are what creates value in the policy.

Before we discuss the practical aspects of life insurance as a charitable gift, following is a brief summary of the basic structure of life insurance policies:

- **Policy** – Life insurance is a legal contract (the "policy") promising to pay a certain amount (the "death benefit") upon the death of an individual (the "insured").

  - The insurance company seeks a large number of people to insure in order to spread the risk of having to pay the death benefit in any one year.

  - The company charges a fee (the "premium") for the policy and uses this money to pay death benefits to the beneficiaries of those insureds who die.

- **Term Life Insurance** – "all life insurance is term insurance"

  - The policy covers one life for a specified period of time (usually one year).

- The amount of the premium increases each year as the likelihood of paying the death benefit during that year increases because the insured is older.

  - **Annual renewable term** – The insurance company promises to renew the coverage each year—but at higher premium for the same death benefit.

  - **Decreasing term** – The insurance company promises to renew the coverage each year for the same premium but with a smaller death benefit.

- **Whole Life Insurance** – The premium stays the same and the coverage stays the same for the life of the insured.

  - In the early years the premium for a whole life is significantly higher than for the same coverage under a term insurance policy.

  - The extra premiums collected in the early years are accumulated and invested to be used to pay the higher cost of insurance in later years when the insured is older.

  - The insurance company guarantees that a specific value in death benefit will be paid as long as premium payments made on time regardless of investment performance, mortality experience, or other vagaries during the life of the insured.

- **Universal or Variable Life Insurance** – Both the premium amount and the value of the death benefit may be adjusted during the course of the policy.

  - Similar to whole life policies, excess premiums are accumulated to be invested and used later to pay the cost of insurance.

  - Most of the variables, including the cost of insurance, mortality assumptions, investment return and value of death benefit, are not guaranteed and can be adjusted from time to time.

  - The policy owner may be provided some opportunity to select the investments owned by the policy.

- **Limited Payment or "Vanishing Premium" Plans**

  - A limited number of annual premiums are projected, after which a sufficient policy value is expected to have accumulated in order to pay the cost of insurance for the lifetime of the insured.

- **Single Premium or "Paid Up" Life Insurance**

  - One very large premium is paid at the time of purchase, most of which is set up as an investment account to pay the cost of insurance for the lifetime of the insured.

LIFE INSURANCE VOCABULARY

Life insurance employs a very specific and technical vocabulary. An understanding of several key terms will be helpful in the evaluation and comparison of charitable life insurance proposals:

Account value	The sum of all premium payments adjusted by periodic charges, credits and partial withdrawals
Annuity	A contract issued by an insurer that promises to periodically pay an amount to a beneficiary (the amount of the annuity can be fixed or variable and continue for the lifetime of the insured or last for a shorter period depending upon the terms of the contract)
Beneficiary	The individual or entity to whom the death benefit or periodic annuity is to be paid
Cash surrender value	The cash value available upon surrender of the insurance contract
Death Benefit	The amount paid upon the death of the insured (the amount of the death benefit can be guaranteed and fixed at the time the policy is issued or it can vary depending upon the terms of the contract, the net amount available may be reduced by loans or withdrawals made before the death of the insured)
Guaranteed value / guaranteed rate	Policy illustrations usually include certain minimum or guaranteed rates of investment return as well as assumed rates of investment return; guaranteed policy values are those projected based upon the guaranteed rates while values based upon the assumed rates are not guaranteed

Insured	The individual upon whose life a policy or annuity is issued
Insurer	The insurance company that issues the policy or annuity
Owner	The individual or entity that owns and controls the policy
Policy	A contract issued by an insurer which promises to pay a death benefit to the beneficiary upon the death of the insured
Policy year	The "fiscal year" of the policy, generally beginning the first day the life insurance coverage is in place; premium payments and other outlays are usually assumed to be made at the beginning of the year while cash values are usually shown as of the end of the policy year
Premium	The amount paid to the insurer in exchange for the contractual promises of the policy (insurance policies usually require periodic payment of premiums during the lifetime of the insured, annuities usually require a single premium payment when the contract is issued)

OUTRIGHT CONTRIBUTIONS OF LIFE INSURANCE

If a charity is named as the "beneficiary" of the policy, the charity will receive the death benefit amount when the insured dies.

If, in addition, the donor assigns "ownership" of the policy to the charity, the donor can receive a current income tax deduction for "interpolated terminal reserve value" (basically the "cash value," subject to certain adjustments) of the policy. In addition, if the donor makes premium payments on the policy after it has been contributed to the charity, he or she can receive an income tax charitable deduction for those amounts too.

Note: | Policy loans, withdrawals, and other obligations may decrease, sometimes significantly, the value of the policy to the charity.

Donors should be advised that the charity, as owner of the policy, has sole discretion to make decisions which will affect the value of the policy to the charity:

Further premium payments – the charity is *not* obligated to make any further premium payments on the policy

Policy loans – the charity can borrow the cash value from the policy

Paid-up insurance – the charity may elect to accept a smaller death benefit and eliminate the need for further premium payments

69

"Wealth Replacement" Life Insurance

Since planned gifts often remove estate assets that would otherwise have gone to surviving heirs, life insurance naming the heirs as the beneficiary can provide a cost-efficient way to replace the assets given to charity.

Those donors who are concerned about estate taxes can work with their financial advisors to ensure that wealth replacement policies are owned by the heirs. Ownership by the heirs can avoid estate taxes on wealth passed to the next generation.

Evaluating Life Insurance Contributions

It seems there is a never-ending array of programs promoting creative applications for life insurance in charitable giving. Before engaging in any life insurance program, the charity should engage in a careful review of the proposal to ensure that there is real value for the charity.

The Partnership for Philanthropic Planning (formerly National Committee on Planned Giving) has published guidelines for the evaluation of life insurance. These guidelines are available from the Partnership's Web site which is listed in the Appendix on A-77. The key elements of the recommended review are:

Complete Analysis – Careful analysis of both the subjective and objective factors is key. Some aspects of charitable life insurance programs lend themselves to quantitative analysis, while other aspects are more qualitative in nature. A worthwhile charitable life insurance program will meet both subjective and objective criteria.

Value and Values – The analysis should guard both the value and the values of the charitable organization today and in the future. Even though a charitable life insurance program may be financially viable, it may still present unwarranted risk to reputation and/or consume unreasonable amounts of valuable staff time and resources.

Nothing is Free – Nothing of value comes without a price. All of the costs of the charitable life insurance program, including the costs of insurance, borrowing, commissions, and on-going administration, must be paid by someone at some point. The charity should have a clear understanding of all of these costs and the sources of the funds to pay these expenses, as well as the ultimate source of the value the charitable organization expects to receive.

Charitable Interest – The charitable life insurance program must respect and serve the charitable interests of the donor.

Obligations and Commitments – Charitable organizations should fully understand the obligations involved in a proposed charitable life insurance program and the impact should the program not unfold as planned. Interest rates, mortality assumptions, and the cost of insurance are all variables that may increase or decrease the charity's out-of-pocket expenses over time.

BARGAIN SALE GIFTS

A "bargain sale" occurs when a donor sells property to a charity for less than its full fair market value. For tax purposes, the transaction is viewed as having two elements; a sale and a gift. The donor is allowed an income tax deduction for the difference between the sale price and the fair market value of the property.

Bargain sale gifts that should be approached with special caution include: appreciated short term property, ordinary income property, mortgaged property, stock redemption plans, and tangible personal property. Although a bargain sale is possible in these situations—and can even be mutually advantageous to both the donor and the charitable institution—the guidance of qualified counsel should be sought before proceeding.

Note:	The donor of a bargain sale gift will owe capital gains tax on the portion of the property that was sold. For example, if a donor owns a property now worth $50,000 with a cost basis of $20,000, the donor has a $30,000 gain in the property ($50,000 sale price minus $20,000 basis). Put another way, 60% of the total value of the property is capital gain, which means that 60 cents of each dollar received in a sale would be capital gain and the remaining 40 cents would be recovery of cost basis. The same ratio applies to the portion sold by the bargain sale donor. If the donor sells the property to charity for $10,000, he or she will be liable for capital gains tax on $6,000 of capital gain (60% of $10,000).

The bargain sale can become even more complex if the property is mortgaged or if the donor has taken accelerated appreciation deductions related to the property. Under the appropriate circumstances, such gifts can be acceptable, however in some cases the donor will incur taxable income in addition to capital gain. Donors should be urged to consult their own tax advisors before completing a bargain sale.

Finally, the charity should carefully evaluate the implications before accepting a bargain sale gift. Two considerations should be paramount:

- Is the property usable and valuable to the charity in its mission? If not, is it readily marketable so that the charity can use the proceeds for its charitable work? Since the charity will be committing financial resources to the purchase, there should be a reasonable likelihood that the transaction will result in additional support for the mission of the charity.

71

- Does the charity have sufficient resources to engage in the purchase? The initial cash purchase may be only the beginning. There may be expenses and costs if the property cannot be sold quickly.

FAMILY FOUNDATIONS

The notion of a "family foundation" can be very appealing to generous individuals. A family foundation is a way to have an impact on an array of organizations over an extended period of time and to provide family members and others with opportunities to influence charitable giving now and in the future. Interestingly, there is no legal definition of "family foundation." Most often a private foundation is the vehicle used to establish a "family foundation", increasingly, however, donors are using a donor advised fund as an alternative way to establish a family foundation.

PRIVATE FOUNDATION

A private foundation is a separate tax-exempt entity, created either as a non-profit corporation or in the form of a trust. The private foundation accepts contributions from one or more donors. The governing board of the private foundation manages and administers its assets and makes distributions, or grants, for charitable purposes.

Private foundations are subject to a number of restrictions—the private foundation rules—which prohibit transactions between the private foundation and its founders, donors, or individuals or parties related to them. As a separate legal entity, a private foundation must provide for its own administration, accounting, and investment management. It must also complete and file its own tax and information returns each year, which must be made available to the public on request.

DONOR ADVISED FUND

Donor advised funds are among the fastest growing vehicles for personal philanthropy. Although donor advised funds are most often created through community foundations, other public charities sometimes sponsor donor advised funds. Several financial institutions, including Fidelity Investments, Vanguard, and Charles Schwab, operate very large donor advised funds.

Through a written agreement with the sponsoring charity, a donor creates a specially named fund account to which contributions are made. The terms of the agreement allow the donor (or others) the privilege of making non-binding recommendations regarding charitable distributions that the sponsoring charity makes from the fund.

Since the donor makes contributions directly to the sponsoring charity, contributions to the fund are charitable contributions to a public charity rather than gifts to a private foundation. Since a charitable contribution must be "complete" in order to qualify for tax deduction purposes, the donor's recommendations as to the use of the contribution must be advisory only and the governing body of the sponsoring charity must have final control over all distributions.

The table below compares several aspects of a donor advised fund and a private foundation.

	Donor Advised Fund	Private Foundation
tax-exempt status	gets public charity status from the sponsoring charity	establish separate tax exempt status as private foundation
charitable deduction limit	50% / 30% of AGI	30% / 20% of AGI
donor control over grant making	donor may recommend distributions but charity makes final decision	donor retains significant control subject to IRS private foundation rules
minimum payout requirements	none (except by policy of sponsoring charity)	at least 5% of asset value each year (regardless of income)
start-up	established by agreement with sponsoring charity	non-profit entity must be established and separate tax exempt status secured
practical minimum size	depends upon policy of sponsoring charity, often as little at $10,000	substantial assets required, typically $1.0 million or more
annual taxes	none	subject to excise tax of up to 2% of net investment gain
annual tax filings and returns	none required, reported as a part of the sponsoring charity's annual return	separate tax and information return must be filed annually along with required schedules
administration and investment management	provided by the sponsoring charity	must establish or secure its own services

Planned Giving in a Nutshell

Advanced Planned Giving Methods

INTRODUCTION

Even though the vast majority of planned gifts are simple charitable bequests, successful development officers still find it well worth their while to maintain at least a conversational knowledge of the more advanced planning giving methods. First of all, these advanced planned gifts are, for the most part, irrevocable, and therefore arguably better for the charitable organization because they cannot be changed or revoked like a simple bequest. In addition, the development officer who has a working knowledge of advanced planned giving methods is in a better position to be of service to his or her donors and can be helpful to them in creating charitable gift plans that benefit the donor and the organization.

LIFE INCOME GIFTS

In the simplest terms, a "life income gift" is a plan that allows a donor to make a contribution to charity and receive an income in return. Depending upon the plan, the income may be fixed or variable and it can go on for one or more lifetimes, a term of years, or a combination of the two. Later we will explore a number of specific plans, however, they have the following features in common:

- are irrevocable once the contribution has been made
- provide a current income tax deduction for the calculated value of the charitable gift
- can be made during lifetime or included in a Will or other testamentary instrument
- subject to both Federal and state laws

Life income gifts offer distinct advantages—and disadvantages—for both the donor and the charity:

- **For the donor** – the ability to receive income, avoid capital gains tax, and shift investment strategies are advantages, however donors must also consider that these gifts are irrevocable and there is very little flexibility should the donor wish to make changes after the gift is made

- **For the charity** – the irrevocability of these gifts is an advantage compared to other planned gifts which can be changed or even revoked without the charity being aware, however the charity must consider that it will need to establish relationships—sometimes lifelong—with the donor and beneficiary and take responsibility for fiscal and fiduciary matters

TYPES OF LIFE INCOME GIFTS

Charitable gift annuity

- Money, property, or other assets are irrevocably given to a charity now in exchange for a contractual promise to pay a fixed amount each year to one or two beneficiaries

- The amount of payment is set at the time the gift is made and cannot be changed

- One or two annuitants are named at the time the gift is made and cannot be changed

- The date of the first annuity payment may be delayed (deferred payment gift annuity)

- Payments are backed by the charitable organization that issues the gift annuity

Charitable remainder trust

- Money, property, or other assets are irrevocably transferred to a trustee with instructions to pay income to one or more income beneficiaries for a period of time and then to transfer the remainder in the trust fund to charity

- Two types:

  - **Annuity trust** – pays a fixed dollar amount to the income beneficiaries

  - **Unitrust** – pays a fixed percentage of the value of the trust fund to the income beneficiaries

- Trustee may be the charity, a trust company, an individual, or others

- Payout method (annuity or percent of trust value), rate or amount of payout, income beneficiary(ies), and other terms of trust are set at the time the gift is made and cannot be changed

Pooled income fund

- Many donors irrevocably contribute money, property, or other assets to a pooled investment fund operated by a charity

76

- Income beneficiaries are paid a share of the fund's net income proportionate to the value of their contribution

- As income beneficiaries die, their share of the fund is withdrawn for use by the charity

BY THE NUMBERS

Since a life income gift donor contributes only a partial interest (the donor retains the right to income), the income tax charitable deduction is less than the fair market value of the property or money contributed. Following is a brief overview of the calculation of the deductible amount:

- In general, the charitable deduction is for the estimated value of the contribution to the charity—the value of the money or property contributed, minus the value of the right of the income beneficiary to receive income

- Formulae, factors, other variables, and a discount rate[8] are specified by U.S. Treasury Regulations

- Charitable Gift Annuity

  - Begin with the value of money or the fair market value of property or other assets contributed

  - Then subtract the present value of a annuity (which is the value retained by the donor)

  - The remainder is the amount of the charitable deduction

- Charitable Remainder Trust or Pooled Income Fund

  - Begin with the value of money or the fair market value of property or other assets contributed

  - Then subtract the present value of the income expected to be paid to the beneficiaries (which is the value retained by the donor)

  - The remainder is the amount of the charitable deduction

- General rules of thumb:

---

[8] The "Applicable Federal Rate" (AFR), sometimes called the "Charitable Midterm Federal Rate" (CMFR) or the "7520 Rate," is the IRS discount rate used to determine the charitable deduction for most planned gifts. It is the assumed rate of return that the gift assets will earn during the gift term. The IRS discount rate changes monthly. It equals 120% of the annualized average yield of U.S. Treasury instruments over the past 30 days that have remaining maturities of 3-9 years. The higher the IRS discount rate, the higher the deduction for charitable remainder trusts and gift annuities, and the lower the deduction for charitable lead trusts and retained life estates. Fluctuations in the IRS discount rate affect unitrust deductions far less than annuity trust and gift annuity deductions.

- **Older beneficiaries, lower payouts = larger deduction** – the older the beneficiary and/or the lower the payout, the larger the deduction because the charity can be expected to pay less to the income beneficiary thus leaving more for charity

- **Younger beneficiaries, higher payouts = smaller deduction** – the younger the beneficiary and/or the higher the payout, the smaller the deduction because the charity can be expected to pay more to the income beneficiary. It is also true that more beneficiaries leads to a smaller deduction.

- Technology to the rescue!

  Fortunately for development officers, readily available software can provide quick and accurate calculations. Programs such as *Planned Giving Manager* software by PG Calc® can calculate deductions and compare different gift plans and options (e.g., sell and reinvest versus make a contribution). In addition, the software can model financial results over time and prepare appealing presentations and formal documentation.

CHARITABLE GIFT ANNUITY

A charitable gift annuity is a contractual promise issued by the charity to pay a fixed dollar amount annually for the lifetime of one or two individuals. The contract is issued in exchange for a contribution. Gift annuity contracts are fully backed by the financial assets of the charity that issues the annuity.

> A sample generic charitable gift annuity contract is in Appendix C on page A-5.

ANNUITY PAYMENTS AND AMOUNT

Payments to the income beneficiary (annuitant) must be at least annual but can be more often. Quarterly is a common payment schedule. Payments can start now or at some fixed date in the future (a "deferred payment gift annuity").

The amount of the annuity is fixed at the time the gift is made and cannot be changed. Although the amount can be negotiated between the charity and the donor, in most cases the amount is set by referring to the rates recommended by the American Council on Gift Annuities. For example, following are the latest (effective since January 1, 2012) recommended rates for a single life gift annuity for various ages:

Age	Rate	Age	Rate	Age	Rate	Age	Rate
5-10	2.0	44-45	3.3	64	4.6	78	6.4
11-15	2.1	46	3.4	65	4.7	79	6.6
16-19	2.2	47	3.5	66-67	4.8	80	6.8
20-23	2.3	48-49	3.6	68	4.9	81	7.0
24-26	2.4	50	3.7	69	5.0	82	7.2
27-29	2.5	51-52	3.8	70	5.1	83	7.4
30-32	2.6	53-54	3.9	71	5.3	84	7.6
33-34	2.7	55	4.0	72	5.4	85	7.8
35-36	2.8	56-57	4.1	73	5.5	86	8.0
37-38	2.9	58	4.2	74	5.7	87	8.2
39-40	3.0	59	4.3	75	5.8	88	8.4
41-42	3.1	60-61	4.4	76	6.0	89	8.7
43	3.2	62-63	4.5	77	6.2	90+	9.0

Current recommended gift annuity rates for both single and two-life gift annuities are available at the American Council on Gift Annuities Web site at http:acga-web.org.

ANNUITANTS (BENEFICIARIES)

There can be no more than two beneficiaries of a charitable gift annuity contract, and they both must be named at the time the gift annuity is issued.

TAXATION OF ANNUITY PAYMENTS

The payment to the beneficiary of a gift annuity is taxed as follows:

- **Part tax-free** – a portion of each payment is deemed to be due to the donor's "investment in the contract," and a return of that which already belongs to the donor which is therefore tax-free

- **Part taxed as capital gain income** – if long term appreciated capital gain property was contributed and the donor is the annuitant (which is usually the case), then the portion of the payment deemed to be "investment in the contract" that is attributable to the capital gain will be taxed as capital gain income. (If the donor is not the annuitant, then the donor must report all of this capital gain in the year of the gift and the tax-free portion of the annuity payments becomes greater.)

- **Ordinary income** – the remainder of the payment is taxed as ordinary income

Payments after the end of the donor's actuarial life expectancy are entirely taxed as ordinary income because the donor is assumed to have recovered his or her entire "investment in the contract."

STATE REGULATION

Charitable gift annuities are subject to regulation under state law. Many states exempt charitable gift annuities from regulation, while others require registration of the gift annuity and some require annual reporting. Some states regulate only the charities in the state, other states take the position that out-of-state charities must comply with state regulations if they make annuity payments to a state resident. The American Council on Gift Annuities is a good resource for current state regulations. Charitable organizations should consult their own advisors before issuing gift annuities, especially if annuitants reside out of state.

REQUIRED DISCLOSURE

The Philanthropy Protection Act (1995) exempts most life income gifts from securities registration requirements provided that (among other things) full and complete disclosure is made to prospective donors prior to the making of a gift. Following is a sample disclosure statement designed to meet these requirements.

Example: Gift Annuity Disclosure Statement

A gift annuity is a simple contract between the donor and Charity. In exchange for the donor's contribution, Charity promises to make fixed, guaranteed payments for life to one or two annuitants (usually, but not necessarily, the donor(s)). The amount paid is based on the age of the annuitant(s), in accordance with Charity's rate schedule.

Not a Commercial Investment

The act of establishing a gift annuity with Charity is not, and should not be viewed as, an investment. Rather, it is a way to receive annuity payments while making a charitable donation. In this respect, a gift annuity issued by Charity is different from a commercial annuity. However, the fact that you are making a charitable gift may provide you with tax benefits, including a current Federal income tax charitable deduction (if you itemize your deductions), annuity payments which are partially tax-free, and future estate tax savings.

Gift Annuity Rates

Generally, the gift annuity rates paid by Charity are those suggested by the American Council on Gift Annuities, which is a national organization of charities that has been in existence since 1927. These rates have been calculated so as to provide attractive payments to the donor and/or other annuitant(s) and also to result in a significant portion of the contribution remaining for the charity. The rates are lower than those available through commercial annuities offered by insurance companies and other financial institutions because a charitable gift is involved.

Assets Backing Annuity

The annuity payments are a general obligation of Charity, and they are backed by all of our assets (subject to security interests). On <date> our total invested funds exceeded $<amount>, and they are invested in <types of investments>. Assets received by Charity for gift annuities are managed internally, in a conservative and disciplined manner. If Charity should ever fail financially, individuals entitled to receive annuities will qualify as general creditors of Charity.

Responsibility for governing Charity, which was established in <year>, is vested in a Board of Directors comprised of <number> persons, who are self-appointed. Common investment funds managed by our organization are exempt from registration requirements of the Federal securities laws, pursuant to the exemption for collective investment funds and similar funds maintained by

---

charitable organizations under the Philanthropy Protection Act of 1995 (P.L. 104-62). Information in this letter is provided to you in accordance with the requirements of that Act.

Points to Remember

A contribution for a gift annuity is irrevocable. The principal you contribute cannot be returned to you.

The right to annuity payments may not be assigned to any person or organization, other than Charity.

CHARITABLE GIFT ANNUITY EXAMPLES

Assume a donor, age 72, wishes to make a contribution of $25,000 in exchange for a charitable gift annuity, naming herself as the annuitant. Following are the results for a contribution of cash:

SUMMARY OF BENEFITS: *5.4% CHARITABLE GIFT ANNUITY*

ASSUMPTIONS:	
Annuitant	72
Cash Donated	$25,000
Annuity Rate	5.4%
Payment Schedule	quarterly at end
BENEFITS:	
Charitable Deduction	**$9,915.50**
Annuity	**$1,350.00**
Tax-free Portion	$1,040.85
Ordinary Income	$309.15

After 14.5 years, the entire annuity becomes ordinary income.

IRS Discount Rate is 1.8%

(The detailed actuarial calculations for this example are in Appendix E1 on page A-11.)

Now assume the donor funds the gift annuity with appreciated securities now worth $25,000 for which she paid $5,000 a number of years ago. Note that the only difference is in the taxation of the annuity payments, a portion of which is now capital gain income.

81

Summary of Benefits: *5.4% Charitable Gift Annuity*

Assumptions:	
Annuitant	72
Principal Donated	$25,000
Cost Basis of Property	$5,000
Annuity Rate	5.4%
Payment Schedule	quarterly at end
Benefits:	
Charitable Deduction	**$9,915.50**
Annuity	**$1,350.00**
Tax-free Portion	$208.17
Capital Gain Income	$832.68
Ordinary Income	$309.15
After 14.5 years, the entire annuity becomes ordinary income.	
IRS Discount Rate is 1.8%	

(The detailed actuarial calculations for this example are in Appendix E2 on page A-13.)

Deferred Payment Gift Annuity

An alternative form of the gift annuity allows the donor to postpone the date of the first payment for a period of time. This "deferred payment gift annuity" can be especially advantageous for donors who are now in their high income years and are interested in making a contribution now that will provide payments to them in the future perhaps when they reach retirement. Since the charity holds the gift for a period before making the first payment, the amount of the annuity can be greater than an annuity that begins payments immediately.

Following is an example of a deferred payment gift annuity, funded with $25,000 in cash, for a donor who is age 55 at the time of the gift and agrees to postpone the first payment for 15 years until he is age 65. Note that the annuity rate, 7.6%, is considerably higher than the 3.7% rate for an immediate annuity for a 50 year-old. The higher rate is because of the 15 year deferral period.

SUMMARY OF BENEFITS: *7.6% DEFERRED CHARITABLE GIFT ANNUITY*

ASSUMPTIONS:	
Annuitant	50
Age at First Payment	65
Cash Donated	$25,000
Annuity Rate	7.6%
Payment Schedule	quarterly at end
BENEFITS:	
Charitable Deduction	**$6,237.00**
Annuity	**$1,900.00**
Tax-free Portion	$942.40
Ordinary Income	$957.60

After 19.9 years from when payments begin, the entire annuity becomes ordinary income.

IRS Discount Rate is 1.8%

(The detailed actuarial calculations for this example are in Appendix E3 on page A-15.)

Finally, assume the donor has decided to fund the deferred payment gift annuity with $25,000 in appreciated property that cost $5,000 a number of years ago. Note that the only difference is the taxation of the annuity payments, which now include a portion of capital gain income.

SUMMARY OF BENEFITS: *7.6% DEFERRED CHARITABLE GIFT ANNUITY*

ASSUMPTIONS:	
Annuitant	50
Age at First Payment	65
Principal Donated	$25,000
Cost Basis of Property	$5,000
Annuity Rate	7.6%
Payment Schedule	quarterly at end
BENEFITS:	
Charitable Deduction	**$6,237.00**
Annuity	**$1,900.00**
Tax-free Portion	$188.48
Capital Gain Income	$753.92
Ordinary Income	$957.60

After 19.9 years, the entire annuity becomes ordinary income.

IRS Discount Rate is 1.8%

(The detailed actuarial calculations for this example are in Appendix E4 on page A-17.)

CHARITABLE REMAINDER TRUSTS

There are many different types of trusts, some with highly specialized uses. In general, trusts function as follows:

- The grantor (or donor) transfers money or property to a trustee along with a legal instrument providing instructions for operation of the trust (the trust agreement)

- The trustee:

  - Holds, sells, invests and reinvests the trust's assets

  - Makes payments to the income to beneficiaries as directed in the trust agreement

  - Then, when the trust ends, distributes the remainder as directed in the trust agreement

A trust can be *inter vivos* (set up during grantor's lifetime) or testamentary (created after death through the Will of the grantor).

Trusts are generally subject to state law.

A charitable remainder trust (CRT) is a special type of trust which is tax-exempt under Federal law. A charitable remainder trust separates the right to receive the income (the income interest) from the right to eventually own the trust assets themselves (the remainder interest). In order to qualify as a CRT, a trust must meet several specific requirements. Among them are:

> A sample charitable remainder unitrust document can be found in Appendix D beginning on page A-7.

- Donor contributes to charity an irrevocable right to the remainder interest

- May not be perpetual, but can last for one or more lifetimes, a term of years (not to exceed 20), or a combination of lifetimes and years, set at the time the trust is created

- The payout percentage for a unitrust must be not less than 5% and the payout amount for an annuity trust must not be less than the equivalent of 5% of the contribution

- The trust agreement must include certain specific provisions, including:

  - Acknowledgement that the trust is irrevocable

  - At least one of the income beneficiaries must be an individual

  - Payments to the income beneficiary must be made at least annually

  - Income interest must be an "annuity trust" or "unitrust" interest

  - Remainder beneficiary must be a charitable organization

There is no capital gains tax on the transfer of capital gain property to the trust and, since charitable remainder trusts are tax exempt entities, the trust does not pay capital gains tax if it sells the appreciated property.

CHARITABLE REMAINDER BENEFICIARY

As noted above, the remainder beneficiary of a qualified charitable remainder trust must be a charitable organization. However, at the time the trust is created the donor may reserve the right to change the specific charity that will receive the remainder. As a consequence, although the donor's contribution to the charitable remainder trust is irrevocable, your organization's position as remainder beneficiary may not be irrevocable.

The sample trust document provided by the Internal Revenue Service in Appendix D beginning on page A-7 names one charity irrevocably (see lines 32-34). This provision could instead reserve for the right to change the specific charity, in which case your organization might or might not receive the remainder. Note that in either case the next sentence (see lines 34-39) ensures that the remainder will be distributed only to a charity even if the donor fails to name a charitable remainder beneficiary or names a charity that is not inexistence when the trust ends.

CHARITABLE REMAINDER TRUST TYPES

There are two types of charitable remainder trusts, which differ in how the amount paid to the income beneficiary is determined:

- **Annuity trust** pays a fixed dollar amount to the income beneficiary. The amount may be determined as a percentage of the amount contributed, but once the dollar amount is determined, it never changes. (For this reason, an annuity trust *may not* accept additional contributions.)

- **Unitrust** pays a fixed percentage of the value of the trust fund, as re-valued each year. Once the percentage is set, it cannot be changed. However, since the value of the trust fund changes each year, the actual amount paid to the income beneficiary will vary. A unitrust *may* accept additional contributions.

Further, there are four types of charitable remainder unitrusts. In each case the trustee values the trust assets each year and applies the unitrust percentage in order to determine the unitrust amount for that year. However, the actual amount paid to the income beneficiaries is determined differently depending upon the type of unitrust.

- **"Basic," "Standard," "Type I," or "SCRUT"** – the trustee pays the unitrust payment amount and can distribute principal if required to make the payment

- **"Net Income," "Type II," or "NICRUT"** – the income beneficiary receives the unitrust payment amount or the trust's net income, whichever is *less*, but the trustee must not distribute principal—for example, if the unitrust payout rate is 5% but the trust earns only 4%, the beneficiary will receive the smaller amount

- **"Net Income with Make-Up," "Type III," or "NIMCRUT"** – pays the unitrust payment amount or the trust's net income, whichever is *less* (just like the Net Income Unitrust), but keeps track of shortfalls and pays make-up payments in years when there is excess income (not likely to occur at today's very low interest rates)

- **"Flip Trust"** – begins as either a "Net Income" or "Net Income with Make-up" type, but then transforms into a "Standard" type upon the occurrence of some event in the future, such as the sale of a piece of real estate or a specific date.

| **Note:** | With the exception of a "Flip" provision, a unitrust cannot change its type once it is created. |

INCOME TAXES TO BENEFICIARIES

Income paid to the beneficiary of a charitable remainder trust is subject to taxation depending upon the source of the funds the trustee uses to make the payment. Since the charitable remainder trust itself is tax-exempt, it pays no income taxes. Essentially, the trust passes through the income tax obligation when it makes distributions to its income beneficiaries. In other words, the dollars paid to the income beneficiary retain the same tax character they would have had if the trust had been required to pay income tax itself. For example, the trust can collect interest income and pay no income tax, however if the trust then distributes that interest income to an income beneficiary, the beneficiary will have to pay income tax on the interest.

The trustee must follow a strict set of rules to determine which funds are used to make payments to the income beneficiaries. The so-called "Four Tier Payout Rule" specifies that the trustee must payout income in the following order:

- First, all "net income" (interest and dividends) and any undistributed net income from previous years—which is taxed as ordinary income to the beneficiary

- Second, all realized long term capital gains income and any undistributed long term capital gains income from previous years—which is taxed as capital gain income

- Third, all tax-exempt income and any undistributed tax-exempt income from previous years—which is tax-exempt to the beneficiary

- Finally, principal of the trust—which is tax-free to the income beneficiary

In categories that include more than one kind of income, the income taxed at the highest rate is distributed first. For example, bond interest and qualified dividends are both forms of ordinary income, but bond interest is taxed at a higher rate than qualified dividends, so all of the bond interest will be distributed before any of the qualified dividends.

> **Example**: **a $25,000 payment from a unitrust might consist of four types of income**
>
> Dividend and interest (ordinary income taxed up to 39.6%) $7,500
>
> Long-term capital gain income (taxed up to 20%) $12,500
>
> Tax-exempt income (tax free) $2,500
>
> Return of principal (tax free) $2,500
>
> TOTAL $25,000
>
> For a beneficiary in the 28% marginal income tax bracket and the 15% long-term capital gain tax bracket, the income tax due on this distribution would be $3,975 ($7,500 x 28% + $12,500 x 15%) compared to $7,000 ($25,000 x 28%) if the entire payment had been taxed as ordinary income.

CAVEAT REGARDING SECURITIES LAWS

Ambiguity regarding the application of securities laws to life income gifts and the necessity to register certain plans with the Securities Exchange Commission as investment securities was resolved by the Philanthropy Protection Act (1995), which exempts life income gifts from securities registration requirements provided that (among other things) full and complete disclosure is made to prospective donors prior to the making of a gift.

CHARITABLE REMAINDER TRUST EXAMPLES

Assume a donor, age 72, decides to create a charitable remainder unitrust which will pay him 5% of the value of the trust fund each year for the rest of his lifetime. Following is a summary of the results:

SUMMARY OF BENEFITS: 5% *CHARITABLE UNITRUST*

ASSUMPTIONS:	
Beneficiary Age	72
Cash Donated	$500,000.00
Payout Rate	5%
Payment Schedule	quarterly 3 months to first payment
BENEFITS:	
Charitable Deduction	$276,805.00
Estimated Income in first full year (future income will vary with trust value)	$25,000.00
IRS Discount Rate is 1.8%	

(The detailed actuarial calculations for this example are in Appendix E6 on page A-21.)

The selection of the charitable remainder payout percentage is a critical element in the creation of a successful charitable remainder trust. Donors are often inclined to select a high payout with the expectation that it will result in larger payments for the income beneficiaries. However, setting the payout too high can cause the trust to erode principal value which not only reduces the amount available for charity but can ultimately reduce the amount paid to the income beneficiaries.

The payout percentage must be set at the time the gift is made and cannot be changed later. By law the percentage cannot be less than 5% and cannot be so high that the resulting charitable deduction is less than 10% of the amount contributed. When discussing the payout with your donor, keep in mind the following points:

- A higher payout percentage reduces the value of the charitable deduction. Depending upon the IRS discount rate in effect at the time of the gift, a 1% increase in a unitrust payout amount can result in a 10% (or more) loss in the charitable deduction as illustrated in the table below:

Charitable Deduction for $500,000 Contribution to a 5% Unitrust

Payout Rate:	5%	6%	7%	8%	9%	10%
One Life 72	$276,805	$248,865	$224,605	$203,475	$185,015	$168,830
Two Lives 72	$220,855	$188,995	$162,170	$139,535	$120,400	$104,180
IRS Discount Rate is 1.8%						

- If the unitrust payout percentage is set higher, the trustee may be forced to select riskier investments in order to produce an investment return sufficient to meet the payout percentage. Riskier investments can bring greater variability in the trust— higher highs, hopefully, but also lower lows.

- Finally, if the unitrust payout percentage is set much higher than the excepted investment return (and the unitrust is not a net income type), the trust may be forced to consume principal in order to make the unitrust payments each year. The following graphs illustrate charitable remainder unitrusts with various payout rates, each earning a net total return of 6%. The higher payout percentage has a dramatic negative impact on the remainder left for charity and, given enough time, can actually result in a smaller payment to the income beneficiaries.

PROJECTED BENEFITS: *CHARITABLE REMAINDER UNITRUSTS*

ASSUMPTIONS:

Projection runs for 20 years
Original principal is $500,000 Cost basis is $100,000
Beneficiary income tax bracket is 43.4%, 23.8% for long-term capital gains
Net Total Return is 6%: 2% income and 4% appreciation

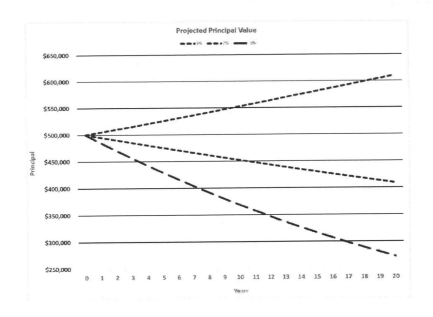

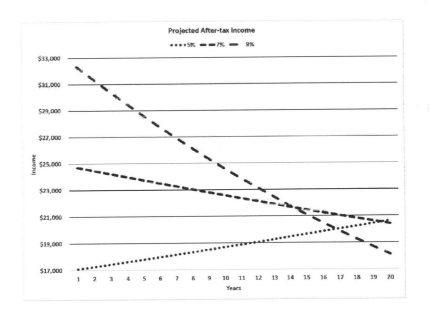

89

Sometimes it can be helpful to provide prospective donors with an illustration of the projected value of a charitable remainder trust over their lifetimes. Following is an example of a life income projection for a charitable remainder unitrust comparing various payout rates and assuming the same investment return in each case:

PROJECTED BENEFITS: *CHARITABLE REMAINDER UNITRUSTS*

ASSUMPTIONS:

Projection runs for 20 years.
Measuring life age 72.
Original principal is $500,000. Cost basis is $100,000.
Donor income tax bracket is 43.3%, 39.6% for tax savings, 23.8% for capital gains.
Beneficiary income tax bracket is 43.4%, 23.8% for long-term capital gains.
Net Total Return is 6%: 2% income and 4% appreciation.
Contributed assets are sold in first year.

	Charitable Unitrust 5%	Charitable Unitrust 7%	Charitable Unitrust 9%
1) Gross Principal	$500,000	$500,000	$500,000
2) Average Annual Beneficiary Payment	$27,524	$31,866	$34,215
3) Charitable Deduction	$276,805	$224,605	$185,015
4) Income Tax Savings	$109,615	$88,944	$73,266
5) After-tax Cost of Gift	$390,385	$411,056	$426,734
6) Total Before Tax Beneficiary Payment	$550,475	$637,326	$684,308
7) Total After-tax Beneficiary Payment	$376,305	$449,952	$491,638
8) Projected Remainder to Charity	$610,095	$408,953	$271,897
9) Total Benefit (7 + 8)	$986,400	$858,905	$763,535
IRS Discount Rate is 1.8%			

Finally, donors might wish to consider a charitable remainder trust as an alternative to selling an appreciated property, paying the capital gains tax, and reinvesting the proceeds. The following example compares the charitable remainder trust with selling and reinvesting (and making no gift at the present time). This example makes the same investment assumptions for both alternatives. Note that the charitable remainder trust results in greater income and a larger amount remaining. The reason is that the capital gains tax is not paid and therefore the trust begins with a larger amount of capital to invest.

ASSUMPTIONS:

Projection runs for 20 years.

Measuring life age 72.

Original principal is $500,000. Cost basis is $100,000.

Donor income tax bracket is 43.4%, 39.6 for tax savings, 23.8% for capital gains.

Beneficiary income tax bracket is 43.4%, 23.8% for capital gains.

	Kept Intact	Sold and Reinvested	Unitrust 5%
1) Gross Principal	$500,000	$500,000	$500,000
2) Net Principal	$500,000	$404,800	$500,000
3) Average Annual Beneficiary Payment	$14,889	$22,283	$27,524
4) Charitable Deduction	0	0	$276,805
5) Income Tax Savings	0	0	$109,615
6) Capital Gains Tax	0	$95,200	0
7) After-tax Cost	$500,000	$500,000	$390,385
Investment Income	2%	5%	2%
Investment Capital Appreciation	4%	1%	4%
8) Total Before Tax Beneficiary Payment	$297,781	$455,665	$550,475
9) Total After-tax Beneficiary Payment	$168,544	$252,246	$376,305
10) Total Left to Heirs	$1,095,562	$493,933	0
11) Remainder to Charity	0	0	$610,095
12) Total Benefit (9 + 10 + 11)	$1,264,105	$746,179	$986,400
IRS Discount Rate is 1.8%			

CHARITABLE LEAD TRUSTS

The charitable lead trust is, essentially, the inverse of a charitable remainder trust. A charitable lead trust pays income to one or more charities and then distributes its remainder to one or more individuals, just the opposite of a charitable remainder trust.

Like the charitable remainder trust, there are two types of charitable lead trusts:

- **Annuity lead trust** – pays a fixed dollar amount each year

- **Unitrust lead trust** – pays a fixed percentage of the trust's value each year

Unlike the charitable remainder trust, there are no "net income" or "flip" options available with a unitrust-type charitable lead trust.

Further, since charitable lead trusts are not tax-exempt, the donor must choose the tax treatment of the trust when it is created. There are two types:

- **Non-grantor lead trust** – The trust's income each year is not taxable to the grantor (donor). The donor receives no income tax deduction for creating the trust, but does receive a gift tax deduction based upon the value of the charity's right to receive income.

- **Grantor lead trust** – The trust's income each year is taxable to the grantor (donor). The donor receives an income tax deduction based upon the charity's right to receive income, but receives no gift tax deduction.

Charitable lead trusts are most often used in sophisticated financial and estate planning as a method to reduce gift and estate taxes. The most common use is a non-grantor charitable lead trust used to eventually pass assets to heirs with reduced gift or estate taxes. While the details of this application are very complex, these are the essential points:

- When a donor creates a charitable lead trust, he or she makes a contribution to charity extending over a number of years, but he or she also makes a gift to the individual who will eventually receive the remainder of the trust.

- Like any other gift to an individual, the gift of the remainder interest is subject to the gift tax. Since the charitable lead trust is irrevocable, the taxable gift is deemed to have been made at the time the trust is funded, even though the individual will not receive the remainder until sometime in the future.

- However, the donor can use the gift tax deduction from the non-grantor charitable lead trust to reduce—or in some cases eliminate—the amount of the taxable gift.

The target audience for charitable lead trusts is highly affluent individuals and families who are most concerned about estate and gift taxes. In order to take maximum advantage of the tax incentives offered by a charitable lead trust, the donor must be able to afford to part with the income from a significant sized asset for a number of years in return for estate and gift tax savings.

CHARITABLE LEAD TRUST EXAMPLE

Assume a wealthy donor is willing to commit $10 million to a charitable lead trust that will pay an annual amount to charity for 20 years before distributing its principal to his or her heirs. If the charitable payout is set high enough, the donor will receive a Federal gift tax deduction equal to the value of the taxable gift of the remainder interest to his or her heirs which will avoid the gift tax due, as illustrated below:

Example: **Charitable Lead Trust eliminates gift taxes**

Assumptions:

- Non-grantor charitable annuity lead trust runs for 20 years.

- Trust is funded with $10 million dollars.

- Trust makes annual payments of $612,500 to charity.

- Remainder is distributed to the donor's heirs.

- Donor's estate will be taxed at the current Federal Estate Tax rates.

Results:

Over the 20 year term of the trust, the charity will receive a total of $12.5 million in equal annual payments of $612,500.

The donor will have made an irrevocable gift to his or her heirs of the remainder interest in the trust. Although this potentially will be a taxable gift, the gift and estate tax deduction resulting from the contribution to the lead trust will off-set and "zero out" the taxable gift, eliminating the possibility of gift or estate tax on this transfer to heirs. Assuming that this gift would otherwise have been taxed at the current 40% estate and gift tax rate, this is a potential tax savings of $4 million.

At the end of the trust, 20 years from now, the heirs will receive whatever is remaining in the trust without additional gift taxes.

Note: | This example assumes that the gift and estate tax system and its rates remain in place for 20 years from now as they stand. If the estate tax is reduced (or eliminated), then a bequest to the heirs might produce a more favorable tax result.

RETAINED LIFE ESTATE

A donor can irrevocably contribute his or her personal residence or farm to charity but retain the right to continue to live in it for his or her lifetime. This gift arrangement is called a "retained life estate."

The donor receives a current income tax deduction for the calculated value of the remainder interest that has been contributed to charity.

The donor continues to be responsible for routine expenses—maintenance fees, insurance, property taxes, repairs, etc.—while retaining the right to live in the property.

If, later on, the donor decides to vacate the property, he or she can simply accelerate the charity's right to fully own the property and receive an additional income tax deduction at that time. Less commonly, the donor may work with the charity to rent all or part of the property to someone else or sell the property in cooperation with the charity.

Once the retained life estate ends, the charity can then sell or use the property for its charitable purposes.

Following is an example of a retained life estate gift funded with a personal residence worth $500,000:

SUMMARY OF BENEFITS: *RETAINED LIFE ESTATE*

ASSUMPTIONS:	
Life Tenant Age	72
Value of Property	$500,000.00
Cost Basis of Property	$100,000.00
Value of Building(s)	$350,000.00
Estimated Useful Life of Building(s)	45 years
Salvage Value of Building(s)	$115,000.00
BENEFITS:	
Charitable Deduction	$349,922.50
IRS Discount Rate is 1.8%.	

(The detailed actuarial calculations for this example are in Appendix E10 on page A-23.)

Note: Retained life estate agreements are not limited to a private residence or home. Any property used by the donor as a "personal residence" can be used, not only a principal residence. Vacation homes and recreational property, for example, make excellent gifts of this type.

A retained life estate in a farm need not be the entire farm property.

Planned Giving in a Nutshell

Organizational Readiness

A successful planned giving program requires more than generous donors and skilled development staff. It also requires a high level of commitment on the part of the charitable organization. Many planned gifts create a responsibility on the part of the charitable organization to provide services to donors and beneficiaries. In some cases the organization will incur fiduciary obligations and enter into relationships that last for one or more lifetimes. In this chapter we review some additional organization considerations including creation of policies and procedures, managing the probate process, verification of legal and tax exempt status, and handling restrictions placed on gifts.

POLICIES AND PROCEDURES

Planned gifts stand apart from other simpler forms of charitable giving. Planned gifts are far more technical and complex, require specialized knowledge, involve long term cultivation of donors, and rely heavily on outside professional advice. The development officer involved in planned gifts must routinely work with attorneys, CPAs, trust officers, life underwriters, financial planners and other professionals. Close ties are often formed with donors and members of their families, and these relationships can endure for lifetimes.

In addition, many planned gifts, by design, involve splitting interests between the charitable organization and the donor. The successful completion of a planned gift often requires negotiation and compromise between the donor and the organization. These "split interest" transactions require that the interests of the parties be carefully balanced. Throughout the course of gift negotiations, the organization may be required to make important decisions which will have an impact on the gift and the organization's obligations. In addition, the split interest environment abounds with potential conflicts of interest for the development officer and his or her organization.

For these reasons it is imperative that the charitable organization have in place a set of well-developed institutional policies and procedures that are strong enough to protect the interests of the organization while still providing flexibility and guidance to encourage the negotiation and acceptance of high quality charitable gifts that benefit both the organization and help the donor fulfill his or her charitable objectives.

POLICY DEVELOPMENT PROCESS

The *process* of developing and adopting policies and procedures is as important as the final product. During a thorough policy development process your organization will engage in a healthy internal dialog regarding alternatives and issues that will inevitably arise as you pursue more complex charitable gift situations. Rather than wrestling with such issues under time pressure and with a contribution hanging in the balance, a workable set of policies and procedures will provide a basis for thoughtful deliberation and good decision making that will serve both the organization and the donor.

The policy development process should not be shortchanged. As tempting as it may be to simply adopt the policies of another organization, the result will be unsatisfactory. The process should be a collaborative effort including the development office, the business office, legal counsel, and leadership. While it will probably fall to the development office to lead the process, the creation of policies and procedures should never be a solitary effort.

You may consider forming a task force or advisory committee. Members should have an understanding of your organization and its processes and expertise or interest in subject areas to be covered by your new policies and procedures such as internal processes, legal affairs, financial records, and marketing. The group may need to meet several times before arriving at a final document ready for presentation to the governing board. Additional staff support may be required for research, distribution of material to committee members, planning agendas, making assignments and managing the process.

Creating your policies and procedures can begin with the materials in this text. You may wish to review the policies of other organizations. However, you should not haphazardly adopt the work of others. Carefully studying your own circumstances and engaging both internal and external stakeholders will help ensure that you settle on a set of policies and procedures that best serve needs of your organization and your donors.

Here is a topic outline typical of a comprehensive set of policies.

> Institution or Organization
>> Legal name and address
>> Documentation of exempt status
>> Statement of charitable purpose
>> Affiliation
>> Governing body
>
> Program Authorization
>> Enabling policy statement authorizing engagement in planned gifts
>> Authorization for negotiation and decision making hierarchy
>> Authorization to sign agreements and contracts
>
> General Policies and Procedures

Conflict of interest
Use of professional counsel
Professional and ethical standards
Confidentiality
Roles and responsibilities: Development Office and Business Office
Investment approach
Limitations
Composition of written proposals
Follow-up procedures

Specific Policies – Gift Acceptance
Minimum ages
Minimum gift size
Gift Restrictions
Difficult to value property
Debt encumbered property
Gifts by Will
Split interest gifts
Charitable Gift Annuity
Charitable Remainder Annuity Trust
Charitable Remainder Unitrust

Record Management and Retention
Mailing lists
Prospect information
Finalized agreements and Wills in probate

Supplementary Information
Directory of key positions / organization chart
Liaison with governing board
Professional counsel
Advisory Council and/or Planned Giving Committee

Additional policy issues you may wish to consider depending upon your organization's circumstances include:

- Care and caution in working with donors who are ill, near death, or incompetent

- Working with the heirs of donors

- Resolution regarding "finder's fees"

- Whether or not proposed contributions of real estate will be considered, under what circumstances

- Clarification of duties and relationships of the development office and business office

- Trustee for charitable split-interest gifts: The organization? Bank or trust company? Individual? Clarification regarding fees and accountability

- Method and approach for counting and crediting planned gifts for donor records, campaign goals, endowment goals, present value, matured value and projecting expectancies

- Relationship of the planned giving program and staff to other fund raising activities of the organization, including capital/endowment campaign

The work of actually drafting of the policy document will most likely fall to you or another staff member; writing by committee is almost never a workable approach. However, you should involve committee members seeking and incorporating their comments and changes. Plan to go through several drafts before you finalize the document. Of course, your chief executive officer, chief business officer and members of the development staff should be kept advised on progress in order to help ensure they are invested in the final product.

Depending upon your organization's governance model, formal adoption of the policies by the governing board may or may not be required. In any case, securing the support of the governing board is important. Planned gifts involve serious commitments on the part of the organization and it is crucial that the governing board be fully aware of the organization's policies and procedures and that they understand and support the representations being made by the staff on behalf of the organization.

Finally, once the policies and procedures are finalized, they should be documented along with other important items in a policy and procedure manual — whether hard-copy or electronic — governing the planned giving program. Following are other documents you may wish to include in this manual:

- Final version of the policy documents

- IRS determination letters certifying the tax exempt status of your organization

- Internal letters, memoranda and minutes which set or affect planned gifts negotiations

- Sample agreement and calculation forms for various types gifts

- Directory of key persons, such as the Planned Giving Committee, Development and Investment Committees of the board, and professional advisors

- Job descriptions for members of the staff

- Index of references and resources

PROBATE AND THE DEVELOPMENT OFFICE

One day in the mail arrives a letter notifying you that a donor, now deceased, has named your organization in his or her Will. Thus begins a potentially long process, one that most often goes smoothly but seldom moves quickly. As a first step, the letter itself can provide a significant important information, including:

- Name of the deceased

- State and county in which the estate will be administered

- Notice of probate

- Probate file number

- Notice of hearing(s)

- Name of the estate administrator

- Notice to creditors

- Name and address of the attorney representing the estate

- Date the Notice was filed

You may also receive a cover letter from the estate administrator or attorney for the estate with additional information and instructions, perhaps with a copy of the Will or other testamentary document.

Okay, but now what do you do? In many organizations there is some degree of confusion as to how best to respond to this initial notice, what follow-up steps should be taken, and whether it is the development office, the business office, or someone else who should be responsible.

One person in your organization should be charged with the responsibility to manage estate gifts and the estate administrator or attorney should be notified to direct communications to that individual. During the course of estate administration there may be numerous contacts among the estate administrator, attorney, and your organization. These communications will be much more efficient if one individual has responsibility for managing the relationship.

Following is an outline of the basic steps and timing for a typical estate administration. Of course each situation is different. Most cases will proceed efficiently and require little involvement on your part, but others may require a great deal of attention.

Response to Initial Notice

- Set up file under name of the deceased donor

- List the estate in your ledger of deferred gift expectancies

- Write to the estate administrator or attorney:

- Provide your IRS determination letter as evidence of tax exempt status — sooner or later the estate administrator will require this information

- Request a copy of the Will or trust if it has not already been provided

- Request a copy of the Inventory and Appraisement when filed and the Federal Estate Tax Return if it is to be filed

- Request a copy of the Final Account when prepared

- Ask for name(s) of closest survivor(s) who may be contacted for purposes of expressing appreciation for the deceased donor's generosity

- Prepare a summary report for your management:

- Provide the name and location of the deceased, with information on his or her past relationship to your organization

- Summarize the anticipated amount of the contribution and note any special circumstances or anticipated problems

- Make note of restrictions and any unusual conditions

- Provide an estimate of how long the probate is expected to take — estimate at least a year unless you have reason to expect otherwise

- As they arise, alert management to specific problems that occur during the course of estate administration

Six Months After Initial Notice

- Request a status report from the estate administrator

- Request copy of Inventory and Appraisement, unless already received

One Year After Initial Notice

- Request a status report from the estate administrator

- Request a copy of the Federal estate tax return if required

Eighteen Months After Initial Notice

- Request a status report

- Request copy of the Final Account

Continue taking follow-up steps until the estate is finally closed and the assets have been distributed. Ordinarily, your organization will be asked to execute a receipt acknowledging payment, usually prepared by the estate administrator.

Finally, make certain to follow-up internally with your business office, program staff and others to make certain that the restrictions and purposes of the bequest are understood and will be honored

Depending upon the specific circumstances, it may be appropriate to contact surviving members of the family to express thanks and steward the bequest.

RIGHTS AND RESPONSIBILITIES

As a beneficiary of an estate, your organization has a right to receive documents and reports from the administrator of the estate. Occasionally you may encounter resistance to your requests for this information. Remember that the responsibility for estate rests with the estate administrator, attorney, and the probate court. While you should avoid becoming a nuisance or an obstacle, you should not be reluctant to follow-up assertively if need be. The deceased donor has entrusted your organization with his or her charitable dreams. You have an obligation to the donor to ensure that the estate moves toward closure.

In most cases the estate administration process moves smoothly, albeit sometimes slowly. However, breakdowns will sometimes occur requiring action on your part. Your goal should be to make sure all of the property and/or funds designated for your organization are distributed in accordance with the wishes of the deceased donor.

As the charitable beneficiary, your organization has the right to protect its interests against fiduciary malfeasance or negligence. Key items to watch are:

- Unexplained delays in payment

- Signs of investment mismanagement or questionable financial conduct

- Loss through avoidable taxation

- Adoption of legal positions or interpretations adverse to the interests of the donor or the charitable organization

It is best to secure a complete copy of the Will, even though the section dealing with your bequest may be only a very brief statement. Other parts of the Will may add, subtract, or otherwise modify the language that mentions your interests. Note that in the case of a trust, your organization may or may not be entitled to a copy of the entire document. If there is any question, qualified legal counsel should study the Will and/or trust and provide your office with a summary and recommendations.

Occasionally the restrictions placed on the bequest may make it unadvisable to accept the contribution. In these cases, you should involve your management and leadership as early as possible so that they can determine what steps to take. Under certain circumstances you may be able to ask the Courts to clarify unreasonable restrictions. Ultimately, your organization may determine that it is best to decline the contribution.

Finally, be aware that most of the proceedings in probate court are a matter of public record and the involvement and behavior of your organization during the administration of the estate may become a matter of public interest. The best starting point for your organization is to respect and trust the legal process. In general, your organization has a right to expect the work of estate administration to be completed on a timely basis, and then to receive for review an accounting of what has been done. The position of your organization ought to be that of an ally of the deceased donor in fulfilling his or her charitable interests.

STEPS TOWARD FINAL RESOLUTION

How should you proceed if you come to suspect that objectionable acts, such as unreasonable delays, neglect, or even malfeasance have occurred?

The first step may be a letter to the estate administrator or attorney expressing concern and requesting clarification. Often this resolves the problem, and the estate administrator will begin to act in a more cautious and responsible manner. Or, you may learn of extenuating circumstances related to the probate over which the estate administrator has no control.

As a next step you may request a meeting with the estate administrator to discuss your concerns. Before going to the meeting be sure to study the record carefully, keeping in mind the sequence of actions over time since the first notice, the positive results that have been achieved thus far, and the specific points of concern to your organization. Following the meeting you should write a letter to the estate administrator clearly stating the substance of your visit, and details the expected outcomes, both in time and action.

If the problem persists, or the acts of the estate administrator could cause imminent harm to the charitable intentions of the deceased donor, you should engage legal counsel.

CHARITIES MUST ACT RESPONSIBLY

The preceding discussion has been one-sided, from the point-of-view of the charitable organization. Unfortunately, the experiences of estate administrators and probate attorneys dealing with charitable beneficiaries are not uniformly positive either. Sometimes charities fail to respond to requests for routine information, procrastinate in making decisions, delay the execution of receipts and other important documents, and worse. Such acts by the charity only cause delay and increase the costs of estate administration ultimately harming the beneficiaries of the estate and delaying the good work the deceased donor envisioned.

One of the best ways to avoid these problems is to make certain that all contacts with family, attorneys, estate administrators, and courts regarding estate gifts are assigned to one individual in the charitable organization and ensuring that this person is well supported and delegated the appropriate authority to act.

In reality, handling your organization's involvement in an estate is a simple matter of good donor relations.

STATEMENT OF LEGAL AND TAX EXEMPT STATUS

It is good practice to maintain and readily make available a document setting forth the legal and tax exempt status of your organization. The document, which might be only a page in length, should include several items:

- The full legal name of your organization or agency
- Address and phone number
- Statement of charitable purpose
- Explanation of governance responsibility
- State of incorporation and identification number (if appropriate)
- IRS Employee Identification Number (Federal EIN)
- The name, title, and phone number of the institutional contact person

You should also have on hand a copy of the letter from the Internal Revenue Service certifying the tax exempt status of your organization. Often this letter is very old, sometimes dating back to the time the organization was founded. Frequently there will be later correspondence from the IRS affirming that the original certification remains valid. This correspondence should clearly state that:

- your organization is exemption from Federal Income Tax under Section 501(c)(3) of the Internal Revenue Code;
- contributions made to your organization are deductible as provided in Section 170 of the Code; and,
- transfers or gifts to or for the use of your organization are deductible for Federal Estate and Gift Tax purposes as provided in Sections 2055, 2106, 2522 of the Code.

GIFT RESTRICTIONS

Gifts made without any restrictions whatsoever, whether current or deferred, are usually the most valuable to the organization because they can be used for whatever purpose the governing board may decide is most appropriate. Unrestricted gifts allow the organization the most flexibility in fulfilling its charitable purpose.

However, donors often have a desire to have some say in how their contribution is used. This is especially true of large gifts and more sophisticated donors. For this reason, most organizations are willing to consider donors' restrictions and accept them as long as they are reasonable.

Donor restrictions are many and quite varied. Most are routine and cause little concern. Some general guidelines to consider when contemplating a donor's proposed restrictions include:

- A restricted gift should never be accepted if the organization cannot realistically expect to honor the restriction.

- The mission and charitable purpose of the organization should govern. The availability of a restricted gift should not diminish the organization's primary mission.

- Consideration should be given to the adequacy of amount of funding. The contribution should be sufficient to accomplish the restriction.

- Sustainability should be determined. It may be appropriate to initiate temporary or limited programs based upon a restricted contribution, but the expectation that the program or initiative will be short-lived should be acceptable to the organization.

- Once accepted, the conditions of the restricted gift must be carefully managed inside the organization so that the funds are used in a timely way and for the purposes agreed upon.

DOCUMENTATION

Depending upon the size of the contribution and the complexity of the restriction, it is a good practice to create a formal written "gift agreement."

For smaller gifts and more general restrictions, you may wish to create special restricted funds to which many like-minded donors may contribute. For example, a general scholarship fund can accept contributions from a great number of donors all of whom agree that general scholarship support is important.

However, as gifts become larger and restrictions more complex a written gift agreement provides solid documentation of the understandings and conditions of the gift. Depending upon your organization's practices the gift agreement can be as simple as an exchange of letters or as formal as a contract drafted by legal counsel. A sample gift agreement is included in Appendix B on page A-3.

DISCRETIONARY CLAUSE

Whenever the purpose of a gift is restricted, it is good practice to include a "discretionary clause" which grants authority to the governing board to alter the restriction at some future date should it become necessary. An example a discretionary clause is:

"The Fund shall at all times be subject to the power of the Board to eliminate or modify any restriction, condition, or limitation imposed with respect to the Fund if, in the judgment of the Board, such restriction, condition, or limitation becomes unnecessary, incapable of fulfillment, or inconsistent with the charitable purposes of Charity Name. In such event the Fund shall be used for purposes as the Board determines are not inconsistent with the charitable intentions of the Donor."

Initially donors may be wary of a discretionary clause fearing that it empowers the charity to arbitrarily ignore their wishes. Donors should understand that the power to modify the restriction is limited to a narrow set of conditions—only if circumstances change such that the purpose becomes unfeasible. Explain to donors that since their gift may not come to be until some point in the future, and no one can know for certain what circumstances will be at that time, it is in their best interests to charge the board of your organization with the discretion to make certain that the donor's charitable objectives are fulfilled.

Finally, your organization may choose to omit the discretionary clause depending upon the circumstances of the gift. However, in the absence of discretionary provisions, if it becomes impossible to follow the restrictions the funds might go unused or your organization might need to seek Court approval to modify the restriction. Sometimes explaining to donors that the ultimate alternative is to seek Court approval can help them appreciate the value of a discretionary clause.

Planned Giving in a Nutshell

Appendices

Appendix A: Worksheet for Estimating the After-tax Cost of a Gift

Key points:

- Income tax savings effectively reduce the donor's cost of giving.

- The charitable deduction reduces taxable income which reduces the total amount of tax owed.

- These are real dollar savings that the donor receives when filing his or her income tax return.

- In addition, donors can avoid capital gains tax by contributing instead of selling appreciated property that has been held long term.

- Focusing on the after-tax cost of giving encourages donors to make gifts and can allow them to make larger gifts than they might otherwise be able to afford.

Gift of Cash

Line	Instructions	
1	Enter the amount of the contribution	$
2	Enter the donor's expected marginal (top) tax rate	%
3	Multiply Line 1 by Line 2	$
4	Subtract the amount on Line 3 from the amount on Line 1 The result is the estimated after-tax cost of this gift	$

Gift of Long-term Appreciated Property

Line	Instructions	
1	Enter the fair market value of the property to be contributed	$
2	Enter the amount the donor paid for the property	$
3	Enter the donor's expected marginal (top) tax rate	%
4	Enter the donor's expected capital gains tax rate	%
5	Multiply Line 1 by Line 3	$
6	Subtract Line 2 from Line 1	$
7	Multiply Line 6 by Line 4	$
8	Subtract the amounts on Lines 5 & Line 7 from the amount on Line 1 The result is the estimated after-tax cost of this gift	$

Appendix B: Sample Permanent Endowment Gift Instrument

<Name of Fund>

<Donor Name>, (the Donor) and the <Name of Charity> (the Charity) agree to establish the <Name of Fund> an endowment fund (the Fund) of the Charity.

NAME: The <Name of Fund>

PURPOSE: The purpose of the Fund is to <insert appropriate language restricting use of funds>.

SOURCE OF FUNDS: A contribution <of cash/stock, by bequest, etc.> in the amount of $<amount> from the Donor to the Charity will provide the initial principal of the Fund. Additional contributions to the Fund may be made by anyone at any time.

AVAILABILITY OF DISTRIBUTIONS: Distributions will be available after the end of the quarter following formal establishment of the Fund. Distributions will be made at such times and in such amounts as determined by the Charity.

DISTRIBUTIONS AND EXPENSES The Fund is a permanent endowment fund and will be administered in accordance with the *<State Statute>* as amended. The amount distributable from the Fund for the purposes described above will be determined in accordance with the endowment spending policy of the Charity as amended.

The Fund will be invested in accordance with the investment policy of the Charity as amended.

The Charity may make a charge to its endowment funds in an amount reasonably calculated to reimburse the direct and indirect costs incurred by the Charity.

The Charity will administer the Fund in a manner intended to maintain the stability of endowment support for the purposes of the Fund and to preserve the purchasing power of the Fund against inflationary pressures. Any investment returns remaining after distributions for the purposes of the Fund and payment of investment management, administrative, and other costs, shall be retained as part of the principal of the Fund.

ADMINISTRATION: The Fund is an "institutional fund" as defined under the *<State Statute>*. The Fund is not a trust and no trust relationship is created by this gift instrument.

This document is a "gift instrument" as defined under <State Statute>. This gift instrument is not a contract and does not create a contractual relationship between the Charity and any party.

This document is the entire gift instrument and contains all terms and conditions of the Fund. Changes or additions can be made only by written amendment to this gift instrument.

The assets of the Fund may be commingled with other assets of the Charity for investment purposes. Separate receipt and disbursement records will be maintained.

AMMENDMENT: The Fund shall at all times be subject to the power of the Board of the Charity to eliminate or modify any restriction, condition, or limitation imposed with respect to the Fund if, in the judgment of the Board of the Charity, such restriction, condition, or limitation becomes unnecessary, incapable of fulfillment, or inconsistent with the charitable purposes of the Charity. In such event the Fund shall be used for purposes as the Board of the Charity determines are not inconsistent with the general charitable intentions of the Donor.

Appendix C: Sample Charitable Gift Annuity

> **NOTE:** DO NOT USE THIS FORM AS-IS. It is presented for illustration only. Consult with legal counsel to develop a gift annuity agreement suitable for your purposes.

This Agreement is made between <donor> of (hereinafter "the Donor"), and <charity name>, of <address> (hereinafter "Charity").

1. Transfer of Property by Donor

Charity certifies that the Donor, as an evidence of his desire to support the work of Charity and to make a charitable gift, on <date of gift> contributed to Charity the property described in Schedule A attached hereto, the fair market value of which is $<gift amount>.

2. Payment of Annuity

In consideration of the property transferred by the Donor, Charity shall pay an annual annuity of $<annual annuity amount> from the date of this Agreement and shall pay such amount to the Donor so long as he is living.

3. Payment Dates; First Installment

The annuity shall be paid in quarterly installments of $<quarterly annuity amount>. The first installment shall be payable on <first payment date> in the amount of $<partial payment amount>, prorated on the basis of the number of days in the initial payment period. Subsequent installments beginning on <first regular payment date> and continuing every quarter thereafter shall be in the full amount of $<quarterly annuity amount>.

4. Birth Date of Donor

The birth date of the Donor is <birth date>.

5. Irrevocability; Non-assignability; Termination

This annuity is irrevocable and non-assignable, except that it may be assigned to Charity. Charity's obligation under this Agreement shall terminate with the regular payment preceding the Donor's death.

6. Entire Agreement; Governing Law

This Agreement, together with Schedule A attached hereto, constitutes the entire agreement of the parties. This Agreement shall be governed by the laws of the State of <state>.

1 **Appendix D: Sample Charitable Remainder Trust Agreement**

NOTE: DO NOT USE THIS FORM AS-IS. It is presented for illustration only.
Consult with legal counsel to develop a trust agreement suitable for your purposes.

2 **<Name> Charitable Remainder Trust**

3 On this <date> day of <month, year>, I, <donor name> (hereinafter "the Donor"), desiring to
4 establish a charitable remainder unitrust within the meaning of Rev. Proc. 2005-52 and §664(d)(2) of
5 the Internal Revenue Code (hereinafter "the Code"), hereby enter into this trust agreement with
6 <trustee name> as the initial trustee (hereinafter "the Trustee"). This trust shall be known as the
7 <name> Charitable Remainder Unitrust.

8 **1. *Funding of Trust.***
9 The Donor hereby transfers and irrevocably assigns, on the above date, to the Trustee the property
10 described in Schedule A, and the Trustee accepts the property and agrees to hold, manage, and
11 distribute the property, and any property subsequently transferred, under the terms set forth in this
12 trust instrument.

13 **2. *Payment of Unitrust Amount.***
14 In each taxable year of the trust during the unitrust period, the Trustee shall pay to <beneficiary
15 name > (hereinafter "the Recipient") a unitrust amount equal to <number> percent of the net fair
16 market value of the assets of the trust valued as of the first day of each taxable year of the trust
17 (hereinafter "the valuation date"). The first day of the unitrust period shall be the date property is
18 first transferred to the trust and the last day of the unitrust period shall be the date of the Recipient's
19 death. The unitrust amount shall be paid in equal quarterly installments at the end of each calendar
20 quarter from income and, to the extent income is not sufficient, from principal. Any income of the
21 trust for a taxable year in excess of the unitrust amount shall be added to principal. If, for any year,
22 the net fair market value of the trust assets is incorrectly determined, then within a reasonable period
23 after the correct value is finally determined, the Trustee shall pay to the Recipient (in the case of an
24 undervaluation) or receive from the Recipient (in the case of an overvaluation) an amount equal to
25 the difference between the unitrust amount(s) properly payable and the unitrust amount(s) actually
26 paid.

27 **3. *Proration of Unitrust Amount.***
28 For a short taxable year and for the taxable year during which the unitrust period ends, the Trustee
29 shall prorate on a daily basis the unitrust amount described in paragraph 2, or, if an additional
30 contribution is made to the trust, the unitrust amount described in paragraph 5.

31 **4. *Distribution to Charity.***
32 At the termination of the unitrust period, the Trustee shall distribute all of the then principal and
33 income of the trust (other than any amount due the Recipient under the terms of this trust) to <charity
34 name> (hereinafter "the Charitable Organization"). If the Charitable Organization is not an
35 organization described in §§170(c), 2055(a), and 2522(a) of the Code at the time when any principal
36 or income of the trust is to be distributed to it, then the Trustee shall distribute the then principal and

37 income to one or more organizations described in §§170(c), 2055(a), and 2522(a) of the Code as the
38 Trustee shall select, and in the proportions as the Trustee shall decide, in the Trustee's sole
39 discretion.

40 *5. Additional Contributions.*
41 If any additional contributions are made to the trust after the initial contribution, the unitrust amount
42 for the year in which any additional contribution is made shall be <same number as paragraph 2>
43 percent of the sum of (a) the net fair market value of the trust assets as of the valuation date
44 (excluding the assets so added and any post-contribution income from, and appreciation on, such
45 assets during that year) and (b) for each additional contribution during the year, the fair market value
46 of the assets so added as of the valuation date (including any post-contribution income from, and
47 appreciation on, such assets through the valuation date) multiplied by a fraction the numerator of
48 which is the number of days in the period that begins with the date of contribution and ends with the
49 earlier of the last day of the taxable year or the last day of the unitrust period and the denominator of
50 which is the number of days in the period that begins with the first day of such taxable year and ends
51 with the earlier of the last day in such taxable year or the last day of the unitrust period. In a taxable
52 year in which an additional contribution is made on or after the valuation date, the assets so added
53 shall be valued as of the date of contribution, without regard to any post-contribution income or
54 appreciation, rather than as of the valuation date.

55 *6. Deferral of the Unitrust Payment Allocable to Testamentary Transfer.*
56 All property passing to the trust by reason of the death of the Donor (hereinafter "the testamentary
57 transfer") shall be considered to be a single contribution that is made on the date of the Donor's
58 death. Notwithstanding the provisions of paragraphs 2 and 5 above, the obligation to pay the unitrust
59 amount with respect to the testamentary transfer shall commence with the date of the Donor's death.
60 Nevertheless, payment of the unitrust amount with respect to the testamentary transfer may be
61 deferred from the date of the Donor's death until the end of the taxable year in which the funding of
62 the testamentary transfer is completed. Within a reasonable time after the end of the taxable year in
63 which the testamentary transfer is completed, the Trustee must pay to the Recipient (in the case of an
64 underpayment) or receive from the Recipient (in the case of an overpayment) the difference between
65 any unitrust amounts allocable to the testamentary transfer that were actually paid, plus interest, and
66 the unitrust amounts allocable to the testamentary transfer that were payable, plus interest. The
67 interest shall be computed for any period at the rate of interest, compounded annually, that the
68 federal income tax regulations under § 664 of the Code prescribe for this computation.

69 *7. Unmarketable Assets.*
70 Whenever the value of a trust asset must be determined, the Trustee shall determine the value of any
71 assets that are not cash, cash equivalents, or other assets that can be readily sold or exchanged for
72 cash or cash equivalents (hereinafter "unmarketable assets"), by either (a) obtaining a current
73 "qualified appraisal" from a "qualified appraiser," as defined in §1.170A-13(c)(3) and §1.170A-
74 13(c)(5) of the Income Tax Regulations, respectively, or (b) ensuring the valuation of these
75 unmarketable assets is performed exclusively by an "independent trustee," within the meaning of
76 §1.664-1(a)(7)(iii) of the Income Tax Regulations.

77 *8. Prohibited Transactions.*

78 The Trustee shall not engage in any act of self-dealing within the meaning of §4941(d) of the Code,
79 as modified by §4947(a)(2)(A) of the Code, and shall not make any taxable expenditures within the
80 meaning of §4945(d) of the Code, as modified by §4947(a)(2)(A) of the Code.

81 *9. Taxable Year.*

82 The taxable year of the trust shall be the calendar year.

83 *10. Governing Law.*

84 The operation of the trust shall be governed by the laws of the State of <name>. However, the
85 Trustee is prohibited from exercising any power or discretion granted under said laws that would be
86 inconsistent with the qualification of the trust as a charitable remainder unitrust under §664(d)(2) of
87 the Code and the corresponding regulations.

88 *11. Limited Power of Amendment.*

89 This trust is irrevocable. However, the Trustee shall have the power, acting alone, to amend the trust
90 from time to time in any manner required for the sole purpose of ensuring that the trust qualifies and
91 continues to qualify as a charitable remainder unitrust within the meaning of §664(d)(2) of the Code.

92 *12. Investment of Trust Assets.*

93 Nothing in this trust instrument shall be construed to restrict the Trustee from investing the trust
94 assets in a manner that could result in the annual realization of a reasonable amount of income or
95 gain from the sale or disposition of trust assets.

96 *13. Definition of Recipient.*

97 References to the Recipient in this trust instrument shall be deemed to include the estate of the
98 Recipient with regard to all provisions in this trust instrument that describe amounts payable to
99 and/or due from the Recipient. The prior sentence shall not apply to the determination of the last day
100 of the unitrust period.

APPENDIX E1 CHARITABLE GIFT ANNUITY, IMMEDIATE PAYMENT, CASH

ACTUARIAL CALCULATIONS: *5.4% CHARITABLE GIFT ANNUITY*

ASSUMPTIONS:		
[1]	Annuitant	72
	Date of Gift	07/01/2016
[2]	Cash Donated	$25,000.00
[3]	Annuity Rate from ACGA2012 Table	5.4%
[4]	Payment Schedule	Quarterly at end
[5]	Discount Rate under IRC Section 7520(a)	1.8%
CALCULATIONS:		
[6]	Annuity ([2] x [3])	$1,350.00
[7]	[a] Value of $1 for age on [1], rate on [5] (Table S in IRS Publication 1457 (5-2009)	11.0993
	[b] Adjustment for schedule on [4], rate on [5] (Table K in IRS Publication 1457 (5-2009))	1.0067
	[c] Adj. Value of $1 ([7a] x [7b])	11.1737
[8]	Investment in Contract ([6] x [7c])	$15,084.50
[9]	**CHARITABLE DEDUCTION** ([2] - [8])	**$9,915.50**
[10]	[a] Expected Return for age on [1] (Table V in Reg. 1.72-9)	14.6
	[b] Adjustment for payment schedule on [5] (Reg. 1.72-5(a)(2)(i))	-0.1
	[c] Expected Return per $1 ([10a] + [10b])	14.5
[11]	Expected Return ([6] x [10c])	$19,575.00
[12]	Exclusion Ratio ([8] / [11]) (Regs. 1.72-4, 1.1011-2(c) Example (8))	0.771

APPENDIX E1 CHARITABLE GIFT ANNUITY, IMMEDIATE PAYMENT, CASH

TAXATION OF GIFT ANNUITY PAYMENTS: *5.4% CHARITABLE GIFT ANNUITY*

ASSUMPTIONS:	
Annuitant	72
Date of Gift	07/01/2016
Cash Donated	$25,000.00
Annuity Rate	5.4%
Payment Schedule	Quarterly at end

CALCULATIONS	
Charitable Deduction	$9,915.50
Number of Payments in First Year	2
Days in First Payment Period	92
Days in First Credit Period	92
Annuity	$1,350.00
Quarterly Payment	$337.50
First Payment (on 9/30/2016)	$337.50

BREAKDOWN OF ANNUITY:

	Tax-free Portion	Ordinary Income	Total Annuity
Year 1	520.43	154.57	675.00
Years 2 through 13	1,040.85	309.15	1,350.00
Year 14	1,033.02	316.98	1,350.00
Years after	0.00	1,350.00	1,350.00

After 14.5 years, the entire annuity becomes ordinary income.

IRS Discount Rate is 1.8%

APPENDIX E2 CHARITABLE GIFT ANNUITY, IMMEDIATE PAYMENT, PROPERTY

ACTUARIAL CALCULATIONS: *5.4% CHARITABLE GIFT ANNUITY*

	ASSUMPTIONS:	
[1]	Annuitant	72
	Date of Gift	07/01/2016
[2]	Principal Donated	$25,000.00
[3]	Cost Basis of Property	$5,000
[4]	Annuity Rate from ACGA2012 Table	5.4%
[5]	Payment Schedule	Quarterly at end
[6]	Discount Rate under IRC Section 7520(a)	1.8%
	CALCULATIONS:	
[7]	Annuity ([2] x [4])	$1,350.00
[8]	[a] Value of $1 for age on [1], rate on [6] (Table S in IRS Publication 1457 (5-2009)	11.0993
	[b] Adjustment for schedule on [5], rate on [6] (Table K in IRS Publication 1457 (5-2009))	1.0067
	[c] Adj. Value of $1 ([8a] x [8b])	11.1737
[9]	Investment in Contract ([7] x [8c])	$15,084.50
[10]	**CHARITABLE DEDUCTION ([2] - [9])**	**$9,915.50**
[11]	[a] Expected Return for age on [1] (Table V in Reg. 1.72-9)	14.6
	[b] Adjustment for payment schedule on [5] (Reg. 1.72-5(a)(2)(i))	-0.1
	[c] Expected Return per $1 ([11a] + [11b])	14.5
[12]	Expected Return ([7] x [11c])	$19,575.00
[13]	Exclusion Ratio ([9] / [12]) (Regs. 1.72-4, 1.1011-2(c) Example (8))	0.771
[14]	Bargain Sale Ratio ([9] / [2]) (Regs. 1.170A-1(d), 1.1011-2(b))	0.60338
[15]	Cost Basis Allocable to Sale Portion ([14 x [3])	$3,016.90
[16]	Total Reportable Capital Gain ([14] x ([2] – [3]))	$12,067.60
[17]	Years to Report Gain (life expectancy age 72) (Reg. 1.1011-2(a)(4)(ii))	14.5

APPENDIX E2 CHARITABLE GIFT ANNUITY, IMMEDIATE PAYMENT, PROPERTY

TAXATION OF GIFT ANNUITY PAYMENTS: *5.4% CHARITABLE GIFT ANNUITY*

ASSUMPTIONS:	
Annuitant	72
Date of Gift	07/01/2016
Principal Donated	$25,000.00
Cost Basis of Property	$5,000
Annuity Rate	5.4%
Payment Schedule	Quarterly at end
CALCULATIONS	
Charitable Deduction	$9,915.50
Number of Payments in First Year	2
Days in First Payment Period	92
Days in First Credit Period	92
Annuity	$1,350.00
Quarterly Payment	$337.50
First Payment (on 9/30/2016)	$337.50

BREAKDOWN OF ANNUITY:	Capital Gain Income	Tax-free Income	Ordinary Income	Total Annuity
Year 1	416.34	104.09	154.57	675.00
Years 2 thru 13	832.68	208.17	309.15	1,350.00
Year 14	826.42	206.60	316.98	1,350.00
Years after	0.00	0.00	1,350.00	1,350.00

After 14.5 years, the entire annuity becomes ordinary income.

IRS Discount Rate is 1.8%

APPENDIX E3 CHARITABLE GIFT ANNUITY, DEFERRED PAYMENT, CASH

ACTUARIAL CALCULATIONS: *7.6% DEFERRED CHARITABLE GIFT ANNUITY*

ASSUMPTIONS:		
[1]	[a] Annuitant	50
	Date of Gift	07/01/2016
	[b] Age at Annuity Starting Date	65 [07/01/2031]
	[c] Age at Date of First Payment	65 [09/30/2031]
[2]	Cash Donated	$25,000.00
[3]	Annuity Rate from ACGA2012 Table	7.6%
[4]	Payment Schedule	Quarterly at end
[5]	Discount Rate under IRC Section 7520(a)	1.8%
CALCULATIONS:		
[6]	Annuity ([2] x [3])	$1,900.00
[7]	[a] Value of $1 for age on [1b], rate on [5] (Table S in IRS Publication 1457 (5-2009)	14.5915
	[b] Adjustment for schedule on [4], rate on [5] (Table K in IRS Publication 1457 (5-2009))	1.0067
	[c] Adj. Value of $1 ([7a] x [7b])	14.6894
	[d] Deferred Discount Factor for [1] and [5]	0.672276
	[e] Value of $1 Deferred ([7c] x [7d])	9.8753
[8]	Investment in Contract ([6] x [7e])	$18, 763.00
[9]	**CHARITABLE DEDUCTION ([2] - [8])**	**$6,237.00**
[10]	[a] Expected Return for age on [1b] (Table V in Reg. 1.72-9)	20.0
	[b] Adjustment for payment schedule on [4] (Reg. 1.72-5(a)(2)(i))	-0.1
	[c] Expected Return per $1 ([10a] + [10b])	19.9
[11]	Expected Return ([6] x [10c])	$37,810.00
[12]	Exclusion Ratio ([8] / [11]) (Regs. 1.72-4, 1.1011-2(c) Example (8))	0.496
[13]	Unadjusted Annuity Rate for age on [1b]	4.7%
[14]	Years of Deferral from 7/1/2016 to 6/30/2031	15.000
[15]	Deferred Interest Factor (1.0325 ^ 15)	1.615663
[16]	Deferred Annuity Rate ([13] x [15] rounded)	7.6%

APPENDIX E3 CHARITABLE GIFT ANNUITY, DEFERRED PAYMENT, CASH

TAXATION OF GIFT ANNUITY PAYMENTS: *7.6% DEFERRED CHARITABLE GIFT ANNUITY*

ASSUMPTIONS:	
Annuitant	50
Date of Gift	07/01/2016
Age at First Payment	65 [9/30/2031]
Cash Donated	$25,000.00
Annuity Rate	7.6%
Payment Schedule	Quarterly at end
CALCULATIONS	
Charitable Deduction	$6,237.00
Number of Payments in First Year	2
Annuity	$1,900.00
Quarterly Payment	$475.00

BREAKDOWN OF ANNUITY:

	Tax-free Portion	Ordinary Income	Total Annuity
Year 1	471.20	478.80	950.00
Years 2 through 20	942.40	957.60	1,900.00
Year 21	386.20	1,513.80	1,900.00
Years after	0.00	1,900.00	1,900.00

After 19.9 years, the entire annuity becomes ordinary income.

IRS Discount Rate is 1.8%

APPENDIX E4 CHARITABLE GIFT ANNUITY, DEFERRED PAYMENT, PROPERTY

ACTUARIAL CALCULATIONS: *7.6% CHARITABLE GIFT ANNUITY*

	ASSUMPTIONS:	
[1]	[a] Annuitant	50
	Date of Gift	7/1/2016
	[b] Age at Annuity Starting Date	65 [07/01/2031]
	[c] Age at Date of First Payment	65 [09/30/2013]
[2]	Principal Donated	$25,000.00
[3]	Cost Basis of Property	$5,000
[4]	Annuity Rate from ACGA2012 Table	7.6%
[5]	Payment Schedule	Quarterly at end
[6]	Discount Rate under IRC Section 7520(a)	1.8%
	CALCULATIONS:	
[7]	Annuity ([2] x [4])	$1,900.00
[8]	[a] Value of $1 for age on [1b], rate on [6] (Table S in IRS Publication 1457 (5-2009)	14.5915
	[b] Adjustment for schedule on [5], rate on [6] (Table K in IRS Publication 1457 (5-2009))	1.0067
	[c] Adj. Value of $1 ([8a] x [8b])	14.6893
	[d] Deferred Discount Factor for [1] and [6]	0.672276
	[e] Value of $1 Deferred ([8c] x [8d])	9.8753
[9]	Investment in Contract ([7] x [8e])	$18,763.00
[10]	**CHARITABLE DEDUCTION** ([2] - [9])	**$6,237.00**
[11]	[a] Expected Return for age on [1b] (Table V in Reg. 1.72-9)	20.0
	[b] Adjustment for payment schedule on [5] (Reg. 1.72-5(a)(2)(i))	-0.1
	[c] Expected Return per $1 ([11a] + [11b])	19.9
[12]	Expected Return ([7] x [11c])	$37,810.00
[13]	Exclusion Ratio ([9] / [12]) (Regs. 1.72-4, 1.1011-2(c) Example (8))	0.496
[14]	Bargain Sale Ratio ([9] / [2]) (Regs. 1.170A-19d), 1.1011-2(b))	0.75052
[15]	Cost Basis Allocable to Sale Portion ([14 x [3])	$3,752.60
[16]	Total Reportable Capital Gain ([14] x ([2] – [3]))	$15,010.40
[17]	Years to Report Gain (life expectancy age 50) (Reg. 1.1011-2(a)(4)(ii))	19.9
[18]	Unadjusted Annuity Rate for age on [1b]	4.7%
[19]	Years of Deferral from 7/1/2016 to 6/30/2031	15.000
[20]	Deferred Interest Factor (1.0325 ^ 14)	1.615663
[21]	Deferred Annuity Rate ([13] x [15] rounded)	7.6%

APPENDIX E4 CHARITABLE GIFT ANNUITY, DEFERRED PAYMENT, PROPERTY

TAXATION OF GIFT ANNUITY PAYMENTS: *7.6% DEFERRED CHARITABLE GIFT ANNUITY*

ASSUMPTIONS:	
Annuitant	50
Date of Gift	07/01/2016
Age at First Payment	65 [09/30/2031}
Principal Donated	$25,000.00
Cost Basis of Property	$5,000
Annuity Rate	7.6%
Payment Schedule	Quarterly at end
CALCULATIONS	
Charitable Deduction	$6,237.00
Number of Payments in First Year	2
Annuity	$1,900.00
Quarterly Payment	$475.00

BREAKDOWN OF ANNUITY:	Capital Gain Income	Tax-free Income	Ordinary Income	Total Annuity
Year 1	376.96	94.24	478.80	950.00
Years 2 thru 20	753.92	188.48	957.60	1,900.00
Year 21	308.96	77.24	1,513.80	1,900.00
Years after	0.00	0.00	1,900.00	1,900.00

After 19.9 years, the entire annuity becomes ordinary income.
IRS Discount Rate is 1.8%

APPENDIX E5 CHARITABLE REMAINDER ANNUITY TRUST

ACTUARIAL CALCULATIONS: *5% CHARITABLE ANNUITY TRUST*

ASSUMPTIONS:		
[1]	Beneficiary Age	75
	Date of Gift	07/01/2016
[2]	Cash Donated	$500,000.00
[3]	Payout Rate	5%
[4]	Payment Schedule	quarterly at end
[5]	Discount Rate under IRC Section 7520(a)	1.8%
CALCULATIONS:		
[6]	Value of $1 for lives/term on [1], years on [11] (Reg. 25.7520-3(b)(2)(v) Example 5)	9.6444
	[a] Adjustment factor for schedule on [4], rate on [5] (Table K in IRS Publication 1457 (5-2009))	1.0067
	[b] Adjusted value of $1 ([6] x [6a]) (Reg. 20.2031-7(d)(2)(iv))	9.7090
[7]	Remainder factor (1.0 - ([6b] x [3]))	0.51455
[8]	Annual Payment ([2] x [3])	$25,000.00
[9]	Value of Life Interest ([6b] x [8])	$242,725.00
[10]	**CHARITABLE DEDUCTION ([2] - [9])**	**$257,275.00**
[11]	Number of Years to Corpus Exhaustion	24.80817
[12]	Probability of Corpus Exhaustion (Passes 5% Probability Test of Rev. Rul. 77-374)	2.48%

APPENDIX E6 CHARITABLE REMAINDER UNITRUST

ACTUARIAL CALCULATIONS: *5% CHARITABLE UNITRUST*

ASSUMPTIONS:		
[1]	Beneficiary Age	72
	Date of Gift	07/01/2016
[2]	Cash Donated	$500,000.00
[3]	Payout Rate	5%
[4]	Payment Schedule	quarterly 3 months to first payment
[5]	Discount Rate under IRC Section 7520(a)	1.8%
CALCULATIONS:		
[6]	Adjustment factor for schedule on [4], rate on [5] (Table F in IRS Publication 1458 (5-2009))	0.988925
[7]	Adjusted unitrust payout rate ([3] x [6]) (Reg. 1.664-4(e)(3))	4.9446%
[8]	Remainder factor for values on [1] and [7] (Table U(1) in IRS Publication 1458 (5-2009))	0.55361
[9]	**CHARITABLE DEDUCTION** ([?] x [8])	**$276,805.00**

APPENDIX E10: RETAINED LIFE ESTATE

ACTUARIAL CALCULATIONS: *RETAINED LIFE ESTATE*

ASSUMPTIONS:		
[1]	Life Tenant Age	72
	Date of Gift	07/01/2016
[2]	Value of Property	$500,000.00
[3]	Cost Basis of Property	$100,000.00
[4]	Value of Building(s)	$350,000.00
[5]	Estimated Useful Life of Building(s)	45 years
[6]	Salvage Value of Building(s)	$115,000.00
[7]	IRS Discount is 1.8%.	
CALCULATIONS:		
[8]	Non-depreciable Factor for [1] and [7] (Reg. 1.170A-12(b)(1))	0.80021
[9]	Remainder Value of Net Non-depreciable Portion ([8] x ([2] – ([4] – [6])))	$212,055.65
[10]	Depreciable Factor for [1], [5] & [7] (Reg. 1.170A-12(b)(2))	0.58624
[11]	Remainder Value of Net Depreciable Portion ([10] x ([4] – [6]))	$137,766.40
[12]	**Charitable Deduction** ([9] + [11])	**$349,822.05**

Form **8283**

(Rev. December 2014)
Department of the Treasury
Internal Revenue Service

Noncash Charitable Contributions

▶ Attach to your tax return if you claimed a total deduction
of over $500 for all contributed property.
▶ Information about Form 8283 and its separate instructions is at *www.irs.gov/form8283*.

OMB No. 1545-0908

Attachment
Sequence No. **155**

Name(s) shown on your income tax return | Identifying number

Note. Figure the amount of your contribution deduction before completing this form. See your tax return instructions.

Section A. Donated Property of $5,000 or Less and Publicly Traded Securities—List in this section **only** items (or groups of similar items) for which you claimed a deduction of $5,000 or less. Also list publicly traded securities even if the deduction is more than $5,000 (see instructions).

Part I | Information on Donated Property—If you need more space, attach a statement.

1	(a) Name and address of the donee organization	(b) If donated property is a vehicle (see instructions), check the box. Also enter the vehicle identification number (unless Form 1098-C is attached).	(c) Description of donated property (For a vehicle, enter the year, make, model, and mileage. For securities, enter the company name and the number of shares.)
A		☐	
B		☐	
C		☐	
D		☐	
E		☐	

Note. If the amount you claimed as a deduction for an item is $500 or less, you do not have to complete columns (c), (f), and (g).

	(d) Date of the contribution	(e) Date acquired by donor (mo., yr.)	(f) How acquired by donor	(g) Donor's cost or adjusted basis	(h) Fair market value (see instructions)	(i) Method used to determine the fair market value
A						
B						
C						
D						
E						

Part II | **Partial Interests and Restricted Use Property**—Complete lines 2a through 2e if you gave less than an entire interest in a property listed in Part I. Complete lines 3a through 3c if conditions were placed on a contribution listed in Part I; also attach the required statement (see instructions).

2a Enter the letter from Part I that identifies the property for which you gave less than an entire interest ▶ _____
If Part II applies to more than one property, attach a separate statement.

b Total amount claimed as a deduction for the property listed in Part I: (1) For this tax year ▶ _____
(2) For any prior tax years ▶ _____

c Name and address of each organization to which any such contribution was made in a prior year (complete only if different from the donee organization above):
Name of charitable organization (donee)

Address (number, street, and room or suite no.)

City or town, state, and ZIP code

d For tangible property, enter the place where the property is located or kept ▶ _____
e Name of any person, other than the donee organization, having actual possession of the property ▶ _____

		Yes	No
3a	Is there a restriction, either temporary or permanent, on the donee's right to use or dispose of the donated property?		
b	Did you give to anyone (other than the donee organization or another organization participating with the donee organization in cooperative fundraising) the right to the income from the donated property or to the possession of the property, including the right to vote donated securities, to acquire the property by purchase or otherwise, or to designate the person having such income, possession, or right to acquire?		
c	Is there a restriction limiting the donated property for a particular use?		

For Paperwork Reduction Act Notice, see separate instructions.   Cat. No. 62299J   Form **8283** (Rev. 12-2014)

Form 8283 (Rev. 12-2014)   Page **2**

Name(s) shown on your income tax return	Identifying number

Section B. Donated Property Over $5,000 (Except Publicly Traded Securities)—Complete this section for one item (or one group of similar items) for which you claimed a deduction of more than $5,000 per item or group (except contributions of publicly traded securities reported in Section A). Provide a separate form for each property donated unless it is part of a group of similar items. An appraisal is generally required for property listed in Section B. See instructions.

Part I	Information on Donated Property—To be completed by the taxpayer and/or the appraiser.

4   Check the box that describes the type of property donated:

- **a** ☐ Art* (contribution of $20,000 or more)
- **b** ☐ Qualified Conservation Contribution
- **c** ☐ Equipment
- **d** ☐ Art* (contribution of less than $20,000)
- **e** ☐ Other Real Estate
- **f** ☐ Securities
- **g** ☐ Collectibles**
- **h** ☐ Intellectual Property
- **i** ☐ Vehicles
- **j** ☐ Other

*Art includes paintings, sculptures, watercolors, prints, drawings, ceramics, antiques, decorative arts, textiles, carpets, silver, rare manuscripts, historical memorabilia, and other similar objects.

**Collectibles include coins, stamps, books, gems, jewelry, sports memorabilia, dolls, etc., but not art as defined above.

Note. In certain cases, you must attach a qualified appraisal of the property. See instructions.

5	(a) Description of donated property (if you need more space, attach a separate statement)	(b) If tangible property was donated, give a brief summary of the overall physical condition of the property at the time of the gift	(c) Appraised fair market value
A			
B			
C			
D			

	(d) Date acquired by donor (mo., yr.)	(e) How acquired by donor	(f) Donor's cost or adjusted basis	(g) For bargain sales, enter amount received	(h) Amount claimed as a deduction	(i) Date of contribution
A						
B						
C						
D						

Column heading for (h) and (i): **See instructions**

Part II	Taxpayer (Donor) Statement—List each item included in Part I above that the appraisal identifies as having a value of $500 or less. See instructions.

I declare that the following item(s) included in Part I above has to the best of my knowledge and belief an appraised value of not more than $500 (per item). Enter identifying letter from Part I and describe the specific item. See instructions. ▶ _____

Signature of taxpayer (donor) ▶ _____   Date ▶ _____

Part III	Declaration of Appraiser

I declare that I am not the donor, the donee, a party to the transaction in which the donor acquired the property, employed by, or related to any of the foregoing persons, or married to any person who is related to any of the foregoing persons. And, if regularly used by the donor, donee, or party to the transaction, I performed the majority of my appraisals during my tax year for other persons.

Also, I declare that I perform appraisals on a regular basis; and that because of my qualifications as described in the appraisal, I am qualified to make appraisals of the type of property being valued. I certify that the appraisal fees were not based on a percentage of the appraised property value. Furthermore, I understand that a false or fraudulent overstatement of the property value as described in the qualified appraisal or this Form 8283 may subject me to the penalty under section 6701(a) (aiding and abetting the understatement of tax liability). In addition, I understand that I may be subject to a penalty under section 6695A if I know, or reasonably should know, that my appraisal is to be used in connection with a return or claim for refund and a substantial or gross valuation misstatement results from my appraisal. I affirm that I have not been barred from presenting evidence or testimony by the Office of Professional Responsibility.

Sign Here

Signature ▶ _____ Title ▶ _____ Date ▶ _____

Business address (including room or suite no.)	Identifying number
City or town, state, and ZIP code	

Part IV	Donee Acknowledgment—To be completed by the charitable organization.

This charitable organization acknowledges that it is a qualified organization under section 170(c) and that it received the donated property as described in Section B, Part I, above on the following date ▶ _____

Furthermore, this organization affirms that in the event it sells, exchanges, or otherwise disposes of the property described in Section B, Part I (or any portion thereof) within 3 years after the date of receipt, it will file **Form 8282,** Donee Information Return, with the IRS and give the donor a copy of that form. This acknowledgment does not represent agreement with the claimed fair market value.

Does the organization intend to use the property for an unrelated use? . . . . ▶ ☐ Yes ☐ No

Name of charitable organization (donee)	Employer identification number
Address (number, street, and room or suite no.)	City or town, state, and ZIP code
Authorized signature	Title	Date

Form **8283** (Rev. 12-2014)

Instructions for Form 8283

(Rev. December 2014)

Noncash Charitable Contributions

Department of the Treasury
Internal Revenue Service

Section references are to the Internal Revenue Code unless otherwise noted.

General Instructions

Future Developments

Information about any future developments affecting Form 8283 (such as legislation enacted after we release it) will be posted at *www.irs.gov/form8283*.

Purpose of Form

Use Form 8283 to report information about noncash charitable contributions.

Do not use Form 8283 to report out-of-pocket expenses for volunteer work or amounts you gave by check or credit card. Treat these items as cash contributions. Also, do not use Form 8283 to figure your charitable contribution deduction. For details on how to figure the amount of the deduction, see your tax return instructions and Pub. 526, Charitable Contributions.

Who Must File

You must file Form 8283 if the amount of your deduction for all noncash gifts is more than $500. For this purpose, "amount of your deduction" means your deduction before applying any income limits that could result in a carryover. The carryover rules are explained in Pub. 526. Make any required reductions to fair market value (FMV) before you determine if you must file Form 8283. See *Fair Market Value (FMV)*, later.

Form 8283 is filed by individuals, partnerships, and corporations.

C corporations. C corporations, other than personal service corporations and closely held corporations, must file Form 8283 only if the amount claimed as a deduction is more than $5,000.

Partnerships and S corporations. A partnership or S corporation that claims a deduction for noncash gifts of more than $500 must file Form 8283 with Form 1065, 1065-B, or 1120S.

If the total deduction for any item or group of similar items is more than $5,000, the partnership or S corporation must complete Section B of Form 8283 even if the amount allocated to each partner or shareholder is $5,000 or less.

The partnership or S corporation must give a completed copy of Form 8283 to each partner or shareholder receiving an allocation of the contribution deduction shown in Section B of the Form 8283 of the partnership or S corporation.

Partners and shareholders. The partnership or S corporation will provide information about your share of the contribution on your Schedule K-1 (Form 1065 or 1120S). If you received a copy of Form 8283 from the partnership or S corporation, attach a copy to your tax return. Use the amount shown on your Schedule K-1, not the amount shown on the Form 8283, to figure your deduction.

If the partnership or S corporation is not required to give you a copy of its Form 8283, combine the amount of noncash contributions shown on your Schedule K-1 with your other noncash contributions to see if you must file Form 8283. If you need to file Form 8283, you do not have to complete all the information requested in Section A for your share of the partnership's or S corporation's contributions. Complete only column (h) of line 1 with your share of the contribution and enter "From Schedule K-1 (Form 1065 or 1120S)" across columns (d)–(g).

When To File

File Form 8283 with your tax return for the year you contribute the property and first claim a deduction.

Which Sections To Complete

Form 8283 has two sections. If you must file Form 8283, you may have to complete Section A, Section B, or both, depending on the type of property donated and the amount claimed as a deduction.

Use Section A to report donations of property for which you claimed a deduction of $5,000 or less per item or group of similar items (defined later). Also use Section A to report donations of publicly traded securities. Use Section B to report donations of property for which you claimed a deduction of more than $5,000 per item or group of similar items.

In figuring whether your deduction for a group of similar items was more than $5,000, consider all items in the group, even if items in the group were donated to more than one donee organization. However, you must file a separate Form 8283, Section B, for each donee organization.

Example. You claimed a deduction of $2,000 for books you gave to College A, $2,500 for books you gave to College B, and $900 for books you gave to College C. You must report these donations in Section B because the total deduction was more than $5,000. You must file a separate Form 8283, Section B, for the donation to each of the three colleges.

Section A. Include in Section A only the following items.

1. Items (or groups of similar items as defined later) for which you claimed a deduction of $5,000 or less per item (or group of similar items).

2. The following publicly traded securities even if the deduction is more than $5,000:

a. Securities listed on an exchange in which quotations are published daily,

b. Securities regularly traded in national or regional over-the-counter markets for which published quotations are available, or

c. Securities that are shares of a mutual fund for which quotations are published on a daily basis in a newspaper of general circulation throughout the United States.

Section B. Include in Section B only items (or groups of similar items) for which you claimed a deduction of more than $5,000. Do not include publicly traded securities reportable in Section A. With certain exceptions, items reportable in Section B require a written appraisal by a qualified appraiser. You must file a separate Form 8283, Section B, for each donee organization and each item of property (or group of similar items).

Similar Items of Property

Similar items of property are items of the same generic category or type, such as coin collections, paintings, books, clothing, jewelry, nonpublicly traded stock, land, or buildings.

Example. You claimed a deduction of $400 for clothing, $7,000 for publicly traded securities (quotations published daily), and $6,000 for a collection of 15 books ($400 each). Report the clothing and securities in Section A and the books (a group of similar items) in Section B.

Special Rule for Certain C Corporations

A special rule applies for deductions taken by certain C corporations under section 170(e)(3) or (4) for certain contributions of inventory or scientific equipment.

To determine if you must file Form 8283 or which section to complete, use the difference between the amount you claimed as a deduction and the amount you would have claimed as cost of goods sold (COGS) had you sold the property instead. This rule is only for purposes of Form 8283. It does not change the amount or method of figuring your contribution deduction.

If you do not have to file Form 8283 because of this rule, you must attach a statement to your tax return (similar to the one in the example below). Also, attach a statement if you must complete Section A, instead of Section B, because of this rule.

Example. You donated clothing from your inventory for the care of the needy. The clothing cost you $5,000 and your claimed charitable deduction is $8,000. Complete Section A instead of Section B because the difference between the amount you claimed as a charitable deduction and the amount that would have been your COGS deduction is $3,000 ($8,000 – $5,000). Attach a statement to Form 8283 similar to the following:

Form 8283—Inventory

Contribution deduction	$8,000
COGS (if sold, not donated)	– 5,000
For Form 8283 filing purposes	=$3,000

Fair Market Value (FMV)

Although the amount of your deduction determines if you have to file Form 8283, you also need to have information about the FMV of your contribution to complete the form.

FMV is the price a willing, knowledgeable buyer would pay a willing, knowledgeable seller when neither has to buy or sell.

You may not always be able to deduct the FMV of your contribution. Depending on the type of property donated, you may have to reduce the FMV to figure the deductible amount, as explained next.

Reductions to FMV. The amount of the reduction (if any) depends on whether the property is ordinary income property or capital gain property. Attach a statement to your tax return showing how you figured the reduction.

Ordinary income property. Ordinary income property is property that would result in ordinary income or short-term capital gain if it were sold at its FMV on the date it was contributed. Examples of ordinary income property are inventory, works of art created by the donor, and capital assets held for 1 year or less. The deduction for a gift of ordinary income property is limited to the FMV minus the amount that would be ordinary income or short-term capital gain if the property were sold.

Capital gain property. Capital gain property is property that would result in long-term capital gain if it were sold at its FMV on the date it was contributed. For purposes of figuring your charitable contribution, capital gain property also includes certain real property and depreciable property used in your trade or business and, generally, held more than 1 year. However, to the extent of any gain from the property that must be recaptured as ordinary income under section 1245, section 1250, or any other Code provision, the property is treated as ordinary income property.

You usually may deduct gifts of capital gain property at their FMV. However, you must reduce the FMV by the amount of any appreciation if any of the following apply.
• The capital gain property is contributed to certain private nonoperating foundations. This rule does not apply to qualified appreciated stock.
• You choose the 50% limit instead of the special 30% limit for capital gain property.
• The contributed property is intellectual property (as defined later).
• The contributed property is certain taxidermy property.
• The contributed property is tangible personal property that is put to an unrelated use (as defined in Pub. 526) by the charity.
• The contributed property is certain tangible personal property with a claimed value of more than $5,000 and is sold, exchanged, or otherwise disposed of by the charity during the year in which you made the contribution, and the charity has not made the required certification of exempt use (such as on Form 8282, Part IV).

Qualified conservation contribution. A qualified conservation contribution is a donation of a qualified real property interest, such as an easement, exclusively for certain conservation purposes. The donee must be a qualified organization as defined in section 170(h)(3) and must have the resources to be able to monitor and enforce the conservation easement or other conservation restrictions. To enable the organization to do this, you must give it documents, such as maps and photographs, that establish the condition of the property at the time of the gift.

If the donation has no material effect on the real property's FMV, or enhances rather than reduces its FMV, no deduction is allowable. For example, little or no deduction may be allowed if the property's use is already restricted, such as by zoning or other law or contract, and the donation does not further restrict how the property can be used.

The FMV of a conservation easement cannot be determined by applying a standard percentage to the FMV of the underlying property. The best evidence of the FMV of an easement is the sales price of a comparable easement. If there are no comparable sales, the before and after method may be used.

Attach a statement that:
* Identifies the conservation purposes furthered by your donation,
* Shows, if before and after valuation is used, the FMV of the underlying property before and after the gift,
* States whether you made the donation in order to get a permit or other approval from a local or other governing authority and whether the donation was required by a contract, and
* If you or a related person has any interest in other property nearby, describes that interest.

If an appraisal is required, it must include the method of valuation (such as the income approach or the market data approach) and the specific basis for the valuation (such as specific comparable sales transactions).

Easements on buildings in historic districts. You cannot claim a deduction for this type of contribution unless the contributed interest includes restrictions preserving the entire exterior of the building (including front, sides, rear, and height) and prohibiting any change to the exterior of the building inconsistent with its historical character. If you claim a deduction for this type of contribution, you must include with your return:
* A signed copy of a qualified appraisal,
* Photographs of the entire exterior of the building, and
* A description of all restrictions on the development of the building. The description of the restrictions can be made by attaching a copy of the easement deed.
If you donate this type of property and claim a deduction of more than $10,000, your deduction will not be allowed unless you pay a $500 filing fee. See Form 8283-V and its instructions.

For more information about qualified conservation contributions, see Pub. 526 and Pub. 561, Determining the Value of Donated Property. Also see section 170(h), Regulations section 1.170A-14, and Notice 2004-41. Notice 2004-41, 2004-28 I.R.B. 31, is available at *www.irs.gov/irb/2004-28_IRB/ar09.html*.

Intellectual property. The FMV of intellectual property must be reduced to figure the amount of your deduction, as explained earlier. Intellectual property means a patent, copyright (other than a copyright described in section 1221(a)(3) or 1231(b)(1)(C)), trademark, trade name,

trade secret, know-how, software (other than software described in section 197(e)(3)(A)(i)), or similar property, or applications or registrations of such property.

However, you may be able to claim additional charitable contribution deductions in the year of the contribution and later years based on a percentage of the donee's net income, if any, from the property. The amount of the donee's net income from the property will be reported to you on Form 8899, Notice of Income From Donated Intellectual Property. See Pub. 526 for details.

Clothing and household items. The FMV of used household items and clothing is usually much lower than when new. A good measure of value might be the price that buyers of these used items actually pay in consignment or thrift shops. You can also review classified ads in the newspaper or on the Internet to see what similar products sell for.

You cannot claim a deduction for clothing or household items you donate unless the clothing or household items are in good used condition or better. However, you can claim a deduction for a contribution of an item of clothing or household item that is not in good used condition or better if you deduct more than $500 for it and include a qualified appraisal of it with your return.

Qualified Vehicle Donations

A qualified vehicle is any motor vehicle manufactured primarily for use on public streets, roads, and highways; a boat; or an airplane. However, property held by the donor primarily for sale to customers, such as inventory of a car dealer, is not a qualified vehicle.

If you donate a qualified vehicle with a claimed value of more than $500, you cannot claim a deduction unless you attach to your return a copy of the contemporaneous written acknowledgment you received from the donee organization. The donee organization may use Copy B of Form 1098-C as the acknowledgment. An acknowledgment is considered contemporaneous if the donee organization furnishes it to you no later than 30 days after the:
* Date of the sale, if the donee organization sold the vehicle in an arm's length transaction to an unrelated party, or
* Date of the contribution, if the donee organization will not sell the vehicle before completion of a material improvement or significant intervening use, or the donee organization will give or sell the vehicle to a needy individual for a price significantly below FMV to directly further the organization's charitable purpose of relieving the poor and distressed or underprivileged who need a means of transportation.

For a donated vehicle with a claimed value of more than $500, you can deduct the smaller of the vehicle's FMV on the date of the contribution or the gross proceeds received from the sale of the vehicle, unless an exception applies as explained below. Form 1098-C (or other acknowledgment) will show the gross proceeds from the sale if no exception applies. If the FMV of the vehicle was more than your cost or other basis, you may have to reduce the FMV to figure the deductible amount, as described under *Reductions to FMV*, earlier.

If any of the following exceptions apply, your deduction is not limited to the gross proceeds received from the sale. Instead, you generally can deduct the vehicle's FMV on the date of the contribution if the donee organization:
• Makes a significant intervening use of the vehicle before transferring it,
• Makes a material improvement to the vehicle before transferring it, or
• Gives or sells the vehicle to a needy individual for a price significantly below FMV to directly further the organization's charitable purpose of relieving the poor and distressed or underprivileged who need a means of transportation.

Form 1098-C (or other acknowledgment) will show if any of these exceptions apply. If the FMV of the vehicle was more than your cost or other basis, you may have to reduce the FMV to figure the deductible amount, as described under *Reductions to FMV*, earlier.

Determining FMV. A used car guide may be a good starting point for finding the FMV of your vehicle. These guides, published by commercial firms and trade organizations, contain vehicle sale prices for recent model years. The guides are sometimes available from public libraries or from a loan officer at a bank, credit union, or finance company. You can also find used car pricing information on the Internet.

An acceptable measure of the FMV of a donated vehicle is an amount not in excess of the price listed in a used vehicle pricing guide for a private party sale of a similar vehicle. However, the FMV may be less than that amount if the vehicle has engine trouble, body damage, high mileage, or any type of excessive wear. The FMV of a donated vehicle is the same as the price listed in a used vehicle pricing guide for a private party sale only if the guide lists a sales price for a vehicle that is the same make, model, and year, sold in the same area, in the same condition, with the same or similar options or accessories, and with the same or similar warranties as the donated vehicle.

Example. Neal donates his car, which he bought new in 2008 for $20,000. A used vehicle pricing guide shows the FMV for his car is $9,000. Neal receives a Form 1098-C showing the car was sold for $7,000. Neal can deduct $7,000 and must attach Form 1098-C to his return.

More information. For details, see Pub. 526 or Notice 2005-44. Notice 2005-44, 2005-25 I.R.B. 1287, is available at *www.irs.gov/irb/2005-25_IRB/ar09.html*.

Additional Information

You may want to see Pub. 526 and Pub. 561. If you contributed depreciable property, see Pub. 544, Sales and Other Disposition of Assets.

Specific Instructions

Identifying number. Individuals must enter their social security number. All other filers should enter their employer identification number.

Section A

Part I, Information on Donated Property
Line 1

Column (b). Check the box if the donated property is a qualified vehicle (defined earlier). If you are not attaching Form 1098-C (or other acknowledgment) to your return, enter the vehicle identification number (VIN) in the spaces provided below the checkbox.

You can find the VIN on the vehicle registration, the title, the proof of insurance, or the vehicle itself. Generally, the VIN is 17 characters made up of numbers and letters.

If the VIN has fewer than 17 characters, enter a zero in each of the remaining entry spaces to the left of the VIN. For example, if the VIN is "555555X555555," enter "0000555555X555555."

Column (c). Describe the property in sufficient detail. The greater the value of the property, the more detail you must provide. For example, a personal computer should be described in more detail than pots and pans.

If the donated property is a vehicle, give the year, make, model, condition, and mileage at the time of the donation (for example, "1963 Studebaker Lark, fair condition, 135,000 miles") regardless of whether you attach a Form 1098-C or other acknowledgment. If you do not know the actual mileage, use a good faith estimate based on car repair records or similar evidence.

For securities, include the following:
• Company name,
• Number of shares,
• Kind of security,
• Whether a share of a mutual fund, and
• Whether regularly traded on a stock exchange or in an over-the-counter market.

Column (d). Enter the date you contributed the property. If you made contributions on various dates, enter each contribution and its date on a separate row.

Note. If the amount you claimed as a deduction for the item is $500 or less, you do not have to complete columns (e), (f), and (g).

Column (e). Enter the approximate date you acquired the property. If it was created, produced, or manufactured by or for you, enter the date it was substantially completed.

If you are donating a group of similar items and you acquired the items on various dates (but have held all the items for at least 12 months), you can enter "Various."

Column (f). State how you acquired the property. This could be by purchase, gift, inheritance, or exchange.

Column (g). Do not complete this column for property held at least 12 months or publicly traded securities. Keep records on cost or other basis.

Note. If you have reasonable cause for not providing the information in columns (e) and (g), attach an explanation.

Column (h). Enter the FMV of the property on the date you donated it. You must attach a statement if:
• You were required to reduce the FMV to figure the amount of your deduction, or
• You gave a qualified conservation contribution for which you claimed a deduction of $5,000 or less. See *Fair Market Value (FMV)*, earlier, for the type of statement to attach.

Column (i). Enter the method(s) you used to determine the FMV.

Examples of entries to make include "Appraisal," "Thrift shop value" (for clothing or household items), "Catalog" (for stamp or coin collections), or "Comparable sales" (for real estate and other kinds of assets). See Pub. 561.

Part II, Partial Interests and Restricted Use Property

If Part II applies to more than one property, attach a separate statement. Give the required information for each property separately. Identify which property listed in Part I the information relates to.

Lines 2a Through 2e

Complete lines 2a–2e only if you contributed less than the entire interest in the donated property during the tax year and claimed a deduction for it of $5,000 or less. On line 2b, enter the amount claimed as a deduction for this tax year and in any prior tax years for gifts of a partial interest in the same property.

Lines 3a Through 3c

Complete lines 3a–3c only if you attached restrictions to the right to the income, use, or disposition of the donated property. An example of a "restricted use" is furniture that you gave only to be used in the reading room of an organization's library. Attach a statement explaining (1) the terms of any agreement or understanding regarding the restriction, and (2) whether the property is designated for a particular use.

Section B

Include in Section B only items (or groups of similar items) for which you claimed a deduction of more than $5,000. File a separate Form 8283, Section B, for:
• Each donee, and
• Each item of property, except for an item that is part of a group of similar items.

Part I, Information on Donated Property

You must get a written appraisal from a qualified appraiser before completing Part I. However, see *Exceptions*, below.

Generally, you do not need to attach the appraisals to your return but you should keep them for your records. But see *Art valued at $20,000 or more*, *Clothing and household items not in good used condition*, *Easements on buildings in historic districts*, and *Deduction of more than $500,000*, later.

Exceptions. You do not need a written appraisal if the property is:

1. Nonpublicly traded stock of $10,000 or less,

2. A vehicle (including a car, boat, or airplane) if your deduction for the vehicle is limited to the gross proceeds from its sale,

3. Intellectual property (as defined earlier),

4. Certain securities considered to have market quotations readily available (see Regulations section 1.170A-13(c)(7)(xi)(B)),

5. Inventory and other property donated by a corporation that are "qualified contributions" for the care of the ill, the needy, or infants, within the meaning of section 170(e)(3)(A), or

6. Stock in trade, inventory, or property held primarily for sale to customers in the ordinary course of your trade or business.

Although a written appraisal is not required for the types of property just listed, you must provide certain information in Part I of Section B (see *Line 5*) and have the donee organization complete Part IV.

Art valued at $20,000 or more. If your total deduction for art is $20,000 or more, you must attach a complete copy of the signed appraisal. For individual objects valued at $20,000 or more, a photograph must be provided upon request. The photograph must be of sufficient quality and size (preferably an 8 x 10 inch color photograph or a color transparency no smaller than 4 x 5 inches) to fully show the object.

Clothing and household items not in good used condition. You must include with your return a qualified appraisal of any single item of clothing or any household item that is not in good used condition or better for which you deduct more than $500. The appraisal is required whether the donation is reportable in Section A or Section B. See *Clothing and household items*, earlier.

Easements on buildings in historic districts. If you claim a deduction for a qualified conservation contribution of an easement on the exterior of a building in a registered historic district, you must include a signed copy of a qualified appraisal, photographs, and certain other information with your return. See *Easements on buildings in historic districts*, under *Fair Market Value (FMV)*, earlier.

Deduction of more than $500,000. If you claim a deduction of more than $500,000 for an item (or group of similar items) donated to one or more donees, you must attach a signed copy of a qualified appraisal of the property to your return unless an exception applies. See *Exceptions*, earlier.

Appraisal Requirements

The appraisal must be made by a qualified appraiser (defined later) in accordance with generally accepted appraisal standards. It also must meet the relevant requirements of Regulations section 1.170A-13(c)(3) and Notice 2006-96. Notice 2006-96, 2006-46 I.R.B. 902, is available at www.irs.gov/irb/2006-46_IRB/ar13.html.

The appraisal must be made not earlier than 60 days before the date you contribute the property. You must receive the appraisal before the due date (including extensions) of the return on which you first claim a deduction for the property. For a deduction first claimed on an amended return, the appraisal must be received before the date the amended return was filed.

A separate qualified appraisal and a separate Form 8283 are required for each item of property except for an item that is part of a group of similar items. Only one appraisal is required for a group of similar items contributed in the same tax year, if it includes all the required information for each item. The appraiser may group similar items with a collective value appraised at $100 or less.

If you gave similar items to more than one donee for which you claimed a total deduction of more than $5,000, you must attach a separate form for each donee.

Example. You claimed a deduction of $2,000 for books given to College A, $2,500 for books given to College B, and $900 for books given to a public library. You must attach a separate Form 8283 for each donee.

Line 4

Check only one box on line 4 of each Form 8283. Complete as many separate Forms 8283 as necessary so that only one box has to be checked on line 4 of each Form 8283.

Vehicles. If you check box "i" to indicate the donated property is a vehicle, you must attach to your return a copy of Form 1098-C (or other acknowledgment) you received from the donee organization.

Line 5

You must complete at least column (a) of line 5 (and column (b) if applicable) before submitting Form 8283 to the donee. You may then complete the remaining columns.

Column (a). Provide a detailed description so a person unfamiliar with the property could be sure the property that was appraised is the property that was contributed. The greater the value of the property, the more detail you must provide.

For a qualified conservation contribution, describe the easement terms in detail, or attach a copy of the easement deed.

A description of donated securities should include the company name and number of shares donated.

Column (c). Include the FMV from the appraisal. If you were not required to get an appraisal, include the FMV you determine to be correct.

Column (d). If you are donating a group of similar items and you acquired the items on various dates (but have held all the items for at least 12 months), you can enter "Various."

Columns (d)–(f). If you have reasonable cause for not providing the information in columns (d), (e), or (f), attach an explanation so your deduction will not automatically be disallowed.

For a qualified conservation contribution, indicate whether you are providing information about the underlying property or about the easement.

Column (g). A bargain sale is a transfer of property that is in part a sale or exchange and in part a contribution. Enter the amount received for bargain sales.

Column (h). Complete column (h) only if you were not required to get an appraisal, as explained earlier.

Column (i). Complete column (i) only if you were not required to get an appraisal, as explained earlier.

Part II, Taxpayer (Donor) Statement

Complete Section B, Part II, for each item included in Section B, Part I, that has an appraised value of $500 or less. Because you do not have to show the value of these items in Section B, Part I, of the donee's copy of Form 8283, clearly identify them for the donee in Section B, Part II. Then, the donee does not have to file Form 8282, Donee Information Return, for the items valued at $500 or less. See the *Note* under *Part IV, Donee Acknowledgment*, for more details about filing Form 8282.

The amount of information you give in Section B, Part II, depends on the description of the donated property you enter in Section B, Part I. If you show a single item as "Property A" in Part I and that item is appraised at $500 or less, then the entry "Property A" in Part II is enough. However, if "Property A" consists of several items and the total appraised value is over $500, list in Part II any item(s) you gave that is valued at $500 or less.

All shares of nonpublicly traded stock or items in a set are considered one item. For example, a book collection by the same author, components of a stereo system, or six place settings of a pattern of silverware are one item for the $500 test.

Example. You donated books valued at $6,000. The appraisal states that one of the items, a collection of books by author "X," is worth $400. On the Form 8283 that you are required to give the donee, you decide not to show the appraised value of all of the books. But you also do not want the donee to have to file Form 8282 if the collection of books is sold within 3 years after the donation. If your description of Property A on line 5 includes all the books, then specify in Part II the "collection of books by X included in Property A." But if your Property A description is "collection of books by X," the only required entry in Part II is "Property A."

In the above example, you may have chosen instead to give a completed copy of Form 8283 to the donee. The donee would then be aware of the value. If you include all the books as Property A on line 5, and enter $6,000 in column (c), you may still want to describe the specific collection in Part II so the donee can sell it without filing Form 8282.

Part III, Declaration of Appraiser

If you had to get an appraisal, you must get it from a qualified appraiser. A qualified appraiser is an individual who meets all the following requirements.

    1. The individual either:

    a. Has earned an appraisal designation from a recognized professional appraiser organization for demonstrated competency in valuing the type of property being appraised, or

    b. Has met certain minimum education and experience requirements.

    2. The individual regularly prepares appraisals for which he or she is paid.

    3. The individual demonstrates verifiable education and experience in valuing the type of property being appraised. To do this, the appraiser can make a declaration that, because of his or her background, experience, education, and membership in professional associations, he or she is qualified to make appraisals of the type of property being valued. The declaration must be part of the appraisal. However, if the appraisal was already completed without this declaration, the declaration can be made separately and associated with the appraisal.

    4. The individual has not been prohibited from practicing before the IRS under section 330(c) of title 31 of the United States Code at any time during the 3-year period ending on the date of the appraisal.

In addition, the appraiser must complete Part III of Form 8283. See section 170(f)(11)(E), Notice 2006-96, and Regulations section 1.170A-13(c)(5) for details.

If you use appraisals by more than one appraiser, or if two or more appraisers contribute to a single appraisal, all the appraisers must sign the appraisal and Part III of Form 8283.

Persons who cannot be qualified appraisers are listed in the Declaration of Appraiser. Generally, a party to the transaction in which you acquired the property being appraised will not qualify to sign the declaration. But a person who sold, exchanged, or gave the property to you may sign the declaration if the property was donated within 2 months of the date you acquired it and the property's appraised value did not exceed its acquisition price.

An appraiser may not be considered qualified if you had knowledge of facts that would cause a reasonable person to expect the appraiser to falsely overstate the value of the property. An example of this is an agreement between you and the appraiser about the property value when you know that the appraised amount exceeds the actual FMV.

Usually, appraisal fees cannot be based on a percentage of the appraised value unless the fees were paid to certain not-for-profit associations. See Regulations section 1.170A-13(c)(6)(ii).

Identifying number. The appraiser's taxpayer identification number (social security number or employer identification number) must be entered in Part III.

Part IV, Donee Acknowledgment

The donee organization that received the property described in Part I of Section B must complete Part IV. Before submitting page 2 of Form 8283 to the donee for acknowledgment, complete at least your name, identifying number, and description of the donated property (line 5, column (a)). If tangible property is donated, also describe its physical condition (line 5, column (b)) at the time of the gift. Complete Part II, if applicable, before submitting the form to the donee. See the instructions for Part II.

The person acknowledging the gift must be an official authorized to sign the tax returns of the organization, or a person specifically designated to sign Form 8283. When you ask the donee to fill out Part IV, you should also ask the donee to provide you with a contemporaneous written acknowledgment required by section 170(f)(8).

After completing Part IV, the organization must return Form 8283 to you, the donor. You must give a copy of Section B of this form to the donee organization. You may then complete any remaining information required in Part I. Also, the qualified appraiser can complete Part III at this time.

In some cases, it may be impossible to get the donee's signature on Form 8283. The deduction will not be disallowed for that reason if you attach a detailed explanation of why it was impossible.

Note. If it is reasonable to expect that donated tangible personal property will be used for a purpose unrelated to the purpose or function of the donee, the donee should check the "Yes" box in Part IV. In this situation, your deduction will be limited. In addition, if the donee (or a successor donee) organization disposes of the property within 3 years after the date the original donee received it, the organization must file Form 8282, Donee Information Return, with the IRS and send a copy to the donor. (As a result of the sale by the donee, the donor's contribution deduction may be limited or part of the prior year contribution deduction may have to be recaptured. See Pub. 526.) An exception applies to items having a value of $500 or less if the donor identified the items and signed the statement in Section B, Part II, of Form 8283. See the instructions for Part II.

Failure To File Form 8283

Your deduction generally will be disallowed if you fail to:
• Attach a required Form 8283 to your return,
• Get a required appraisal and complete Section B of Form 8283, or
• Attach to your return a required appraisal of clothing or household items not in good used condition, an easement on a building in a registered historic district, or property for which you claimed a deduction of more than $500,000. However, your deduction will not be disallowed if your failure was due to reasonable cause and not willful neglect

or was due to a good-faith omission. If the IRS asks you to submit the form, you have 90 days to send a completed Section B of Form 8283 before your deduction is disallowed. However, your deduction will not be allowed if you did not get a required appraisal within the required period.

Paperwork Reduction Act Notice. We ask for the information on this form to carry out the Internal Revenue laws of the United States. You are required to give us the information. We need it to ensure that you are complying with these laws and to allow us to figure and collect the right amount of tax.

You are not required to provide the information requested on a form that is subject to the Paperwork Reduction Act unless the form displays a valid OMB control number. Books or records relating to a form or its instructions must be retained as long as their contents may become material in the administration of any Internal Revenue law. Generally, tax returns and return information are confidential, as required by section 6103.

The time needed to complete and file this form will vary depending on individual circumstances. The estimated burden for individual taxpayers filing this form is approved under OMB control number 1545-0074 and is included in the estimates shown in the instructions for their individual income tax return. The estimated burden for all other taxpayers who file this form is shown below.

Recordkeeping	19 min.
Learning about the law or the form	29 min.
Preparing the form	1 hr 4 min.
Copying, assembling, and sending the form to the IRS	34 min.

If you have comments concerning the accuracy of these time estimates or suggestions for making this form simpler, we would be happy to hear from you. See the instructions for the tax return with which this form is filed.

-8-

Form **8282**
(Rev. April 2009)
Department of the Treasury
Internal Revenue Service

Donee Information Return

(Sale, Exchange, or Other Disposition of Donated Property)

▶ See instructions.

OMB No. 1545-0908

Give a Copy to Donor

Parts To Complete

- If the organization is an **original donee,** complete *Identifying Information,* Part I (lines 1a–1d and, if applicable, lines 2a–2d), and Part III.
- If the organization is a **successor donee,** complete *Identifying Information,* Part I, Part II, and Part III.

Identifying Information

Print or Type	Name of charitable organization (donee)	Employer identification number
	Address (number, street, and room or suite no.) (or P.O. box no. if mail is not delivered to the street address)	
	City or town, state, and ZIP code	

Part I   Information on ORIGINAL DONOR and SUCCESSOR DONEE Receiving the Property

1a Name of original donor of the property	1b Identifying number(s)
1c Address (number, street, and room or suite no.) (P.O. box no. if mail is not delivered to the street address)	
1d City or town, state, and ZIP code	

Note. Complete lines 2a–2d only if the organization gave this property to another charitable organization (successor donee).

2a Name of charitable organization	2b Employer identification number
2c Address (number, street, and room or suite no.) (or P.O. box no. if mail is not delivered to the street address)	
2d City or town, state, and ZIP code	

Part II   Information on PREVIOUS DONEES. Complete this part only if the organization was not the first donee to receive the property. See the instructions before completing lines 3a through 4d.

3a Name of original donee	3b Employer identification number
3c Address (number, street, and room or suite no.) (or P.O. box no. if mail is not delivered to the street address)	
3d City or town, state, and ZIP code	

4a Name of preceding donee	4b Employer identification number
4c Address (number, street, and room or suite no.) (or P.O. box no. if mail is not delivered to the street address)	
4d City or town, state, and ZIP code	

For Paperwork Reduction Act Notice, see page 4.   Cat. No. 62307Y   Form **8282** (Rev. 4-2009)

Part III   Information on DONATED PROPERTY

1. Description of the donated property sold, exchanged, or otherwise disposed of and how the organization used the property. (If you need more space, attach a separate statement.)	2. Did the disposition involve the organization's entire interest in the property?		3. Was the use related to the organization's exempt purpose or function?		4. Information on use of property. • If you answered "Yes" to question 3 and the property was tangible personal property, describe how the organization's use of the property furthered its exempt purpose or function. Also complete Part IV below. • If you answered "No" to question 3 and the property was tangible personal property, describe the organization's intended use (if any) at the time of the contribution. Also complete Part IV below, if the intended use at the time of the contribution was related to the organization's exempt purpose or function and it became impossible or infeasible to implement.
	Yes	No	Yes	No	
A					
B					
C					
D					

		Donated Property			
		A	**B**	**C**	**D**
5	Date the organization received the donated property (MM/DD/YY)	/ /	/ /	/ /	/ /
6	Date the original donee received the property (MM/DD/YY)	/ /	/ /	/ /	/ /
7	Date the property was sold, exchanged, or otherwise disposed of (MM/DD/YY)	/ /	/ /	/ /	/ /
8	Amount received upon disposition	$	$	$	$

Part IV   Certification

You must sign the certification below if any property described in Part III above is tangible personal property and:
- You answered "Yes" to question 3 above, or
- You answered "No" to question 3 above and the intended use of the property became impossible or infeasible to implement.

Under penalties of perjury and the penalty under section 6720B, I certify that either: (1) the use of the property that meets the above requirements, and is described above in Part III, was substantial and related to the donee organization's exempt purpose or function; or (2) the donee organization intended to use the property for its exempt purpose or function, but the intended use has become impossible or infeasible to implement.

▶ _____ | _____ ▶ _____
Signature of officer   Title   Date

Sign Here

Under penalties of perjury, I declare that I have examined this return, including accompanying schedules and statements, and to the best of my knowledge and belief, it is true, correct, and complete.

▶ _____ | _____ ▶ _____
Signature of officer   Title   Date

_____
Type or print name

Form **8282** (Rev. 4-2009)

General Instructions

Section references are to the Internal Revenue Code.

Purpose of Form

Donee organizations use Form 8282 to report information to the IRS and donors about dispositions of certain charitable deduction property made within 3 years after the donor contributed the property.

Definitions

 For Form 8282 and these instructions, the term "donee" includes all donees, unless specific reference is made to "original" or "successor" donees.

Original donee. The first donee to or for which the donor gave the property. The original donee is required to sign Form 8283, Noncash Charitable Contributions, *Section B. Donated Property Over $5,000 (Except Certain Publicly Traded Securities),* presented by the donor for charitable deduction property.

Successor donee. Any donee of property other than the original donee.

Charitable deduction property. Any donated property (other than money and publicly traded securities) if the claimed value exceeds $5,000 per item or group of similar items donated by the donor to one or more donee organizations. This is the property listed in Section B on Form 8283.

Who Must File

Original and successor donee organizations must file Form 8282 if they sell, exchange, consume, or otherwise dispose of (with or without consideration) charitable deduction property (or any portion) within 3 years after the date the original donee received the property. See *Charitable deduction property* above.

If the organization sold, exchanged, or otherwise disposed of motor vehicles, airplanes, or boats, see Pub. 526, Charitable Contributions.

Exceptions. There are two situations where Form 8282 does not have to be filed.

1. Items valued at $500 or less. The organization does not have to file Form 8282 if, at the time the original donee signed Section B of Form 8283, the donor had signed a statement on Form 8283 that the appraised value of the specific item was not more than $500. If Form 8283 contains more than one item, this exception applies only to those items that are clearly identified as having a value of $500 or less. However, for purposes of the donor's determination of whether the appraised value of the item exceeds $500, all shares of nonpublicly traded stock, or items that form a set, are considered one item. For example, a collection of books written by the same author, components of a stereo system, or six place settings of a pattern of silverware are considered one item.

2. Items consumed or distributed for charitable purpose. The organization does not have to file Form 8282 if an item is consumed or distributed, without consideration, in fulfilling your purpose or function as a tax-exempt organization. For example, no reporting is required for medical supplies consumed or distributed by a tax-exempt relief organization in aiding disaster victims.

When To File

If the organization disposes of charitable deduction property within 3 years of the date the original donee received it and the organization does not meet exception 1 or 2 above, the organization must file Form 8282 within 125 days after the date of disposition.

Exception. If the organization did not file because it had no reason to believe the substantiation requirements applied to the donor, but the organization later becomes aware that the substantiation requirements did apply, the organization must file Form 8282 within 60 days after the date it becomes aware it was liable. For example, this exception would apply where Section B of Form 8283 is furnished to a successor donee after the date that donee disposes of the charitable deduction property.

Missing information. If Form 8282 is filed by the due date, enter the organization's name, address, and employer identification number (EIN) and complete at least Part III, columns 1, 2, 3, and 4; and Part IV. The organization does not have to complete the remaining items if the information is not available. For example, the organization may not have the information necessary to complete all entries if the donor did not make Section B of Form 8283 available.

Where To File

Send Form 8282 to the Department of Treasury, Internal Revenue Service Center, Ogden, UT 84201-0027.

Other Requirements

Information the organization must give a successor donee. If the property is transferred to another charitable organization within the 3-year period discussed earlier, the organization must give the successor donee all of the following information.

1. The name, address, and EIN of the organization.

2. A copy of Section B of Form 8283 that the organization received from the donor or a preceding donee. The preceding donee is the one who gave the organization the property.

3. A copy of this Form 8282, within 15 days after the organization files it.

The organization must furnish items 1 and 2 above within 15 days after the latest of the date:

● The organization transferred the property,

● The original donee signed Section B of Form 8283, or

● The organization received a copy of Section B of Form 8283 from the preceding donee if the organization is also a successor donee.

Information the successor donee must give the organization. The successor donee organization to whom the organization transferred this property is required to give the organization its name, address, and EIN within 15 days after the later of:

● The date the organization transferred the property, or

● The date the successor donee received a copy of Section B of Form 8283.

Information the organization must give the donor. The organization must give a copy of Form 8282 to the original donor of the property.

Recordkeeping. The organization must keep a copy of Section B of Form 8283 in its records.

Penalties

Failure to file penalty. The organization may be subject to a penalty if it fails to file this form by the due date, fails to include all of the information required to be shown on the filed form, or includes incorrect information on the filed form. The penalty is generally $50 per form. For more details, see section 6721 and 6724.

Fraudulent identification of exempt use property. A $10,000 penalty may apply to any person who identifies in Part III tangible personal property the organization sold, exchanged, or otherwise disposed of, as having a use that is related to a purpose or function knowing that such property was not intended for such a use. For more details, see section 6720B.

Specific Instructions
Part I

Line 1a. Enter the name of the original donor.

Line 1b. The donor's identifying number may be either an employer identification number or a social security number, and should be the same number provided on page 2 of Form 8283.

Line 1c and 1d. Enter the last known address of the original donor.

Lines 2a–2d. Complete these lines if the organization gave the property to another charitable organization successor donee (defined earlier). If the organization is an original donee, skip Part II and go to Part III.

Part II

Complete Part II only if the organization is a successor donee. If the organization is the original donee, do not complete any lines in Part II; go directly to Part III.

If the organization is the **second donee,** complete lines 3a through 3d. If the organization is the **third or later donee,** complete lines 3a through 4d. On lines 4a through 4d, give information on the preceding donee.

Part III

Column 1. For charitable deduction property that the organization sold, exchanged, or otherwise disposed of within 3 years of the original contribution, describe each item in detail. For a motor vehicle, include the vehicle identification number. For a boat, include the hull identification number. For an airplane, include the aircraft identification number. Additionally, for the period of time the organization owned the property, explain how it was used. If additional space is needed, attach a statement.

Column 3. Check "Yes" if the organization's use of the charitable deduction property was related to its exempt purpose or function. Check "No" if the organization sold, exchanged, or otherwise disposed of the property without using it.

Signature

Form 8282 is not valid unless it is signed by an officer of the organization. Be sure to include the title of the person signing the form and the date the form was signed.

How To Get Tax Help

Internet

You can access the IRS website 24 hours a day, 7 days a week at *www.irs.gov/eo* to:

- Download forms, instructions, and publications;

- Order IRS products online;

- Research your tax questions online;

- Search publications online by topic or keyword;

- View Internal Revenue Bulletins (IRBs) published in the last few years; and

- Sign up to receive local and national tax news by email. To subscribe, visit *www.irs.gov/eo.*

DVD

You can order Publication 1796, IRS Tax Products DVD, and obtain:

- Current-year forms, instructions, and publications.

- Prior-year forms, instructions, and publications.

- Tax Map: an electronic research tool and finding aid.

- Tax law frequently asked questions.

- Tax topics from the IRS telephone response system.

- Fill-in, print, and save features for most tax forms.

- IRBs.

- Toll-free and email technical support.

- Two releases during the year.

Purchase the DVD from National Technical Information Service (NTIS) at *www.irs.gov/cdorders* for $30 (no handling fee) or call **1-877-CDFORMS** (1-877-233-6767) toll-free to buy the DVD for $30 (plus a $6 handling fee). Price is subject to change.

By Phone

You can order forms and publications by calling 1-800-TAX-FORM (1-800-829-3676). You can also get most forms and publications at your local IRS office. If you have questions and/or need help completing this form, please call 1-877-829-5500. This toll free telephone service is available Monday thru Friday.

Paperwork Reduction Act Notice. We ask for the information on this form to carry out the Internal Revenue laws of the United States. You are required to give us the information. We need it to ensure that you are complying with these laws and to allow us to figure and collect the right amount of tax.

You are not required to provide the information requested on a form that is subject to the Paperwork Reduction Act unless the form displays a valid OMB control number. Books or records relating to a form or its instructions must be retained as long as their contents may become material in the administration of any Internal Revenue law. Generally, tax returns and return information are confidential, as required by section 6103.

The time needed to complete this form will vary depending on individual circumstances. The estimated average time is:

Recordkeeping . . . . 3 hr., 35 min.

Learning about the law or the form . . . . 12 min.

Preparing and sending the form to the IRS . . . . 15 min.

If you have comments concerning the accuracy of these time estimates or suggestions for making this form simpler, we would be happy to hear from you. You can write to the Internal Revenue Service, Tax Products Coordinating Committee, SE:W:CAR:MP:T:T:SP, 1111 Constitution Ave. NW, IR-6526, Washington, DC 20224. Do not send the form to this address. Instead, see *Where To File* on page 3.

NOTE: IRS updates this publication annually, most current version is at http://irs.gov

Department
of the
Treasury

**Internal
Revenue
Service**

Publication 526
Cat. No. 15050A

Charitable Contributions

For use in preparing

2015 Returns

Get forms and other information faster and easier at:
- *IRS.gov* (English)
- *IRS.gov/Korean* (한국어)
- *IRS.gov/Spanish* (Español)
- *IRS.gov/Russian* (Русский)
- *IRS.gov/Chinese* (中文)
- *IRS.gov/Vietnamese* (TiếngViệt)

Contents

Future Developments

For the latest information about developments related to Pub. 526 (such as legislation enacted after we release it), go to *www.irs.gov/pub526*.

What's New

Limit on itemized deductions. For 2015, you may have to reduce the total amount of certain itemized deductions, including charitable contributions, if your adjusted gross income is more than:

- $154,950 if married filing separately,
- $258,250 if single,
- $284,050 if head of household, or
- $309,900 if married filing jointly or qualifying widow(er).

For more information and a worksheet, see the instructions for Schedule A (Form 1040).

Slain Officer Family Support Act of 2015. A special rule applies to cash contributions made between January 1, 2015, and April 15, 2015, to benefit the families of slain New York Detectives Wenjian Liu or Rafael Ramos. See *Contributions You Can Deduct*.

Reminders

Disaster relief. You can deduct contributions for flood relief, hurricane relief, or other disaster relief to a qualified organization (defined under *Organizations That Qualify To Receive Deductible Contributions*). However, you can't deduct contributions earmarked for relief of a particular individual or family.

Pub. 3833, Disaster Relief, Providing Assistance through Charitable Organizations, has more information about disaster relief, including how to establish a new charitable organization. You can also find more information on IRS.gov. Enter "disaster relief" in the search box.

Photographs of missing children. The IRS is a proud partner with the National Center for Missing and Exploited Children. Photographs of missing children selected by the Center may appear in this publication on pages that would otherwise be blank. You can help bring these children home by looking at the photographs and calling 1-800-THE-LOST (1-800-843-5678) if you recognize a child.

Introduction

This publication explains how to claim a deduction for your charitable contributions. It discusses the types of organizations to which you can make deductible charitable contributions and the types of contributions you can deduct. It also discusses how much you can deduct, what records you must keep, and how to report charitable contributions.

A charitable contribution is a donation or gift to, or for the use of, a qualified organization. It is voluntary and is made without getting, or expecting to get, anything of equal value.

Qualified organizations. Qualified organizations include nonprofit groups that are religious, charitable, educational, scientific, or literary in purpose, or that work to prevent cruelty to children or animals. You will find descriptions of these organizations under *Organizations That Qualify To Receive Deductible Contributions*.

Form 1040 required. To deduct a charitable contribution, you must file Form 1040 and itemize deductions on Schedule A (Form 1040). The amount of your deduction may be limited if certain rules and limits explained in this publication apply to you.

Comments and suggestions. We welcome your comments about this publication and your suggestions for future editions.

You can send us comments from *www.irs.gov/formspubs*. Click on "More Information" and then on "Give us feedback."

Or you can write to:

Internal Revenue Service
Tax Forms and Publications
1111 Constitution Ave. NW, IR-6526
Washington, DC 20224

We respond to many letters by telephone. Therefore, it would be helpful if you would include your daytime phone number, including the area code, in your correspondence.

Although we can't respond individually to each comment received, we do appreciate your feedback and will consider your comments as we revise our tax products.

Ordering forms and publications. Visit *www.irs.gov/formspubs* to download forms and publications. Otherwise, you can go to

www.irs.gov/orderforms to order current and prior-year forms and instructions. Your order should arrive within 10 business days.

Tax questions. If you have a tax question not answered by this publication, check IRS.gov and *How To Get Tax Help* at the end of this publication.

Useful Items

You may want to see:

Publication

❏ **561** Determining the Value of Donated Property

Forms (and Instructions)

❏ **Schedule A (Form 1040)** Itemized Deductions

❏ **8283** Noncash Charitable Contributions

See *How To Get Tax Help* near the end of this publication for information about getting these publications and forms.

Organizations That Qualify To Receive Deductible Contributions

You can deduct your contributions only if you make them to a qualified organization. Most organizations, other than churches and governments, must apply to the IRS to become a qualified organization.

Table 1. **Examples of Charitable Contributions—A Quick Check**

Use the following lists for a quick check of whether you can deduct a contribution. See the rest of this publication for more information and additional rules and limits that may apply.

Deductible As Charitable Contributions	Not Deductible As Charitable Contributions
Money or property you give to: • Churches, synagogues, temples, mosques, and other religious organizations • Federal, state, and local governments, if your contribution is solely for public purposes (for example, a gift to reduce the public debt or maintain a public park) • Nonprofit schools and hospitals • The Salvation Army, American Red Cross, CARE, Goodwill Industries, United Way, Boy Scouts of America, Girl Scouts of America, Boys and Girls Clubs of America, etc. • War veterans' groups	Money or property you give to: • Civic leagues, social and sports clubs, labor unions, and chambers of commerce • Foreign organizations (except certain Canadian, Israeli, and Mexican charities) • Groups that are run for personal profit • Groups whose purpose is to lobby for law changes • Homeowners' associations • Individuals • Political groups or candidates for public office
Expenses paid for a student living with you, sponsored by a qualified organization	Cost of raffle, bingo, or lottery tickets
Out-of-pocket expenses when you serve a qualified organization as a volunteer	Dues, fees, or bills paid to country clubs, lodges, fraternal orders, or similar groups
	Tuition
	Value of your time or services
	Value of blood given to a blood bank

How to check whether an organization can receive deductible charitable contributions. You can ask any organization whether it is a qualified organization, and most will be able to tell you. Or go to IRS.gov. Click on "Tools" and then on "Exempt Organizations Select Check" (*www.irs.gov/Charities-&-Non-Profits/Exempt-Organizations-Select-Check*). This online tool will enable you to search for qualified organizations.

Types of Qualified Organizations

Generally, only the following types of organizations can be qualified organizations.

1. A community chest, corporation, trust, fund, or foundation organized or created in or under the laws of the United States, any state, the District of Columbia, or any possession of the United States (including Puerto Rico). It must, however, be organized and operated only for charitable, religious, scientific, literary, or educational purposes, or for the prevention of cruelty to children or animals. Certain organizations that foster national or international amateur sports competition also qualify.

2. War veterans' organizations, including posts, auxiliaries, trusts, or foundations, organized in the United States or any of its possessions (including Puerto Rico).

3. Domestic fraternal societies, orders, and associations operating under the lodge system. (Your contribution to this type of organization is deductible only if it is to be used solely for charitable, religious, scientific, literary, or educational purposes, or

for the prevention of cruelty to children or animals.)

4. Certain nonprofit cemetery companies or corporations. (Your contribution to this type of organization isn't deductible if it can be used for the care of a specific lot or mausoleum crypt.)

5. The United States or any state, the District of Columbia, a U.S. possession (including Puerto Rico), a political subdivision of a state or U.S. possession, or an Indian tribal government or any of its subdivisions that perform substantial government functions. (Your contribution to this type of organization is deductible only if it is to be used solely for public purposes.)

Example 1. You contribute cash to your city's police department to be used as a reward for information about a crime. The city police department is a qualified organization, and your contribution is for a public purpose. You can deduct your contribution.

Example 2. You make a voluntary contribution to the social security trust fund, not earmarked for a specific account. Because the trust fund is part of the U.S. Government, you contributed to a qualified organization. You can deduct your contribution.

Examples. The following list gives some examples of qualified organizations.

- Churches, a convention or association of churches, temples, synagogues, mosques, and other religious organizations.
- Most nonprofit charitable organizations such as the American Red Cross and the United Way.
- Most nonprofit educational organizations, including the Boy Scouts of America, Girl Scouts of America, colleges, and museums. This also includes nonprofit daycare centers that provide childcare to the general public if substantially all the childcare is provided to enable parents and guardians to be gainfully employed. However, if your contribution is a substitute for tuition or other enrollment fee, it isn't deductible as a charitable contribution, as explained later under *Contributions You Can't Deduct.*
- Nonprofit hospitals and medical research organizations.
- Utility company emergency energy programs, if the utility company is an agent for a charitable organization that assists individuals with emergency energy needs.
- Nonprofit volunteer fire companies.
- Nonprofit organizations that develop and maintain public parks and recreation facilities.
- Civil defense organizations.

Canadian charities. You may be able to deduct contributions to certain Canadian charitable organizations covered under an income tax treaty with Canada. To deduct your contribution to a Canadian charity, you generally must have income from sources in Canada. See Pub. 597, Information on the United States-Canada In-

come Tax Treaty, for information on how to figure your deduction.

Mexican charities. Under the U.S.-Mexico income tax treaty, a contribution to a Mexican charitable organization may be deductible, but only if and to the extent the contribution would have been treated as a charitable contribution to a public charity created or organized under U.S. law. To deduct your contribution to a Mexican charity, you must have income from sources in Mexico. The limits described in *Limits on Deductions,* later, apply and are figured using your income from Mexican sources.

Israeli charities. Under the U.S.-Israel income tax treaty, a contribution to an Israeli charitable organization is deductible if and to the extent the contribution would have been treated as a charitable contribution if the organization had been created or organized under U.S. law. To deduct your contribution to an Israeli charity, you must have income from sources in Israel. The limits described in *Limits on Deductions,* later, apply. The deduction is also limited to 25% of your adjusted gross income from Israeli sources.

Contributions You Can Deduct

Generally, you can deduct contributions of money or property you make to, or for the use of, a qualified organization. A contribution is "for the use of" a qualified organization when it is held in a legally enforceable trust for the qualified organization or in a similar legal arrangement.

The contributions must be made to a qualified organization and not set aside for use by a specific person.

Slain Officer Family Support Act of 2015. If you made a contribution for the relief of the families of slain New York Police Department Detectives Liu Wenjian or Rafael Ramos you may be able to treat that contribution as made in 2014. If you want to treat the contribution as made in 2014, it must have been made:

- In cash,
- Between January 1 and April 15, 2015, and
- For the relief of the families of the slain detectives.

 If you treat the contribution as made in 2014 instead of 2015, you may need to file an amended return for 2014.

 If you made your contribution by phone, keep your phone bill showing the name of who you made the donation to, the date you made the contribution, and the amount of the contribution. See Records To Keep.

If you give property to a qualified organization, you generally can deduct the fair market value of the property at the time of the contribution. See *Contributions of Property,* later.

Your deduction for charitable contributions generally can't be more than 50% of your adjusted gross income (AGI), but in some cases 20% and 30% limits may apply.

In addition, the total of your charitable contributions deduction and certain other itemized deductions may be limited. See *Limits on Deductions,* later.

Table 1 in this publication gives examples of contributions you can and can't deduct.

Contributions From Which You Benefit

If you receive a benefit as a result of making a contribution to a qualified organization, you can deduct only the amount of your contribution that is more than the value of the benefit you receive. Also see *Contributions From Which You Benefit* under *Contributions You Can't Deduct,* later.

If you pay more than fair market value to a qualified organization for goods or services, the excess may be a charitable contribution. For the excess amount to qualify, you must pay it with the intent to make a charitable contribution.

Example 1. You pay $65 for a ticket to a dinner dance at a church. Your entire $65 payment goes to the church. The ticket to the dinner dance has a fair market value of $25. When you buy your ticket, you know its value is less than your payment. To figure the amount of your charitable contribution, subtract the value of the benefit you receive ($25) from your total payment ($65). You can deduct $40 as a charitable contribution to the church.

Example 2. At a fundraising auction conducted by a charity, you pay $600 for a week's stay at a beach house. The amount you pay is no more than the fair rental value. You haven't made a deductible charitable contribution.

Athletic events. If you make a payment to, or for the benefit of, a college or university and, as a result, you receive the right to buy tickets to an athletic event in the athletic stadium of the college or university, you can deduct 80% of the payment as a charitable contribution.

If any part of your payment is for tickets (rather than the right to buy tickets), that part isn't deductible. Subtract the price of the tickets from your payment. You can deduct 80% of the remaining amount as a charitable contribution.

Example 1. You pay $300 a year for membership in a university's athletic scholarship program. The only benefit of membership is that you have the right to buy one season ticket for a seat in a designated area of the stadium at the university's home football games. You can deduct $240 (80% of $300) as a charitable contribution.

Example 2. The facts are the same as in *Example 1* except your $300 payment includes the purchase of one season ticket for the stated ticket price of $120. You must subtract the usual price of a ticket ($120) from your $300 payment. The result is $180. Your deductible charitable contribution is $144 (80% of $180).

Charity benefit events. If you pay a qualified organization more than fair market value for the right to attend a charity ball, banquet, show, sporting event, or other benefit event, you can deduct only the amount that is more than the value of the privileges or other benefits you receive.

If there is an established charge for the event, that charge is the value of your benefit. If there is no established charge, the reasonable value of the right to attend the event is the value of your benefit. Whether you use the tickets or other privileges has no effect on the amount you can deduct. However, if you return the ticket to the qualified organization for resale, you can deduct the entire amount you paid for the ticket.

 Even if the ticket or other evidence of payment indicates that the payment is a "contribution," this doesn't mean you can deduct the entire amount. If the ticket shows the price of admission and the amount of the contribution, you can deduct the contribution amount.

Example. You pay $40 to see a special showing of a movie for the benefit of a qualified organization. Printed on the ticket is "Contribution–$40." If the regular price for the movie is $8, your contribution is $32 ($40 payment – $8 regular price).

Membership fees or dues. You may be able to deduct membership fees or dues you pay to a qualified organization. However, you can deduct only the amount that is more than the value of the benefits you receive.

You can't deduct dues, fees, or assessments paid to country clubs and other social organizations. They aren't qualified organizations.

Certain membership benefits can be disregarded. Both you and the organization can disregard the following membership benefits if you get them in return for an annual payment of $75 or less.

1. Any rights or privileges, other than those discussed under *Athletic events,* earlier, that you can use frequently while you are a member, such as:
   a. Free or discounted admission to the organization's facilities or events,
   b. Free or discounted parking,
   c. Preferred access to goods or services, and
   d. Discounts on the purchase of goods and services.
2. Admission, while you are a member, to events open only to members of the organization if the organization reasonably projects that the cost per person (excluding any allocated overhead) isn't more than $10.50.

Token items. You don't have to reduce your contribution by the value of any benefit you receive if both of the following are true.

1. You receive only a small item or other benefit of token value.
2. The qualified organization correctly determines that the value of the item or benefit you received isn't substantial and informs you that you can deduct your payment in full.

The organization determines whether the value of an item or benefit is substantial by using Revenue Procedures 90-12 and 92-49 and the inflation adjustment in Revenue Procedure 2014-61.

Written statement. A qualified organization must give you a written statement if you make a payment of more than $75 that is partly a contribution and partly for goods or services. The statement must say you can deduct only the amount of your payment that is more than the value of the goods or services you received. It must also give you a good faith estimate of the value of those goods or services.

The organization can give you the statement either when it solicits or when it receives a payment from you.

Exception. An organization won't have to give you this statement if one of the following is true.

1. The organization is:
   a. A governmental organization described in (5) under *Types of Qualified Organizations,* earlier, or
   b. An organization formed only for religious purposes, and the only benefit you receive is an intangible religious benefit (such as admission to a religious ceremony) that generally isn't sold in commercial transactions outside the donative context.
2. You receive only items whose value isn't substantial as described under *Token items,* earlier.
3. You receive only membership benefits that can be disregarded, as described under *Membership fees or dues,* earlier.

Expenses Paid for Student Living With You

You may be able to deduct some expenses of having a student live with you. You can deduct qualifying expenses for a foreign or American student who:

1. Lives in your home under a written agreement between you and a qualified organization (defined later) as part of a program of the organization to provide educational opportunities for the student,
2. Isn't your relative (defined later) or dependent (also defined later), and
3. Is a full-time student in the twelfth or any lower grade at a school in the United States.

 You can deduct up to $50 a month for each full calendar month the student lives with you. Any month when conditions (1) through (3) are met for 15 or more days counts as a full month.

Qualified organization. For these purposes, a qualified organization can be any of the organizations described earlier under *Types of Qualified Organizations,* except those in (4) and (5). For example, if you are providing a home for a student as part of a state or local government program, you can't deduct your expenses as charitable contributions. But see *Foster parents* under *Out-of-Pocket Expenses in Giving Services,* later, if you provide the home as a foster parent.

Relative. The term "relative" means any of the following persons.
- Your child, stepchild, foster child, or a descendant of any of them (for example, your grandchild). A legally adopted child is considered your child.
- Your brother, sister, half brother, half sister, stepbrother, or stepsister.
- Your father, mother, grandparent, or other direct ancestor.
- Your stepfather or stepmother.
- A son or daughter of your brother or sister.
- A brother or sister of your father or mother.
- Your son-in-law, daughter-in-law, father-in-law, mother-in-law, brother-in-law, or sister-in-law.

Dependent. For this purpose, the term "dependent" means:

1. A person you can claim as a dependent, or
2. A person you could have claimed as a dependent except that:
   a. He or she received gross income of $4,000 or more,
   b. He or she filed a joint return, or
   c. You, or your spouse if filing jointly, could be claimed as a dependent on someone else's 2015 return.

 Foreign students brought to this country under a qualified international education exchange program and placed in American homes for a temporary period generally aren't U.S. residents and can't be claimed as dependents.

Qualifying expenses. You may be able to deduct the cost of books, tuition, food, clothing, transportation, medical and dental care, entertainment, and other amounts you actually spend for the well-being of the student.

Expenses that don't qualify. You can't deduct depreciation on your home, the fair market value of lodging, and similar items not considered amounts actually spent by you. Nor can you deduct general household expenses, such as taxes, insurance, and repairs.

Reimbursed expenses. In most cases, you can't claim a charitable contribution

Table 2. **Volunteers' Questions and Answers**

If you volunteer for a qualified organization, the following questions and answers may apply to you. All of the rules explained in this publication also apply. See, in particular, *Out-of-Pocket Expenses in Giving Services*.

Question	Answer
I volunteer 6 hours a week in the office of a qualified organization. The receptionist is paid $10 an hour for the same work. Can I deduct $60 a week for my time?	No, you can't deduct the value of your time or services.
The office is 30 miles from my home. Can I deduct any of my car expenses for these trips?	Yes, you can deduct the costs of gas and oil that are directly related to getting to and from the place where you volunteer. If you don't want to figure your actual costs, you can deduct 14 cents for each mile.
I volunteer as a Red Cross nurse's aide at a hospital. Can I deduct the cost of the uniforms I must wear?	Yes, you can deduct the cost of buying and cleaning your uniforms if the hospital is a qualified organization, the uniforms aren't suitable for everyday use, and you must wear them when volunteering.
I pay a babysitter to watch my children while I volunteer for a qualified organization. Can I deduct these costs?	No, you can't deduct payments for childcare expenses as a charitable contribution, even if you would be unable to volunteer without childcare. (If you have childcare expenses so you can work for pay, see Pub. 503, Child and Dependent Care Expenses.)

deduction if you are compensated or reimbursed for any part of having a student live with you. However, you may be able to claim a charitable contribution deduction for the unreimbursed portion of your expenses if you are reimbursed only for an extraordinary one-time item, such as a hospital bill or vacation trip, you paid in advance at the request of the student's parents or the sponsoring organization.

Mutual exchange program. You can't deduct the costs of a foreign student living in your home under a mutual exchange program through which your child will live with a family in a foreign country.

Reporting expenses. For a list of what you must file with your return if you deduct expenses for a student living with you, see *Reporting expenses for student living with you* under *How To Report*, later.

Out-of-Pocket Expenses in Giving Services

Although you can't deduct the value of your services given to a qualified organization, you may be able to deduct some amounts you pay in giving services to a qualified organization. The amounts must be:

- Unreimbursed,
- Directly connected with the services,
- Expenses you had only because of the services you gave, and
- Not personal, living, or family expenses.

Table 2 contains questions and answers that apply to some individuals who volunteer their services.

Underprivileged youths selected by charity. You can deduct reasonable unreimbursed out-of-pocket expenses you pay to allow underprivileged youths to attend athletic events, movies, or dinners. The youths must be selected by a charitable organization whose goal is to reduce juvenile delinquency. Your own similar expenses in accompanying the youths aren't deductible.

Conventions. If a qualified organization selects you to attend a convention as its representative, you can deduct your unreimbursed expenses for travel, including reasonable amounts for meals and lodging, while away from home overnight for the convention. However, see *Travel*, later.

You can't deduct personal expenses for sightseeing, fishing parties, theater tickets, or nightclubs. You also can't deduct travel, meals and lodging, and other expenses for your spouse or children.

You can't deduct your travel expenses in attending a church convention if you go only as a member of your church rather than as a chosen representative. You can, however, deduct unreimbursed expenses that are directly connected with giving services for your church during the convention.

Uniforms. You can deduct the cost and upkeep of uniforms that aren't suitable for everyday use and that you must wear while performing donated services for a charitable organization.

Foster parents. You may be able to deduct as a charitable contribution some of the costs of being a foster parent (foster care provider) if you have no profit motive in providing the foster care and aren't, in fact, making a profit. A qualified organization must select the individuals you take into your home for foster care.

You can deduct expenses that meet both of the following requirements.

1. They are unreimbursed out-of-pocket expenses to feed, clothe, and care for the foster child.

2. They are incurred primarily to benefit the qualified organization.

Unreimbursed expenses that you can't deduct as charitable contributions may be considered support provided by you in determining whether you can claim the foster child as a dependent. For details, see Pub. 501, Exemptions, Standard Deduction, and Filing Information.

Example. You cared for a foster child because you wanted to adopt her, not to benefit the agency that placed her in your home. Your

unreimbursed expenses aren't deductible as charitable contributions.

Church deacon. You can deduct as a charitable contribution any unreimbursed expenses you have while in a permanent diaconate program established by your church. These expenses include the cost of vestments, books, and transportation required in order to serve in the program as either a deacon candidate or an ordained deacon.

Car expenses. You can deduct as a charitable contribution any unreimbursed out-of-pocket expenses, such as the cost of gas and oil, directly related to the use of your car in giving services to a charitable organization. You can't deduct general repair and maintenance expenses, depreciation, registration fees, or the costs of tires or insurance.

If you don't want to deduct your actual expenses, you can use a standard mileage rate of 14 cents a mile to figure your contribution.

You can deduct parking fees and tolls whether you use your actual expenses or the standard mileage rate.

You must keep reliable written records of your car expenses. For more information, see *Car expenses* under *Records To Keep*, later.

Travel. Generally, you can claim a charitable contribution deduction for travel expenses necessarily incurred while you are away from home performing services for a charitable organization only if there is no significant element of personal pleasure, recreation, or vacation in the travel. This applies whether you pay the expenses directly or indirectly. You are paying the expenses indirectly if you make a payment to the charitable organization and the organization pays for your travel expenses.

The deduction for travel expenses won't be denied simply because you enjoy providing services to the charitable organization. Even if you enjoy the trip, you can take a charitable contribution deduction for your travel expenses if you are on duty in a genuine and substantial sense throughout the trip. However, if you have only nominal duties, or if for significant parts of the trip you don't have any duties, you can't deduct your travel expenses.

Example 1. You are a troop leader for a tax-exempt youth group and you take the group on a camping trip. You are responsible for overseeing the setup of the camp and for providing adult supervision for other activities during the entire trip. You participate in the activities of the group and enjoy your time with them. You oversee the breaking of camp and you transport the group home. You can deduct your travel expenses.

Example 2. You sail from one island to another and spend 8 hours a day counting whales and other forms of marine life. The project is sponsored by a charitable organization. In most circumstances, you can't deduct your expenses.

Example 3. You work for several hours each morning on an archeological dig sponsored by a charitable organization. The rest of the day is free for recreation and sightseeing. You can't take a charitable contribution deduction even though you work very hard during those few hours.

Example 4. You spend the entire day attending a charitable organization's regional meeting as a chosen representative. In the evening you go to the theater. You can claim your travel expenses as charitable contributions, but you can't claim the cost of your evening at the theater.

Daily allowance (per diem). If you provide services for a charitable organization and receive a daily allowance to cover reasonable travel expenses, including meals and lodging while away from home overnight, you must include in income any part of the allowance that is more than your deductible travel expenses. You may be able to deduct any necessary travel expenses that are more than the allowance.

Deductible travel expenses. These include:
- Air, rail, and bus transportation,
- Out-of-pocket expenses for your car,
- Taxi fares or other costs of transportation between the airport or station and your hotel,
- Lodging costs, and
- The cost of meals.

Because these travel expenses aren't business-related, they aren't subject to the same limits as business related expenses. For information on business travel expenses, see *Travel* in Pub. 463, Travel, Entertainment, Gift, and Car Expenses.

Expenses of Whaling Captains

You may be able to deduct as a charitable contribution any reasonable and necessary whaling expenses you pay during the year to carry out sanctioned whaling activities. The deduction is limited to $10,000 a year. To claim the deduction, you must be recognized by the Alaska Eskimo Whaling Commission as a whaling captain charged with the responsibility of maintaining and carrying out sanctioned whaling activities.

Sanctioned whaling activities are subsistence bowhead whale hunting activities conducted under the management plan of the Alaska Eskimo Whaling Commission.

Whaling expenses include expenses for:
- Acquiring and maintaining whaling boats, weapons, and gear used in sanctioned whaling activities,
- Supplying food for the crew and other provisions for carrying out these activities, and
- Storing and distributing the catch from these activities.

 You must keep records showing the time, place, date, amount, and nature of the expenses. For details, see Revenue Procedure 2006-50, which is on page 944 of Internal Revenue Bulletin 2006-47 at *www.irs.gov/pub/irs-irbs/irb06-47.pdf.*

Contributions You Can't Deduct

There are some contributions you can't deduct and others you can deduct only in part.

You can't deduct as a charitable contribution:

1. A contribution to a specific individual,
2. A contribution to a nonqualified organization,
3. The part of a contribution from which you receive or expect to receive a benefit,
4. The value of your time or services,
5. Your personal expenses,
6. A qualified charitable distribution from an individual retirement arrangement (IRA),
7. Appraisal fees,
8. Certain contributions to donor-advised funds, or
9. Certain contributions of partial interests in property.

Detailed discussions of these items follow.

Contributions to Individuals

You can't deduct contributions to specific individuals, including the following.
- Contributions to fraternal societies made for the purpose of paying medical or burial expenses of members.
- Contributions to individuals who are needy or worthy. You can't deduct these contributions even if you make them to a qualified organization for the benefit of a specific person. But you can deduct a contribution to a qualified organization that helps needy or worthy individuals if you don't indicate that your contribution is for a specific person.
- Payments to a member of the clergy that can be spent as he or she wishes, such as for personal expenses.
- Expenses you paid for another person who provided services to a qualified organization.

Example. Your son does missionary work. You pay his expenses. You can't claim a deduction for your son's unreimbursed expenses related to his contribution of services.
- Payments to a hospital that are for a specific patient's care or for services for a specific patient. You can't deduct these payments even if the hospital is operated by a city, state, or other qualified organization.

 If you made a contribution for the relief of the families of slain New York Police Department Detectives Wenjian Liu or Rafael Ramos on or after December 20, 2014, this contribution isn't considered a contribution to a specific individual. See Slain Officer Family Support Act of 2015.

Contributions to Nonqualified Organizations

You can't deduct contributions to organizations that aren't qualified to receive tax-deductible contributions, including the following.

1. Certain state bar associations if:
   a. The bar isn't a political subdivision of a state,
   b. The bar has private, as well as public, purposes, such as promoting the professional interests of members, and
   c. Your contribution is unrestricted and can be used for private purposes.
2. Chambers of commerce and other business leagues or organizations.
3. Civic leagues and associations.
4. Country clubs and other social clubs.
5. Foreign organizations other than certain Canadian, Israeli, or Mexican charitable organizations. (See *Canadian charities, Mexican charities,* and *Israeli charities* under *Organizations That Qualify To Receive Deductible Contributions,* earlier.) Also, you can't deduct a contribution you made to any qualifying organization if the contribution is earmarked to go to a foreign organization. However, certain contributions to a qualified organization for use in a program conducted by a foreign charity may be deductible as long as they aren't earmarked to go to the foreign charity. For the contribution to be deductible, the qualified organization must approve the program as furthering its own exempt purposes and must keep control over the use of the contributed funds. The contribution is also deductible if the foreign charity is only an administrative arm of the qualified organization.
6. Homeowners' associations.
7. Labor unions. But you may be able to deduct union dues as a miscellaneous itemized deduction, subject to the 2%-of-adjusted-gross-income limit, on Schedule A (Form 1040). See Pub. 529, Miscellaneous Deductions.
8. Political organizations and candidates.

Contributions From Which You Benefit

If you receive or expect to receive a financial or economic benefit as a result of making a contribution to a qualified organization, you can't deduct the part of the contribution that represents the value of the benefit you receive. See *Contributions From Which You Benefit* under *Contributions You Can Deduct*, earlier. These contributions include the following.

- Contributions for lobbying. This includes amounts you earmark for use in, or in connection with, influencing specific legislation.
- Contributions to a retirement home for room, board, maintenance, or admittance. Also, if the amount of your contribution depends on the type or size of apartment you will occupy, it isn't a charitable contribution.
- Costs of raffles, bingo, lottery, etc. You can't deduct as a charitable contribution amounts you pay to buy raffle or lottery tickets or to play bingo or other games of chance. For information on how to report gambling winnings and losses, see *Deductions Not Subject to the 2% Limit* in Pub. 529.
- Dues to fraternal orders and similar groups. However, see *Membership fees or dues* under *Contributions From Which You Benefit*, earlier.
- Tuition, or amounts you pay instead of tuition. You can't deduct as a charitable contribution amounts you pay as tuition even if you pay them for children to attend parochial schools or qualifying nonprofit daycare centers. You also can't deduct any fixed amount you must pay in addition to, or instead of, tuition to enroll in a private school, even if it is designated as a "donation."
- Contributions connected with split-dollar insurance arrangements. You can't deduct any part of a contribution to a charitable organization if, in connection with the contribution, the organization directly or indirectly pays, has paid, or is expected to pay any premium on any life insurance, annuity, or endowment contract for which you, any member of your family, or any other person chosen by you (other than a qualified charitable organization) is a beneficiary.

    Example. You donate money to a charitable organization. The charity uses the money to purchase a cash value life insurance policy. The beneficiaries under the insurance policy include members of your family. Even though the charity may eventually get some benefit out of the insurance policy, you can't deduct any part of the donation.

Qualified Charitable Distributions

A qualified charitable distribution (QCD) is a distribution made directly by the trustee of your individual retirement arrangement (IRA), other than a SEP or SIMPLE IRA, to certain qualified organizations. You must have been at least age 70½ when the distribution was made. Your total

QCDs for the year can't be more than $100,000. If all the requirements are met, a QCD is nontaxable, but you can't claim a charitable contribution deduction for a QCD. See Pub. 590-B, Distributions from Individual Retirement Arrangements (IRAs), for more information about QCDs.

Value of Time or Services

You can't deduct the value of your time or services, including:

- Blood donations to the American Red Cross or to blood banks, and
- The value of income lost while you work as an unpaid volunteer for a qualified organization.

Personal Expenses

You can't deduct personal, living, or family expenses, such as the following items.

- The cost of meals you eat while you perform services for a qualified organization, unless it is necessary for you to be away from home overnight while performing the services.
- Adoption expenses, including fees paid to an adoption agency and the costs of keeping a child in your home before adoption is final. However, you may be able to claim a tax credit for these expenses. Also, you may be able to exclude from your gross income amounts paid or reimbursed by your employer for your adoption expenses. See Form 8839, Qualified Adoption Expenses, and its instructions, for more information. You also may be able to claim an exemption for the child. See *Exemptions for Dependents* in Pub. 501 for more information.

Appraisal Fees

You can't deduct as a charitable contribution any fees you pay to find the fair market value of donated property. But you can claim them, subject to the 2%-of-adjusted-gross-income limit, as a miscellaneous itemized deduction on Schedule A (Form 1040). See *Deductions Subject to the 2% Limit* in Pub. 529 for more information.

Contributions to Donor-Advised Funds

You can't deduct a contribution to a donor-advised fund if:

- The qualified organization that sponsors the fund is a war veterans' organization, a fraternal society, or a nonprofit cemetery company, or
- You don't have an acknowledgment from that sponsoring organization that it has exclusive legal control over the assets contributed.

There are also other circumstances in which you can't deduct your contribution to a donor-advised fund.

Generally, a donor-advised fund is a fund or account in which a donor can, because of being

a donor, advise the fund how to distribute or invest amounts held in the fund. For details, see Internal Revenue Code section 170(f)(18).

Partial Interest in Property

Generally, you can't deduct a contribution of less than your entire interest in property. For details, see *Partial Interest in Property* under *Contributions of Property*, later.

Contributions of Property

If you contribute property to a qualified organization, the amount of your charitable contribution is generally the fair market value of the property at the time of the contribution. However, if the property has increased in value, you may have to make some adjustments to the amount of your deduction. See *Giving Property That Has Increased in Value*, later.

For information about the records you must keep and the information you must furnish with your return if you donate property, see *Records To Keep* and *How To Report*, later.

Contributions Subject to Special Rules

Special rules apply if you contribute:

- Clothing or household items,
- A car, boat, or airplane,
- Taxidermy property,
- Property subject to a debt,
- A partial interest in property,
- A fractional interest in tangible personal property,
- A qualified conservation contribution,
- A future interest in tangible personal property,
- Inventory from your business, or
- A patent or other intellectual property.

These special rules are described next.

Clothing and Household Items

You can't take a deduction for clothing or household items you donate unless the clothing or household items are in good used condition or better.

Exception. You can take a deduction for a contribution of an item of clothing or a household item that isn't in good used condition or better if you deduct more than $500 for it and include a qualified appraisal of it with your return.

Household items. Household items include:

- Furniture and furnishings,
- Electronics,
- Appliances,
- Linens, and
- Other similar items.

Household items don't include:

- Food,
- Paintings, antiques, and other objects of art,
- Jewelry and gems, and
- Collections.

Fair market value. To determine the fair market value of these items, use the rules under *Determining Fair Market Value*, later.

Cars, Boats, and Airplanes

The following rules apply to any donation of a qualified vehicle.

A qualified vehicle is:

- A car or any motor vehicle manufactured mainly for use on public streets, roads, and highways,
- A boat, or
- An airplane.

Deduction more than $500. If you donate a qualified vehicle with a claimed fair market value of more than $500, you can deduct the smaller of:

- The gross proceeds from the sale of the vehicle by the organization, or
- The vehicle's fair market value on the date of the contribution. If the vehicle's fair market value was more than your cost or other basis, you may have to reduce the fair market value to figure the deductible amount, as described under *Giving Property That Has Increased in Value*, later.

Form 1098-C. You must attach to your return Copy B of the Form 1098-C, Contributions of Motor Vehicles, Boats, and Airplanes, (or other statement containing the same information as Form 1098-C) you received from the organization. The Form 1098-C (or other statement) will show the gross proceeds from the sale of the vehicle.

If you e-file your return, you must:

- Attach Copy B of Form 1098-C to Form 8453, U.S. Individual Income Tax Transmittal for an IRS *e-file* Return, and mail the forms to the IRS, or
- Include Copy B of Form 1098-C as a pdf attachment if your software program allows it.

If you don't attach Form 1098-C (or other statement), you can't deduct your contribution. You must get Form 1098-C (or other statement) within 30 days of the sale of the vehicle. But if exception 1 or 2 (described later) applies, you must get Form 1098-C (or other statement) within 30 days of your donation.

Filing deadline approaching and still no Form 1098-C. If the filing deadline is approaching and you still don't have a Form 1098-C, you have two choices.

1. Request an automatic 6-month extension of time to file your return. You can get this extension by filing Form 4868, Application for Automatic Extension of Time To File U.S. Individual Income Tax Return. For more information, see the instructions for Form 4868.

2. File the return on time without claiming the deduction for the qualified vehicle. After receiving the Form 1098-C, file an amended return, Form 1040X, Amended U.S. Individual Income Tax Return, claiming the deduction. Attach Copy B of Form 1098-C (or other statement) to the amended return.

Exceptions. There are two exceptions to the rules just described for deductions of more than $500.

Exception 1—vehicle used or improved by organization. If the qualified organization makes a significant intervening use of or material improvement to the vehicle before transferring it, you generally can deduct the vehicle's fair market value at the time of the contribution. But if the vehicle's fair market value was more than your cost or other basis, you may have to reduce the fair market value to get the deductible amount, as described under *Giving Property That Has Increased in Value*, later. The Form 1098-C (or other statement) will show whether this exception applies.

Exception 2—vehicle given or sold to needy individual. If the qualified organization will give the vehicle, or sell it for a price well below fair market value, to a needy individual to further the organization's charitable purpose, you generally can deduct the vehicle's fair market value at the time of the contribution. But if the vehicle's fair market value was more than your cost or other basis, you may have to reduce the fair market value to get the deductible amount, as described under *Giving Property That Has Increased in Value*, later. The Form 1098-C (or other statement) will show whether this exception applies.

This exception doesn't apply if the organization sells the vehicle at auction. In that case, you can't deduct the vehicle's fair market value.

Example. Anita donates a used car to a qualified organization. She bought it 3 years ago for $9,000. A used car guide shows the fair market value for this type of car is $6,000. However, Anita gets a Form 1098-C from the organization showing the car was sold for $2,900. Neither exception 1 nor exception 2 applies. If Anita itemizes her deductions, she can deduct $2,900 for her donation. She must attach Form 1098-C and Form 8283 to her return.

Deduction $500 or less. If the qualified organization sells the vehicle for $500 or less and exceptions 1 and 2 don't apply, you can deduct the smaller of:

- $500, or
- The vehicle's fair market value on the date of the contribution. But if the vehicle's fair market value was more than your cost or other basis, you may have to reduce the fair market value to get the deductible amount, as described under *Giving Property That Has Increased in Value*, later.

If the vehicle's fair market value is at least $250 but not more than $500, you must have a written statement from the qualified organization acknowledging your donation. The statement must contain the information and meet the tests for an acknowledgment described under

Deductions of At Least $250 But Not More Than $500 under *Records To Keep*, later.

Fair market value. To determine a vehicle's fair market value, use the rules described under *Determining Fair Market Value*, later.

Donations of inventory. The vehicle donation rules just described don't apply to donations of inventory. For example, these rules don't apply if you are a car dealer who donates a car you had been holding for sale to customers. See *Inventory*, later.

Taxidermy Property

If you donate taxidermy property to a qualified organization, your deduction is limited to your basis in the property or its fair market value, whichever is less. This applies if you prepared, stuffed, or mounted the property or paid or incurred the cost of preparing, stuffing, or mounting the property.

Your basis for this purpose includes only the cost of preparing, stuffing, and mounting the property. Your basis doesn't include transportation or travel costs. It also doesn't include the direct or indirect costs for hunting or killing an animal, such as equipment costs. In addition, it doesn't include the value of your time.

Taxidermy property means any work of art that:

- Is the reproduction or preservation of an animal, in whole or in part,
- Is prepared, stuffed, or mounted to recreate one or more characteristics of the animal, and
- Contains a part of the body of the dead animal.

Property Subject to a Debt

If you contribute property subject to a debt (such as a mortgage), you must reduce the fair market value of the property by:

1. Any allowable deduction for interest you paid (or will pay) that is attributable to any period after the contribution, and

2. If the property is a bond, the lesser of:

   a. Any allowable deduction for interest you paid (or will pay) to buy or carry the bond that is attributable to any period before the contribution, or

   b. The interest, including bond discount, receivable on the bond that is attributable to any period before the contribution, and that isn't includible in your income due to your accounting method.

This prevents you from deducting the same amount as both investment interest and a charitable contribution.

If the recipient (or another person) assumes the debt, you must also reduce the fair market value of the property by the amount of the outstanding debt assumed.

The amount of the debt is also treated as an amount realized on the sale or exchange of

Page A-46

property for purposes of figuring your taxable gain (if any). For more information, see *Bargain Sales* under *Giving Property That Has Increased in Value*, later.

Partial Interest in Property

Generally, you can't deduct a charitable contribution of less than your entire interest in property.

Right to use property. A contribution of the right to use property is a contribution of less than your entire interest in that property and isn't deductible.

Example 1. You own a 10-story office building and donate rent-free use of the top floor to a charitable organization. Because you still own the building, you have contributed a partial interest in the property and can't take a deduction for the contribution.

Example 2. Mandy White owns a vacation home at the beach that she sometimes rents to others. For a fund-raising auction at her church, she donated the right to use the vacation home for 1 week. At the auction, the church received and accepted a bid from Lauren Green equal to the fair rental value of the home for 1 week. Mandy can't claim a deduction because of the partial interest rule. Lauren can't claim a deduction either, because she received a benefit equal to the amount of her payment. See *Contributions From Which You Benefit*, earlier.

Exceptions. You can deduct a charitable contribution of a partial interest in property only if that interest represents one of the following items.

- A remainder interest in your personal home or farm. A remainder interest is one that passes to a beneficiary after the end of an earlier interest in the property.

  Example. You keep the right to live in your home during your lifetime and give your church a remainder interest that begins upon your death. You can deduct the value of the remainder interest.

- An undivided part of your entire interest. This must consist of a part of every substantial interest or right you own in the property and must last as long as your interest in the property lasts. But see *Fractional Interest in Tangible Personal Property*, later.

  Example. You contribute voting stock to a qualified organization but keep the right to vote the stock. The right to vote is a substantial right in the stock. You haven't contributed an undivided part of your entire interest and can't deduct your contribution.

- A partial interest that would be deductible if transferred to certain types of trusts.

- A qualified conservation contribution (defined later).

For information about how to figure the value of a contribution of a partial interest in property, see *Partial Interest in Property Not in Trust* in Pub. 561.

Fractional Interest in Tangible Personal Property

You can't deduct a charitable contribution of a fractional interest in tangible personal property unless all interests in the property are held immediately before the contribution by:

- You, or
- You and the qualifying organization receiving the contribution.

If you make an additional contribution later, the fair market value of that contribution will be determined by using the smaller of:

- The fair market value of the property at the time of the initial contribution, or
- The fair market value of the property at the time of the additional contribution.

Tangible personal property is defined later under *Future Interest in Tangible Personal Property*. A fractional interest in property is an undivided portion of your entire interest in the property.

Example. An undivided one-quarter interest in a painting that entitles an art museum to possession of the painting for 3 months of each year is a fractional interest in the property.

Recapture of deduction. You must recapture your charitable contribution deduction by including it in your income if both of the following statements are true.

1. You contributed a fractional interest in tangible personal property after August 17, 2006.

2. You don't contribute the rest of your interests in the property to the original recipient or, if it no longer exists, another qualified organization on or before the earlier of:

   a. The date that is 10 years after the date of the initial contribution, or

   b. The date of your death.

Recapture is also required if the qualified organization hasn't taken substantial physical possession of the property and used it in a way related to the organization's purpose during the period beginning on the date of the initial contribution and ending on the earlier of:

1. The date that is 10 years after the date of the initial contribution, or

2. The date of your death.

Additional tax. If you must recapture your deduction, you must also pay interest and an additional tax equal to 10% of the amount recaptured.

Qualified Conservation Contribution

A qualified conservation contribution is a contribution of a qualified real property interest to a qualified organization to be used only for conservation purposes.

Qualified organization. For purposes of a qualified conservation contribution, a qualified organization is:

- A governmental unit,
- A publicly supported charity, or
- An organization controlled by, and operated for the exclusive benefit of, a governmental unit or a publicly supported charity.

The organization also must have a commitment to protect the conservation purposes of the donation and must have the resources to enforce the restrictions.

A publicly supported charity is an organization of the type described in (1) under *Types of Qualified Organizations*, earlier, that normally receives a substantial part of its support, other than income from its exempt activities, from direct or indirect contributions from the general public or from governmental units.

Qualified real property interest. This is any of the following interests in real property.

1. Your entire interest in real estate other than a mineral interest (subsurface oil, gas, or other minerals, and the right of access to these minerals).

2. A remainder interest.

3. A restriction (granted in perpetuity) on the use that may be made of the real property.

Conservation purposes. Your contribution must be made only for one of the following conservation purposes.

- Preserving land areas for outdoor recreation by, or for the education of, the general public.
- Protecting a relatively natural habitat of fish, wildlife, or plants, or a similar ecosystem.
- Preserving open space, including farmland and forest land, if it yields a significant public benefit. The open space must be preserved either for the scenic enjoyment of the general public or under a clearly defined federal, state, or local governmental conservation policy.
- Preserving a historically important land area or a certified historic structure.

Building in registered historic district. If a building in a registered historic district is a certified historic structure, a contribution of a qualified real property interest that is an easement or other restriction on the exterior of the building is deductible only if it meets all of the following conditions.

1. The restriction must preserve the entire exterior of the building (including its front, sides, rear, and height) and must prohibit any change to the exterior of the building that is inconsistent with its historical character.

2. You and the organization receiving the contribution must enter into a written agreement certifying, under penalty of perjury, that the organization:

   a. Is a qualified organization with a purpose of environmental protection, land conservation, open space preservation, or historic preservation, and

b. Has the resources to manage and enforce the restriction and a commitment to do so.

3. You must include with your return:

   a. A qualified appraisal,

   b. Photographs of the building's entire exterior, and

   c. A description of all restrictions on development of the building, such as zoning laws and restrictive covenants.

If you claimed the rehabilitation credit for the building for any of the 5 years before the year of the contribution, your charitable deduction is reduced. For more information, see Form 3468, Investment Credit, and Internal Revenue Code section 170(f)(14).

If you claim a deduction of more than $10,000, your deduction won't be allowed unless you pay a $500 filing fee. See Form 8283-V, Payment Voucher for Filing Fee Under Section 170(f)(13), and its instructions. You may be able to deduct the filing fee as a miscellaneous itemized deduction, subject to the 2%-of-adjusted-gross-income limit, on Schedule A (Form 1040). See *Deductions Subject to the 2% Limit* in Pub. 529 for more information.

More information. For information about determining the fair market value of qualified conservation contributions, see Pub. 561. For information about the limits that apply to deductions for this type of contribution, see *Limits on Deductions*, later. For more information about qualified conservation contributions, see Regulations section 1.170A-14.

Future Interest in Tangible Personal Property

You can't deduct the value of a charitable contribution of a future interest in tangible personal property until all intervening interests in and rights to the actual possession or enjoyment of the property have either expired or been turned over to someone other than yourself, a related person, or a related organization. But see *Fractional Interest in Tangible Personal Property*, earlier, and *Tangible personal property put to unrelated use*, later.

Related persons include your spouse, children, grandchildren, brothers, sisters, and parents. Related organizations may include a partnership or corporation in which you have an interest, or an estate or trust with which you have a connection.

Tangible personal property. This is any property, other than land or buildings, that can be seen or touched. It includes furniture, books, jewelry, paintings, and cars.

Future interest. This is any interest that is to begin at some future time, regardless of whether it is designated as a future interest under state law.

Example. You own an antique car that you contribute to a museum. You give up ownership, but retain the right to keep the car in your garage with your personal collection. Because

you keep an interest in the property, you can't deduct the contribution. If you turn the car over to the museum in a later year, giving up all rights to its use, possession, and enjoyment, you can take a deduction for the contribution in that later year.

Inventory

If you contribute inventory (property you sell in the course of your business), the amount you can deduct is the smaller of its fair market value on the day you contributed it or its basis. The basis of contributed inventory is any cost incurred for the inventory in an earlier year that you would otherwise include in your opening inventory for the year of the contribution. You must remove the amount of your charitable contribution deduction from your opening inventory. It isn't part of the cost of goods sold.

If the cost of donated inventory isn't included in your opening inventory, the inventory's basis is zero and you can't claim a charitable contribution deduction. Treat the inventory's cost as you would ordinarily treat it under your method of accounting. For example, include the purchase price of inventory bought and donated in the same year in the cost of goods sold for that year.

A special rule applies to certain donations of food inventory. See *Food Inventory*, later.

Patents and Other Intellectual Property

If you donate intellectual property to a qualified organization, your deduction is limited to the basis of the property or the fair market value of the property, whichever is smaller. Intellectual property means any of the following:

- Patents.

- Copyrights (other than a copyright described in Internal Revenue Code sections 1221(a)(3) or 1231(b)(1)(C)).

- Trademarks.

- Trade names.

- Trade secrets.

- Know-how.

- Software (other than software described in Internal Revenue Code section 197(e)(3)(A)(i)).

- Other similar property or applications or registrations of such property.

Additional deduction based on income. You may be able to claim additional charitable contribution deductions in the year of the contribution and years following, based on the income, if any, from the donated property.

The following table shows the percentage of income from the property that you can deduct for each of your tax years ending on or after the date of the contribution. In the table, "tax year 1," for example, means your first tax year ending on or after the date of the contribution. However, you can take the additional deduction only to the extent the total of the amounts figured using this table is more than the amount of the deduction claimed for the original donation of the property.

After the legal life of the intellectual property ends, or after the 10th anniversary of the donation, whichever is earlier, no additional deduction is allowed.

The additional deductions can't be taken for intellectual property donated to certain private foundations.

Tax year	Deductible percentage
1	100%
2	100%
3	90%
4	80%
5	70%
6	60%
7	50%
8	40%
9	30%
10	20%
11	10%
12	10%

Reporting requirements. You must inform the organization at the time of the donation that you intend to treat the donation as a contribution subject to the provisions just discussed.

The organization is required to file an information return showing the income from the property, with a copy to you. This is done on Form 8899, Notice of Income From Donated Intellectual Property.

Determining Fair Market Value

This section discusses general guidelines for determining the fair market value of various types of donated property. Pub. 561 contains a more complete discussion.

Fair market value is the price at which property would change hands between a willing buyer and a willing seller, neither having to buy or sell, and both having reasonable knowledge of all the relevant facts.

Used clothing. The fair market value of used clothing and other personal items is usually far less than the price you paid for them. There are no fixed formulas or methods for finding the value of items of clothing.

You should claim as the value the price that buyers of used items actually pay in used clothing stores, such as consignment or thrift shops.

Also see *Clothing and Household Items*, earlier.

Example. Kristin donated a coat to a thrift store operated by her church. She paid $300 for the coat 3 years ago. Similar coats in the thrift store sell for $50. The fair market value of the coat is $50. Kristin's donation is limited to $50.

Household items. The fair market value of used household items, such as furniture, appliances, and linens, is usually much lower than the price paid when new. These items may have little or no market value because they are in a worn condition, out of style, or no longer useful. For these reasons, formulas (such as using a percentage of the cost to buy a new replacement item) aren't acceptable in determining value.

You should support your valuation with photographs, canceled checks, receipts from your purchase of the items, or other evidence. Magazine or newspaper articles and photographs that describe the items and statements by the recipients of the items are also useful. Don't include any of this evidence with your tax return.

If the property is valuable because it is old or unique, see the discussion under *Paintings, Antiques, and Other Objects of Art* in Pub. 561.

Also see *Clothing and Household Items*, earlier.

Cars, boats, and airplanes. If you contribute a car, boat, or airplane to a charitable organization, you must determine its fair market value.

Boats. Except for small, inexpensive boats, the valuation of boats should be based on an appraisal by a marine surveyor or appraiser because the physical condition is critical to the value.

Cars. Certain commercial firms and trade organizations publish used car pricing guides, commonly called "blue books," containing complete dealer sale prices or dealer average prices for recent model years. The guides may be published monthly or seasonally, and for different regions of the country. These guides also provide estimates for adjusting for unusual equipment, unusual mileage, and physical condition. The prices aren't "official" and these publications aren't considered an appraisal of any specific donated property. But they do provide clues for making an appraisal and suggest relative prices for comparison with current sales and offerings in your area.

These publications are sometimes available from public libraries, or from the loan officer at a bank, credit union, or finance company. You can also find used car pricing information on the Internet.

To find the fair market value of a donated car, use the price listed in a used car guide for a private party sale, not the dealer retail value. However, the fair market value may be less if the car has engine trouble, body damage, high mileage, or any type of excessive wear. The fair market value of a donated car is the same as the price listed in a used car guide for a private party sale only if the guide lists a sales price for a car that is the same make, model, and year, sold in the same area, in the same condition, with the same or similar options or accessories, and with the same or similar warranties as the donated car.

Example. You donate a used car in poor condition to a local high school for use by students studying car repair. A used car guide shows the dealer retail value for this type of car in poor condition is $1,600. However, the guide shows the price for a private party sale of the car is only $750. The fair market value of the car is considered to be $750.

Large quantities. If you contribute a large number of the same item, fair market value is the price at which comparable numbers of the item are being sold.

Example. You purchase 500 bibles for $1,000. The person who sells them to you says the retail value of these bibles is $3,000. If you contribute the bibles to a qualified organization, you can claim a deduction only for the price at which similar numbers of the same bible are currently being sold. Your charitable contribution is $1,000, unless you can show that similar numbers of that bible were selling at a different price at the time of the contribution.

Giving Property That Has Decreased in Value

If you contribute property with a fair market value that is less than your basis in it, your deduction is limited to its fair market value. You can't claim a deduction for the difference between the property's basis and its fair market value.

Your basis in property is generally what you paid for it. If you need more information about basis, see Pub. 551. You may want to see Pub. 551 if you contribute property that you:

• Received as a gift or inheritance,

• Used in a trade, business, or activity conducted for profit, or

• Claimed a casualty loss deduction for.

Common examples of property that decreases in value include clothing, furniture, appliances, and cars.

Giving Property That Has Increased in Value

If you contribute property with a fair market value that is more than your basis in it, you may have to reduce the fair market value by the amount of appreciation (increase in value) when you figure your deduction.

Your basis in property is generally what you paid for it. If you need more information about basis, see Pub. 551.

Different rules apply to figuring your deduction, depending on whether the property is:
• Ordinary income property, or
• Capital gain property.

Ordinary Income Property

Property is ordinary income property if you would have recognized ordinary income or short-term capital gain had you sold it at fair market value on the date it was contributed. Examples of ordinary income property are inventory, works of art created by the donor, manuscripts prepared by the donor, and capital assets (defined later, under *Capital Gain Property*) held 1 year or less.

Property used in a trade or business. Property used in a trade or business is considered ordinary income property to the extent of any gain that would have been treated as ordinary income because of depreciation had the property been sold at its fair market value at the time of contribution. See chapter 3 of Pub. 544, Sales and Other Dispositions of Assets, for the kinds of property to which this rule applies.

Amount of deduction. The amount you can deduct for a contribution of ordinary income property is its fair market value minus the amount that would be ordinary income or short-term capital gain if you sold the property for its fair market value. Generally, this rule limits the deduction to your basis in the property.

Example. You donate stock you held for 5 months to your church. The fair market value of the stock on the day you donate it is $1,000, but you paid only $800 (your basis). Because the $200 of appreciation would be short-term capital gain if you sold the stock, your deduction is limited to $800 (fair market value minus the appreciation).

Exception. Don't reduce your charitable contribution if you include the ordinary or capital gain income in your gross income in the same year as the contribution. See *Ordinary or capital gain income included in gross income* under *Capital Gain Property*, later, if you need more information.

Capital Gain Property

Property is capital gain property if you would have recognized long-term capital gain had you sold it at fair market value on the date of the contribution. Capital gain property includes capital assets held more than 1 year.

Capital assets. Capital assets include most items of property you own and use for personal purposes or investment. Examples of capital assets are stocks, bonds, jewelry, coin or stamp collections, and cars or furniture used for personal purposes.

For purposes of figuring your charitable contribution, capital assets also include certain real property and depreciable property used in your trade or business and, generally, held more than 1 year. You may, however, have to treat this property as partly ordinary income property and partly capital gain property. See *Property used in a trade or business* under *Ordinary Income Property*, earlier.

Real property. Real property is land and generally anything built on, growing on, or attached to land.

Depreciable property. Depreciable property is property used in business or held for the production of income and for which a depreciation deduction is allowed.

For more information about what is a capital asset, see chapter 2 of Pub. 544.

Amount of deduction—general rule. When figuring your deduction for a contribution of capital gain property, you generally can use the fair market value of the property.

Exceptions. However, in certain situations, you must reduce the fair market value by any amount that would have been long-term capital gain if you had sold the property for its fair market value. Generally, this means reducing the fair market value to the property's cost or other basis. You must do this if:

1. The property (other than qualified appreciated stock) is contributed to certain private nonoperating foundations,

2. You choose the 50% limit instead of the special 30% limit for capital gain property, discussed later,

3. The contributed property is intellectual property (as defined earlier under *Patents and Other Intellectual Property*),

4. The contributed property is certain taxidermy property as explained earlier, or

5. The contributed property is tangible personal property (defined earlier) that:

   a. Is put to an unrelated use (defined later) by the charity, or

   b. Has a claimed value of more than $5,000 and is sold, traded, or otherwise disposed of by the qualified organization during the year in which you made the contribution, and the qualified organization hasn't made the required certification of exempt use (such as on Form 8282, Donee Information Return, Part IV). See also *Recapture if no exempt use*, later.

Contributions to private nonoperating foundations. The reduced deduction applies to contributions to all private nonoperating foundations other than those qualifying for the 50% limit, discussed later.

However, the reduced deduction doesn't apply to contributions of qualified appreciated stock. Qualified appreciated stock is any stock in a corporation that is capital gain property and for which market quotations are readily available on an established securities market on the day of the contribution. But stock in a corporation doesn't count as qualified appreciated stock to the extent you and your family contributed more than 10% of the value of all the outstanding stock in the corporation.

Tangible personal property put to unrelated use. Tangible personal property is defined earlier under *Future Interest in Tangible Personal Property*.

Unrelated use. The term "unrelated use" means a use unrelated to the exempt purpose or function of the charitable organization. For a governmental unit, it means the use of the contributed property for other than exclusively public purposes.

Example. If a painting contributed to an educational institution is used by that organization for educational purposes by being placed in its library for display and study by art students, the use isn't an unrelated use. But if the painting is sold and the proceeds are used by the organization for educational purposes, the use is an unrelated use.

Deduction limited. Your deduction for a contribution of tangible personal property may be limited. See (5) under *Exceptions*, earlier.

Recapture if no exempt use. You must recapture part of your charitable contribution deduction by including it in your income if all the following statements are true.

1. You donate tangible personal property with a claimed value of more than $5,000, and your deduction is more than your basis in the property.

2. The organization sells, trades, or otherwise disposes of the property after the year it was contributed but within 3 years of the contribution.

3. The organization doesn't provide a written statement (such as on Form 8282, Part IV), signed by an officer of the organization under penalty of perjury, that either:

   a. Certifies its use of the property was substantial and related to the organization's purpose, or

   b. Certifies its intended use of the property became impossible.

If all the preceding statements are true, include in your income:

1. The deduction you claimed for the property, minus

2. Your basis in the property when you made the contribution.

Include this amount in your income for the year the qualified organization disposes of the property. Report the recaptured amount on Form 1040, line 21.

Ordinary or capital gain income included in gross income. You don't reduce your charitable contribution if you include the ordinary or capital gain income in your gross income in the same year as the contribution. This may happen when you transfer installment or discount obligations or when you assign income to a charitable organization. If you contribute an obligation received in a sale of property that is reported under the installment method, see Pub. 537, Installment Sales.

Example. You donate an installment note to a qualified organization. The note has a fair market value of $10,000 and a basis to you of $7,000. As a result of the donation, you have a short-term capital gain of $3,000 ($10,000 − $7,000), which you include in your income for the year. Your charitable contribution is $10,000.

Food Inventory

Special rules apply to certain donations of food inventory to a qualified organization. These rules apply if all the following conditions are met.

1. You made a contribution of apparently wholesome food from your trade or business. Apparently wholesome food is food intended for human consumption that meets all quality and labeling standards imposed by federal, state, and local laws and regulations even though the food may not be readily marketable due to appearance, age, freshness, grade, size, surplus, or other conditions.

2. The food is to be used only for the care of the ill, the needy, or infants.

3. The use of the food is related to the organization's exempt purpose or function.

4. The organization doesn't transfer the food for money, other property, or services.

5. You receive a written statement from the organization stating it will comply with requirements (2), (3), and (4).

6. The organization isn't a private nonoperating foundation.

7. The food satisfies any applicable requirements of the Federal Food, Drug, and Cosmetic Act and regulations on the date of transfer and for the previous 180 days.

If all the conditions just described are met, use the following worksheet to figure your deduction.

Worksheet 1.
Donations of Food Inventory
See separate Worksheet instructions.
(Keep for your records)

1. Enter fair market value of the donated food .... _____
2. Enter basis of the donated food .... _____
3. Subtract line 2 from line 1. If the result is zero or less, stop here. Don't complete the rest of this worksheet. Your charitable contribution deduction for food is the amount on line 1 .... _____
4. Enter one-half of line 3 .... _____
5. Subtract line 4 from line 1 .... _____
6. Multiply line 2 by 2.0 .... _____
7. Subtract line 6 from line 5. If the result is less than zero, enter -0- .... _____
8. Add lines 4 and 7 .... _____
9. Compare line 3 and line 8. Enter the smaller amount .... _____
10. Subtract line 9 from line 1 .... _____
11. Enter 10% of your total net income for the year from all trades or businesses from which food inventory was donated .... _____
12. Compare line 10 and line 11. Enter the smaller amount. This is your charitable contribution deduction for the food .... _____

Worksheet instructions. Enter on line 11 of the worksheet 10% of your net income for the year from all sole proprietorships, S corporations, or partnerships (or other entity that isn't a C corporation) from which contributions of food inventory were made. Figure net income before any deduction for a charitable contribution of food inventory.

If you made more than one contribution of food inventory, complete a separate worksheet for each contribution. Complete lines 11 and 12 on only one worksheet. On that worksheet, complete line 11. Then compare line 11 and the total of the line 10 amounts on all worksheets and enter the smaller of those amounts on line 12.

More information. See *Inventory*, earlier, for information about determining the basis of donated inventory and the effect on cost of goods sold. For additional details, see section 170(e)(3) of the Internal Revenue Code.

Bargain Sales

A bargain sale of property is a sale or exchange for less than the property's fair market value. A bargain sale to a qualified organization is partly a charitable contribution and partly a sale or exchange.

Part that is a sale or exchange. The part of the bargain sale that is a sale or exchange may result in a taxable gain. For more information on figuring the amount of any taxable gain, see *Bargain sales to charity* in chapter 1 of Pub. 544.

Part that is a charitable contribution. Figure the amount of your charitable contribution in three steps.

Step 1. Subtract the amount you received for the property from the property's fair market value at the time of sale. This gives you the fair market value of the contributed part.

Step 2. Find the adjusted basis of the contributed part. It equals:

$$\text{Adjusted basis of entire property} \times \frac{\text{Fair market value of contributed part}}{\text{Fair market value of entire property}}$$

Step 3. Determine whether the amount of your charitable contribution is the fair market value of the contributed part (which you found in *Step 1*) or the adjusted basis of the contributed part (which you found in *Step 2*). Generally, if the property sold was capital gain property, your charitable contribution is the fair market value of the contributed part. If it was ordinary income property, your charitable contribution is the adjusted basis of the contributed part. See *Ordinary Income Property* and *Capital Gain Property*, both earlier, for more information.

Example. You sell ordinary income property with a fair market value of $10,000 to a church for $2,000. Your basis is $4,000 and your adjusted gross income is $20,000. You make no other contributions during the year. The fair market value of the contributed part of the property is $8,000 ($10,000 – $2,000). The adjusted basis of the contributed part is $3,200 ($4,000 × ($8,000 ÷ $10,000)). Because the property is ordinary income property, your charitable deduction is limited to the adjusted basis of the contributed part. You can deduct $3,200.

Penalty

You may be liable for a penalty if you overstate the value or adjusted basis of contributed property.

20% penalty. The penalty is 20% of the amount by which you underpaid your tax because of the overstatement, if:

1. The value or adjusted basis claimed on your return is 150% or more of the correct amount, and

2. You underpaid your tax by more than $5,000 because of the overstatement.

40% penalty. The penalty is 40%, rather than 20%, if:

1. The value or adjusted basis claimed on your return is 200% or more of the correct amount, and

2. You underpaid your tax by more than $5,000 because of the overstatement.

When To Deduct

You can deduct your contributions only in the year you actually make them in cash or other property (or in a later carryover year, as explained under *How To Figure Your Deduction When Limits Apply*, later). This applies whether you use the cash or an accrual method of accounting.

Time of making contribution. Usually, you make a contribution at the time of its unconditional delivery.

Checks. A check you mail to a charity is considered delivered on the date you mail it.

Text message. Contributions made by text message are deductible in the year you send the text message if the contribution is charged to your telephone or wireless account.

Credit card. Contributions charged on your bank credit card are deductible in the year you make the charge.

Pay-by-phone account. Contributions made through a pay-by-phone account are considered delivered on the date the financial institution pays the amount. This date should be shown on the statement the financial institution sends you.

Stock certificate. A properly endorsed stock certificate is considered delivered on the date of mailing or other delivery to the charity or to the charity's agent. However, if you give a stock certificate to your agent or to the issuing corporation for transfer to the name of the charity, your contribution isn't delivered until the date the stock is transferred on the books of the corporation.

Promissory note. If you issue and deliver a promissory note to a charity as a contribution, it isn't a contribution until you make the note payments.

Option. If you grant a charity an option to buy real property at a bargain price, it isn't a contribution until the charity exercises the option.

Borrowed funds. If you contribute borrowed funds, you can deduct the contribution in the year you deliver the funds to the charity, regardless of when you repay the loan.

Conditional gift. If your contribution depends on a future act or event to become effective, you can't take a deduction unless there is only a negligible chance the act or event won't take place.

If your contribution would be undone by a later act or event, you can't take a deduction unless there is only a negligible chance the act or event will take place.

Example 1. You contribute cash to a local school board, which is a political subdivision of a state, to help build a school gym. The school board will refund the money to you if it doesn't collect enough to build the gym. You can't deduct your contribution until there is no chance (or only a negligible chance) of a refund.

Example 2. You donate land to a city for as long as the city uses it for a public park. The city plans to use the land for a park, and there is no chance (or only a negligible chance) of the land being used for any different purpose. You can deduct your charitable contribution.

Limits on Deductions

For 2015, the total of your charitable contributions deduction and certain other itemized deductions may be limited if your adjusted gross income is more than:

* $154,950 if married filing separately,
* $258,250 if single,
* $284,050 if head of household, or
* $309,900 if married filing jointly or qualifying widow(er).

This is in addition to the other limits described here. See the instructions for Schedule A (Form 1040) for more information about this limit.

If your total contributions for the year are 20% or less of your adjusted gross income, you don't need to read the rest of this section. The limits discussed in this section don't apply to you.

The amount you can deduct for charitable contributions can't be more than 50% of your adjusted gross income. Your deduction may be further limited to 30% or 20% of your adjusted gross income, depending on the type of property you give and the type of organization you give it to. A higher limit applies to certain qualified conservation contributions. These limits are described in detail in this section.

Your adjusted gross income is the amount on Form 1040, line 38.

If your contributions are more than any of the limits that apply, see *Carryovers* under *How To Figure Your Deduction When Limits Apply*, later.

Out-of-pocket expenses. Amounts you spend performing services for a charitable organization may be deductible as a contribution to a qualified organization. If so, your deduction is subject to the limit applicable to donations to that organization. For example, the 50% limit applies to amounts you spend on behalf of a church, a 50% limit organization.

50% Limit

The 50% limit applies to the total of all charitable contributions you make during the year. This means that your deduction for charitable contributions can't be more than 50% of your adjusted gross income for the year. But there is a higher limit, discussed later, for certain qualified conservation contributions.

Only limit for 50% organizations. The 50% limit is the only percentage limit that applies to contributions to organizations listed under *50% Limit Organizations*. But there is one exception.

Exception. A special 30% limit applies to contributions of capital gain property if you figure your deduction using fair market value without reduction for appreciation. (See *Special 30% Limit for Capital Gain Property*, later.)

50% Limit Organizations

You can ask any organization whether it is a 50% limit organization, and most will be able to tell you. Also see *How to check whether an organization can receive deductible charitable contributions*, earlier.

Only the following types of organizations are 50% limit organizations.

1. Churches and conventions or associations of churches.

2. Educational organizations with a regular faculty and curriculum that normally have a regularly enrolled student body attending classes on site.

3. Hospitals and certain medical research organizations associated with these hospitals.

4. Organizations that are operated only to receive, hold, invest, and administer property and to make expenditures to or for the benefit of state and municipal colleges and universities and that normally receive substantial support from the United States or any state or their political subdivisions, or from the general public.

5. The United States or any state, the District of Columbia, a U.S. possession (including Puerto Rico), a political subdivision of a state or U.S. possession, or an Indian tribal government or any of its subdivisions that perform substantial government functions.

6. Publicly supported charities, defined earlier under *Qualified Conservation Contribution*.

7. Organizations that may not qualify as "publicly supported" but that meet other tests showing they respond to the needs of the general public, not a limited number of donors or other persons. They must normally receive more than one-third of their support either from organizations described in (1) through (6), or from persons other than "disqualified persons."

8. Most organizations operated or controlled by, and operated for the benefit of, those organizations described in (1) through (7).

9. Private operating foundations.

10. Private nonoperating foundations that make qualifying distributions of 100% of contributions within 2½ months following the year they receive the contribution. A deduction for charitable contributions to any of these private nonoperating foundations must be supported by evidence from the foundation confirming it made the qualifying distributions timely. Attach a copy of this supporting data to your tax return.

11. A private foundation whose contributions are pooled into a common fund, if the foundation would be described in (8) but for the right of substantial contributors to name the public charities that receive contributions from the fund. The foundation must distribute the common fund's income within 2½ months following the tax year in which it was realized and must distribute the corpus not later than 1 year after the donor's death (or after the death of the donor's surviving spouse if the spouse can name the recipients of the corpus).

30% Limit

A 30% limit applies to the following contributions.

- Contributions to all qualified organizations other than 50% limit organizations. This includes contributions to veterans' organizations, fraternal societies, nonprofit cemeteries, and certain private nonoperating foundations.

- Contributions for the use of any qualified organization.

However, if these contributions are of capital gain property, they are subject to the 20% limit, described later, rather than the 30% limit.

Student living with you. Deductible amounts you spend on behalf of a student living with you are subject to the 30% limit. These amounts are considered a contribution for the use of a qualified organization. See *Expenses Paid for Student Living With You*, earlier.

Special 30% Limit for Capital Gain Property

A special 30% limit applies to contributions of capital gain property to 50% limit organizations. (For contributions of capital gain property to other organizations, see *20% Limit*, next.) However, the special 30% limit doesn't apply when you choose to reduce the fair market value of the property by the amount that would have been long-term capital gain if you had sold the property. Instead, only the 50% limit applies. See *Capital Gain Property*, earlier, and *Capital gain property election* under *How To Figure Your Deduction When Limits Apply*, later.

Also, the special 30% limit doesn't apply to qualified conservation contributions, discussed later.

Two separate 30% limits. This special 30% limit for capital gain property is separate from the other 30% limit. Therefore, the deduction of a contribution subject to one 30% limit doesn't reduce the amount you can deduct for contributions subject to the other 30% limit. However, the total you deduct can't be more than 50% of your adjusted gross income.

Example. Your adjusted gross income is $50,000. During the year, you gave capital gain property with a fair market value of $15,000 to a 50% limit organization. You don't choose to reduce the property's fair market value by its appreciation in value. You also gave $10,000 cash to a qualified organization that isn't a 50% limit organization. The $15,000 contribution of property is subject to the special 30% limit. The $10,000 cash contribution is subject to the other 30% limit. Both contributions are fully deductible because neither is more than the 30% limit that applies ($15,000 in each case) and together they aren't more than the 50% limit ($25,000).

20% Limit

The 20% limit applies to all contributions of capital gain property to or for the use of qualified organizations (other than contributions of capital gain property to 50% limit organizations).

Special 50% Limit for Qualified Conservation Contributions

Your deduction for qualified conservation contributions (QCCs) is limited to 50% of your adjusted gross income minus your deduction for all other charitable contributions. You can carry over any contributions you aren't able to deduct for 2015 because of this limit. See *Carryovers*, later.

100% limit for QCCs of farmers and ranchers. If you are a qualified farmer or rancher, your deduction for QCCs is limited to 100%, rather than 50%, of your adjusted gross income minus your deduction for all other charitable contributions. However, if the donated property is used in agriculture or livestock production (or is available for such production), the contribution must be subject to a restriction that the property remain available for such production. If not, the limit is 50%.

Qualified farmer or rancher. You are a qualified farmer or rancher if your gross income from the trade or business of farming is more than 50% of your gross income for the year.

How To Figure Your Deduction When Limits Apply

If your contributions are subject to more than one of the limits just discussed, deduct them as follows.

1. Contributions subject only to the 50% limit, up to 50% of your adjusted gross income.

2. Contributions subject to the 30% limit, up to the lesser of:

   a. 30% of adjusted gross income, or

b. 50% of adjusted gross income minus your contributions to 50% limit organizations, including contributions of capital gain property subject to the special 30% limit.

3. Contributions of capital gain property subject to the special 30% limit, up to the lesser of:

   a. 30% of adjusted gross income, or

   b. 50% of adjusted gross income minus your other contributions to 50% limit organizations.

4. Contributions subject to the 20% limit, up to the lesser of:

   a. 20% of adjusted gross income,

   b. 30% of adjusted gross income minus your contributions subject to the 30% limit,

   c. 30% of adjusted gross income minus your contributions of capital gain property subject to the special 30% limit, or

   d. 50% of adjusted gross income minus the total of your contributions to 50% limit organizations and your contributions subject to the 30% limit.

5. Qualified conservation contributions (QCCs) subject to the special 50% limit, up to 50% of adjusted gross income minus any contributions in (1) through (4).

6. QCCs subject to the 100% limit for farmers and ranchers, up to 100% of adjusted gross income minus any contributions in (1) through (5).

You also may want to use Worksheet 2, later, to figure your deduction and your carryover.

Example. Your adjusted gross income is $50,000. In March, you gave your church $2,000 cash and land with a fair market value of $28,000 and a basis of $22,000. You held the land for investment purposes. You don't choose to reduce the fair market value of the land by the appreciation in value. You also gave $5,000 cash to a private foundation to which the 30% limit applies.

The $2,000 cash donated to the church is considered first and is fully deductible. Your contribution to the private foundation is considered next. Because your contributions to 50% limit organizations ($2,000 + $28,000) are more than $25,000 (50% of $50,000), your contribution to the private foundation isn't deductible for the year. It can be carried over to later years. See *Carryovers*, later. The contribution of land is considered next. Your deduction for the land is limited to $15,000 (30% × $50,000). The unused part of the contribution ($13,000) can be carried over. For this year, your deduction is limited to $17,000 ($2,000 + $15,000).

Capital gain property election. You may choose the 50% limit for contributions of capital gain property to 50% limit organizations instead of the 30% limit that would otherwise apply. If you make this choice, you must reduce the fair market value of the property contributed by the appreciation in value that would have been long-term capital gain if the property had been sold.

This choice applies to all capital gain property contributed to 50% limit organizations during a tax year. It also applies to carryovers of this kind of contribution from an earlier tax year. For details, see *Carryover of capital gain property*, later.

You must make the choice on your original return or on an amended return filed by the due date for filing the original return.

Example. In the previous example, if you choose to have the 50% limit apply to the land

(the 30% capital gain property) given to your church, you must reduce the fair market value of the property by the appreciation in value. Therefore, the amount of your charitable contribution for the land would be its basis to you of $22,000. You add this amount to the $2,000 cash contributed to the church. You can now deduct $1,000 of the amount donated to the private foundation because your contributions to 50% limit organizations ($2,000 + $22,000) are $1,000 less than the 50%-of-adjusted-gross-income limit. Your total deduction for the year is $25,000 ($2,000 cash to your church, $22,000 for property donated to your church, and $1,000 cash to the private foundation). You can carry over to later years the part of your contribution to the private foundation that you couldn't deduct ($4,000).

Instructions for Worksheet 2

You can use Worksheet 2 if you made charitable contributions during the year, and one or more of the limits described in this publication under *Limits on Deductions* apply to you. You can't use this worksheet if you have a carryover of a charitable contribution from an earlier year. If you have a carryover from an earlier year, see *Carryovers*, next.

The following list gives instructions for completing the worksheet.
* The terms used in the worksheet are explained earlier in this publication.
* If the result on any line is less than zero, enter zero.
* For contributions of property, enter the property's fair market value unless you elected (or were required) to reduce the fair market value as explained under *Giving Property That Has Increased in Value*. In that case, enter the reduced amount.

Worksheet 2. **Applying the Deduction Limits**   *Keep for your records*
If the result on any line is less than zero, enter zero. For other instructions, see *Instructions for Worksheet 2.*

Step 1. Enter any qualified conservation contributions (QCCs).

1. If you are a qualified farmer or rancher, enter any QCCs eligible for the 100% limit **1**
2. Enter any QCCs not entered on line 1. Don't include this amount on line 3, 4, 5, 6, or 8 . . . . . **2**

Step 2. List your other charitable contributions made during the year.

3. Enter your contributions to 50% limit organizations. (Include contributions of capital gain property if you reduced the property's fair market value. Don't include contributions of capital gain property deducted at fair market value.) **Don't** include any contributions you entered on line 1 or 2 . . . . **3**
4. Enter your contributions to 50% limit organizations of capital gain property deducted at fair market value **4**
5. Enter your contributions (other than of capital gain property) to qualified organizations that aren't 50% limit organizations **5**
6. Enter your contributions "for the use of" any qualified organization. (But don't enter here any amount that must be entered on line 8.) **6**
7. Add lines 5 and 6 . . . . **7**
8. Enter your contributions of capital gain property to or for the use of any qualified organization. (But don't enter here any amount entered on line 3 or 4.) **8**

Step 3. Figure your deduction for the year and your carryover to the next year.

9. Enter your adjusted gross income **9**
10. Multiply line 9 by 0.5. This is your 50% limit **10**

			Carryover
Contributions to 50% limit organizations			
11. Enter the smaller of line 3 or line 10 . . . . **11**			
12. Subtract line 11 from line 3 . . . . **12**			
13. Subtract line 11 from line 10 . . . . **13**			
Contributions not to 50% limit organizations			
14. Add lines 3 and 4 . . . . **14**			
15. Multiply line 9 by 0.3. This is your 30% limit **15**			
16. Subtract line 14 from line 10 . . . . **16**			
17. Enter the smallest of line 7, 15, or 16 . . . . **17**			
18. Subtract line 17 from line 7 . . . . **18**			
19. Subtract line 17 from line 15 . . . . **19**			
Contributions of capital gain property to 50% limit organizations			
20. Enter the smallest of line 4, 13, or 15 . . . . **20**			
21. Subtract line 20 from line 4 . . . . **21**			
22. Subtract line 17 from line 16 . . . . **22**			
23. Subtract line 20 from line 15 . . . . **23**			
Other contributions			
24. Multiply line 9 by 0.2. This is your 20% limit **24**			
25. Enter the smallest of line 8, 19, 22, 23, or 24 . . . . . . **25**			
26. Subtract line 25 from line 8 . . . . **26**			
27. Add lines 11, 17, 20, and 25 . . . . **27**			
28. Subtract line 27 from line 10 . . . . **28**			
29. Enter the smaller of line 2 or line 28 . . . . **29**			
30. Subtract line 29 from line 2 . . . . **30**			
31. Subtract line 27 from line 9 . . . . **31**			
32. Enter the smaller of line 1 or line 31 . . . . **32**		
33. Add lines 27, 29, and 32. Enter the total here and on Schedule A (Form 1040), line 16 or line 17, whichever is appropriate **33**		
34. Subtract line 32 from line 1 . . . . **34**		
35. Add lines 12, 18, 21, 26, 30, and 34. Carry this amount forward to Schedule A (Form 1040) next year **35**		

Publication 526 (2015)

Carryovers

You can carry over any contributions you can't deduct in the current year because they exceed your adjusted-gross-income limits. You may be able to deduct the excess in each of the next 5 years until it is used up, but not beyond that time. Your total charitable deduction for the year to which you carry your contributions can't exceed 50% of your adjusted gross income for that year.

A carryover of a qualified conservation contribution can be carried forward for 15 years.

Contributions you carry over are subject to the same percentage limits in the year to which they are carried. For example, contributions subject to the 20% limit in the year in which they are made are 20% limit contributions in the year to which they are carried.

For each category of contributions, you deduct carryover contributions only after deducting all allowable contributions in that category for the current year. If you have carryovers from 2 or more prior years, use the carryover from the earlier year first.

Note. A carryover of a contribution to a 50% limit organization must be used before contributions in the current year to organizations other than 50% limit organizations. See *Example 2.*

Example 1. Last year, you made cash contributions of $11,000 to which the 50% limit applies, but because of the limit you deducted only $10,000 and carried over $1,000 to this year. This year, your adjusted gross income is $20,000 and you made cash contributions of $9,500 to which the 50% limit applies. You can deduct $10,000 (50% of $20,000) this year. Consequently, in addition to your contribution of $9,500 for this year, you can deduct $500 of your carryover contribution from last year. You can carry over the $500 balance of your carryover from last year to next year.

Example 2. This year, your adjusted gross income is $24,000. You make cash contributions of $6,000 to which the 50% limit applies and $3,000 to which the 30% limit applies. You have a contribution carryover from last year of $5,000 for capital gain property contributed to a 50% limit organization and subject to the special 30% limit for contributions of capital gain property.

Your contribution deduction for this year is limited to $12,000 (50% of $24,000). Your 50% limit cash contributions of $6,000 are fully deductible.

The deduction for your 30% limit contributions of $3,000 is limited to $1,000. This is the lesser of:

1. $7,200 (30% of $24,000), or

2. $1,000 ($12,000 minus $11,000).

(The $12,000 amount is 50% of $24,000, your adjusted gross income. The $11,000 amount is the sum of your current and carryover contributions to 50% limit organizations, $6,000 + $5,000.)

The deduction for your $5,000 carryover is subject to the special 30% limit for contributions of capital gain property. This means it is limited to the smaller of:

1. $7,200 (your 30% limit), or

2. $6,000 ($12,000, your 50% limit, minus $6,000, the amount of your cash contributions to 50% limit organizations this year).

Because your $5,000 carryover is less than both $7,200 and $6,000, you can deduct it in full.

Your deduction is $12,000 ($6,000 + $1,000 + $5,000). You carry over the $2,000 balance of your 30% limit contributions for this year to next year.

Carryover of capital gain property. If you carry over contributions of capital gain property subject to the special 30% limit and you choose in the next year to use the 50% limit and take appreciation into account, you must refigure the carryover. Reduce the fair market value of the property by the appreciation and reduce that result by the amount actually deducted in the previous year.

Example. Last year, your adjusted gross income was $50,000 and you contributed capital gain property valued at $27,000 to a 50% limit organization and didn't choose to use the 50% limit. Your basis in the property was $20,000. Your deduction was limited to $15,000 (30% of $50,000), and you carried over $12,000. This year, your adjusted gross income is $60,000 and you contribute capital gain property valued at $25,000 to a 50% limit organization. Your basis in the property is $24,000 and you choose to use the 50% limit. You must refigure your carryover as if you had taken appreciation into account last year as well as this year. Because the amount of your contribution last year would have been $20,000 (the property's basis) instead of the $15,000 you actually deducted, your refigured carryover is $5,000 ($20,000 – $15,000). Your total deduction this year is $29,000 (your $24,000 current contribution plus your $5,000 carryover).

Additional rules for carryovers. Special rules exist for computing carryovers if you:

- Are married in some years but not others,

- Have different spouses in different years,

- Change from a separate return to a joint return in a later year,

- Change from a joint return to a separate return in a later year,

- Have a net operating loss,

- Claim the standard deduction in a carryover year, or

- Become a widow or widower.

Because of their complexity and the limited number of taxpayers to whom these additional rules apply, they aren't discussed in this publication. If you need to figure a carryover and you are in one of these situations, you may want to consult with a tax practitioner.

Records To Keep

You must keep records to prove the amount of the contributions you make during the year. The kind of records you must keep depends on the amount of your contributions and whether they are:

- Cash contributions,

- Noncash contributions, or

- Out-of-pocket expenses when donating your services.

Note. An organization generally must give you a written statement if it receives a payment from you that is more than $75 and is partly a contribution and partly for goods or services. (See *Contributions From Which You Benefit* under *Contributions You Can Deduct*, earlier.) Keep the statement for your records. It may satisfy all or part of the recordkeeping requirements explained in the following discussions.

Cash Contributions

Cash contributions include those paid by cash, check, electronic funds transfer, debit card, credit card, or payroll deduction.

You can't deduct a cash contribution, regardless of the amount, unless you keep one of the following.

1. A bank record that shows the name of the qualified organization, the date of the contribution, and the amount of the contribution. Bank records may include:

   a. A canceled check,

   b. A bank or credit union statement, or

   c. A credit card statement.

2. A receipt (or a letter or other written communication) from the qualified organization showing the name of the organization, the date of the contribution, and the amount of the contribution.

3. The payroll deduction records described next.

Payroll deductions. If you make a contribution by payroll deduction, you must keep:

1. A pay stub, Form W-2, or other document furnished by your employer that shows the date and amount of the contribution, and

2. A pledge card or other document prepared by or for the qualified organization that shows the name of the organization.

If your employer withheld $250 or more from a single paycheck, see *Contributions of $250 or More*, next.

Contributions of $250 or More

You can claim a deduction for a contribution of $250 or more only if you have an acknowledgment of your contribution from the qualified organization or certain payroll deduction records.

If you made more than one contribution of $250 or more, you must have either a separate acknowledgment for each or one acknowledgment that lists each contribution and the date of each contribution and shows your total contributions.

Amount of contribution. In figuring whether your contribution is $250 or more, don't combine separate contributions. For example, if you gave your church $25 each week, your weekly payments don't have to be combined. Each payment is a separate contribution.

If contributions are made by payroll deduction, the deduction from each paycheck is treated as a separate contribution.

If you made a payment that is partly for goods and services, as described earlier under *Contributions From Which You Benefit*, your contribution is the amount of the payment that is more than the value of the goods and services.

Acknowledgment. The acknowledgment must meet these tests.

1. It must be written.
2. It must include:
   a. The amount of cash you contributed,
   b. Whether the qualified organization gave you any goods or services as a result of your contribution (other than certain token items and membership benefits),
   c. A description and good faith estimate of the value of any goods or services described in (b) (other than intangible religious benefits), and
   d. A statement that the only benefit you received was an intangible religious benefit, if that was the case. The acknowledgment doesn't need to describe or estimate the value of an intangible religious benefit. An intangible religious benefit is a benefit that generally isn't sold in commercial transactions outside a donative (gift) context. An example is admission to a religious ceremony.
3. You must get it on or before the earlier of:
   a. The date you file your return for the year you make the contribution, or
   b. The due date, including extensions, for filing the return.

If the acknowledgment doesn't show the date of the contribution, you must also have a bank record or receipt, as described earlier, that does show the date of the contribution. If the acknowledgment shows the date of the contribution and meets the other tests just described, you don't need any other records.

Payroll deductions. If you make a contribution by payroll deduction and your employer withholds $250 or more from a single paycheck, you must keep:

1. A pay stub, Form W-2, or other document furnished by your employer that shows the amount withheld as a contribution, and
2. A pledge card or other document prepared by or for the qualified organization that shows the name of the organization and

states the organization doesn't provide goods or services in return for any contribution made to it by payroll deduction.

A single pledge card may be kept for all contributions made by payroll deduction regardless of amount as long as it contains all the required information.

If the pay stub, Form W-2, pledge card, or other document doesn't show the date of the contribution, you must have another document that does show the date of the contribution. If the pay stub, Form W-2, pledge card, or other document shows the date of the contribution, you don't need any other records except those just described in (1) and (2).

Noncash Contributions

For a contribution not made in cash, the records you must keep depend on whether your deduction for the contribution is:

1. Less than $250,
2. At least $250 but not more than $500,
3. Over $500 but not more than $5,000, or
4. Over $5,000.

Amount of deduction. In figuring whether your deduction is $500 or more, combine your claimed deductions for all similar items of property donated to any charitable organization during the year.

If you received goods or services in return, as described earlier in *Contributions From Which You Benefit*, reduce your contribution by the value of those goods or services. If you figure your deduction by reducing the fair market value of the donated property by its appreciation, as described earlier in *Giving Property That Has Increased in Value*, your contribution is the reduced amount.

Deductions of Less Than $250

If you make any noncash contribution, you must get and keep a receipt from the charitable organization showing:

1. The name of the charitable organization,
2. The date and location of the charitable contribution, and
3. A reasonably detailed description of the property.

A letter or other written communication from the charitable organization acknowledging receipt of the contribution and containing the information in (1), (2), and (3) will serve as a receipt.

You aren't required to have a receipt where it is impractical to get one (for example, if you leave property at a charity's unattended drop site).

Additional records. You must also keep reliable written records for each item of contributed property. Your written records must include the following information.

1. The name and address of the organization to which you contributed.

2. The date and location of the contribution.
3. A description of the property in detail reasonable under the circumstances. For a security, keep the name of the issuer, the type of security, and whether it is regularly traded on a stock exchange or in an over-the-counter market.
4. The fair market value of the property at the time of the contribution and how you figured the fair market value. If it was determined by appraisal, you should also keep a copy of the signed appraisal.
5. The cost or other basis of the property, if you must reduce its fair market value by appreciation. Your records should also include the amount of the reduction and how you figured it. If you choose the 50% limit instead of the special 30% limit on certain capital gain property (discussed under *Capital gain property election*, earlier), you must keep a record showing the years for which you made the choice, contributions for the current year to which the choice applies, and carryovers from preceding years to which the choice applies.
6. The amount you claim as a deduction for the tax year as a result of the contribution, if you contribute less than your entire interest in the property during the tax year. Your records must include the amount you claimed as a deduction in any earlier years for contributions of other interests in this property. They must also include the name and address of each organization to which you contributed the other interests, the place where any such tangible property is located or kept, and the name of any person in possession of the property, other than the organization to which you contributed it.
7. The terms of any conditions attached to the contribution of property.

Deductions of At Least $250 But Not More Than $500

If you claim a deduction of at least $250 but not more than $500 for a noncash charitable contribution, you must get and keep an acknowledgment of your contribution from the qualified organization. If you made more than one contribution of $250 or more, you must have either a separate acknowledgment for each or one acknowledgment that shows your total contributions.

The acknowledgment must contain the information in items (1) through (3) under *Deductions of Less Than $250*, earlier, and your written records must include the information listed in that discussion under *Additional records*.

The acknowledgment must also meet these tests.

1. It must be written.
2. It must include:
   a. A description (but not necessarily the value) of any property you contributed,

b. Whether the qualified organization gave you any goods or services as a result of your contribution (other than certain token items and membership benefits), and

c. A description and good faith estimate of the value of any goods or services described in (b). If the only benefit you received was an intangible religious benefit (such as admission to a religious ceremony) that generally isn't sold in a commercial transaction outside the donative context, the acknowledgment must say so and doesn't need to describe or estimate the value of the benefit.

3. You must get it on or before the earlier of:

a. The date you file your return for the year you make the contribution, or

b. The due date, including extensions, for filing the return.

Deductions Over $500 But Not Over $5,000

If you claim a deduction over $500 but not over $5,000 for a noncash charitable contribution, you must have the acknowledgment and written records described under *Deductions of At Least $250 But Not More Than $500*. Your records must also include:

- How you got the property, for example, by purchase, gift, bequest, inheritance, or exchange,
- The approximate date you got the property or, if created, produced, or manufactured by or for you, the approximate date the property was substantially completed, and
- The cost or other basis, and any adjustments to the basis, of property held less than 12 months and, if available, the cost or other basis of property held 12 months or more. This requirement, however, doesn't apply to publicly traded securities.

If you have reasonable cause for being unable to provide information about the date you got the property or the cost basis of the property, attach a statement of explanation to your return.

Deductions Over $5,000

If you claim a deduction of over $5,000 for a noncash charitable contribution of one item or a group of similar items, you must have the acknowledgment and the written records described under *Deductions Over $500 But Not Over $5,000*. Generally, you must also obtain a qualified written appraisal of the donated property from a qualified appraiser. See *Deductions of More Than $5,000* in Pub. 561 for more information.

In figuring whether your deduction is over $5,000, combine your claimed deductions for all similar items donated to any charitable organization during the year.

Qualified Conservation Contribution

If the contribution was a qualified conservation contribution, your records must also include the fair market value of the underlying property before and after the contribution and the conservation purpose furthered by the contribution.

For more information, see *Qualified Conservation Contribution*, earlier, and in Pub. 561.

Out-of-Pocket Expenses

If you give services to a qualified organization and have unreimbursed out-of-pocket expenses related to those services, the following two rules apply.

1. You must have adequate records to prove the amount of the expenses.

2. If any of your unreimbursed out-of-pocket expenses, considered separately, are $250 or more (for example, you pay $250 for an airline ticket to attend a convention of a qualified organization as a chosen representative), you must get an acknowledgment from the qualified organization that contains:

a. A description of the services you provided,

b. A statement of whether or not the organization provided you any goods or services to reimburse you for the expenses you incurred,

c. A description and a good faith estimate of the value of any goods or services (other than intangible religious benefits) provided to reimburse you, and

d. A statement that the only benefit you received was an intangible religious benefit, if that was the case. The acknowledgment doesn't need to describe or estimate the value of an intangible religious benefit (defined earlier under *Acknowledgment*).

You must get the acknowledgment on or before the earlier of:

1. The date you file your return for the year you make the contribution, or

2. The due date, including extensions, for filing the return.

Car expenses. If you claim expenses directly related to use of your car in giving services to a qualified organization, you must keep reliable written records of your expenses. Whether your records are considered reliable depends on all the facts and circumstances. Generally, they may be considered reliable if you made them regularly and at or near the time you had the expenses.

For example, your records might show the name of the organization you were serving and the dates you used your car for a charitable purpose. If you use the standard mileage rate of 14 cents a mile, your records must show the miles you drove your car for the charitable purpose. If you deduct your actual expenses, your records

must show the costs of operating the car that are directly related to a charitable purpose.

See *Car expenses* under *Out-of-Pocket Expenses in Giving Services*, earlier, for the expenses you can deduct.

How To Report

Report your charitable contributions on lines 16 through 19 of Schedule A (Form 1040).

If you made noncash contributions, you may also be required to fill out parts of Form 8283. See *Noncash contributions*, later.

Cash contributions and out-of-pocket expenses. Enter your cash contributions, including out-of-pocket expenses, on Schedule A (Form 1040), line 16.

Reporting expenses for student living with you. If you claim amounts paid for a student who lives with you, as described earlier under *Expenses Paid for Student Living With You*, you must submit with your return:

1. A copy of your agreement with the organization sponsoring the student placed in your household,

2. A summary of the various items you paid to maintain the student, and

3. A statement that gives:

a. The date the student became a member of your household,

b. The dates of his or her full-time attendance at school, and

c. The name and location of the school.

Noncash contributions. Enter your noncash contributions on Schedule A (Form 1040), line 17.

Total deduction over $500. If your total deduction for all noncash contributions for the year is over $500, you must complete Form 8283 and attach it to your Form 1040. Use Section A of Form 8283 to report noncash contributions for which you claimed a deduction of $5,000 or less per item (or group of similar items). Also use Section A to report contributions of publicly traded securities. See *Deduction over $5,000 for one item*, next, for the items you must report on Section B.

The IRS may disallow your deduction for noncash charitable contributions if it is more than $500 and you don't submit Form 8283 with your return.

Deduction over $5,000 for one item. You must complete Section B of Form 8283 for each item or group of similar items for which you claim a deduction of over $5,000. (However, if you contributed publicly traded securities, complete Section A instead.) In figuring whether your deduction for a group of similar items was more than $5,000, consider all items in the group, even if items in the group were donated to more than one organization. However, you must file a separate Form 8283, Section B, for each organization. The organization that received the property must complete and sign Part IV of Section B.

Vehicle donations. If you donated a car, boat, airplane, or other vehicle, you may have to attach a copy of Form 1098-C (or other statement) to your return. For details, see *Cars, Boats, and Airplanes*, earlier.

Clothing and household items not in good used condition. You must include with your return a qualified appraisal of any single donated item of clothing or any donated household item that isn't in good used condition or better and for which you deduct more than $500. See *Clothing and Household Items*, earlier.

Easement on building in historic district. If you claim a deduction for a qualified conservation contribution for an easement on the exterior of a building in a registered historic district, you must include a qualified appraisal, photographs, and certain other information with your return. See *Qualified Conservation Contribution*, earlier.

Deduction over $500,000. If you claim a deduction of more than $500,000 for a contribution of property, you must attach a qualified appraisal of the property to your return. This doesn't apply to contributions of cash, inventory, publicly traded stock, or intellectual property.

In figuring whether your deduction is over $500,000, combine the claimed deductions for all similar items donated to any charitable organization during the year.

If you don't attach the appraisal, you can't deduct your contribution, unless your failure to attach it is due to reasonable cause and not to willful neglect.

Form 8282. An organization must file Form 8282 if, within 3 years of receiving property for which it was required to sign a Form 8283, it sells, exchanges, consumes, or otherwise disposes of the property. The organization must also send you a copy of the form. However, the organization need not file Form 8282 to report the sale of an item if you signed a statement on Section B of Form 8283 stating that the appraised value of the item, or a specific item within a group of similar items, was $500 or less. For this purpose, all shares of nonpublicly traded stock or securities, or items that form a set (such as a collection of books written by the same author or a group of place settings), are considered to be one item.

How To Get Tax Help

If you have questions about a tax issue, need help preparing your tax return, or want to download free publications, forms, or instructions, go to IRS.gov and find resources that can help you right away.

Preparing and filing your tax return. Find free options to prepare and file your return on IRS.gov or in your local community if you qualify.

- Go to IRS.gov and click on the Filing tab to see your options.

- Enter "Free File" in the search box to see whether you can use brand-name software to prepare and e-file your federal tax return for free.
- Enter "VITA" in the search box, download the free IRS2Go app, or call 1-800-906-9887 to find the nearest Volunteer Income Tax Assistance or Tax Counseling for the Elderly (TCE) location for free tax preparation.
- Enter "TCE" in the search box, download the free IRS2Go app, or call 1-888-227-7669 to find the nearest Tax Counseling for the Elderly location for free tax preparation.

The Volunteer Income Tax Assistance (VITA) program offers free tax help to people who generally make $54,000 or less, persons with disabilities, the elderly, and limited-English-speaking taxpayers who need help preparing their own tax returns. The Tax Counseling for the Elderly (TCE) program offers free tax help for all taxpayers, particularly those who are 60 years of age and older. TCE volunteers specialize in answering questions about pensions and retirement-related issues unique to seniors.

 Getting answers to your tax law questions. On IRS.gov, get answers to your tax questions anytime, anywhere.

- Go to *www.irs.gov/Help-&-Resources* for a variety of tools that will help you with your taxes.
- Enter "ITA" in the search box on IRS.gov for the Interactive Tax Assistant, a tool that will ask you questions on a number of tax law topics and provide answers. You can print the entire interview and the final response.
- Enter "Pub 17" in the search box on IRS.gov to get Pub. 17, Your Federal Income Tax for Individuals, which features details on tax-saving opportunities, 2015 tax changes, and thousands of interactive links to help you find answers to your questions.
- Additionally, you may be able to access tax law information in your electronic filing software.

Tax forms and publications. You can download or print all of the forms and publications you may need on *www.irs.gov/formspubs*. Otherwise, you can go to *www.irs.gov/orderforms* to place an order and have forms mailed to you. You should receive your order within 10 business days.

Direct Deposit. The fastest way to receive a tax refund is by combining direct deposit and IRS e-file. Direct deposit securely and electronically transfers your refund directly into your financial account. Eight in 10 taxpayers use direct deposit to receive their refund. The majority of refunds are received within 21 days or less.

Getting a transcript or copy of a return.
- Go to *www.irs.gov/Individuals/Get-Transcript*.
- Call the transcript toll-free line at 1-800-908-9946.

- Mail Form 4506-T or Form 4506T-EZ (both available on IRS.gov).

Using online tools to help prepare your return. Go to IRS.gov and click on the Tools bar to use these and other self-service options.
- The *Earned Income Tax Credit Assistant* determines if you are eligible for the EIC.
- The *Online EIN Application* helps you get an employer identification number.
- The *IRS Withholding Calculator* estimates the amount you should have withheld from your paycheck for federal income tax purposes.
- The *Electronic Filing PIN Request* helps to verify your identity when you do not have your prior year AGI or prior year self-selected PIN available.
- The *First Time Homebuyer Credit Account Look-up* tool provides information on your repayments and account balance.

For help with the alternative minimum tax, go to IRS.gov/AMT.

Understanding identity theft issues.
- Go to *www.irs.gov/uac/Identity-Protection* for information and videos.
- If your SSN has been lost or stolen or you suspect you are a victim of tax-related identity theft, visit *www.irs.gov/identitytheft* to learn what steps you should take.

Checking on the status of a refund.
- Go to *www.irs.gov/refunds*.
- Download the free IRS2Go app to your smart phone and use it to check your refund status.
- Call the automated refund hotline at 1-800-829-1954.

Making a tax payment. The IRS uses the latest encryption technology so electronic payments are safe and secure. You can make electronic payments online, by phone, or from a mobile device. Paying electronically is quick, easy, and faster than mailing in a check or money order. Go to *www.irs.gov/payments* to make a payment using any of the following options.
- *IRS Direct Pay* (for individual taxpayers who have a checking or savings account).
- **Debit or credit card** (approved payment processors online or by phone).
- **Electronic Funds Withdrawal** (available during e-file).
- **Electronic Federal Tax Payment System** (best option for businesses; enrollment required).
- **Check or money order.**

IRS2Go provides access to mobile-friendly payment options like IRS Direct Pay, offering you a free, secure way to pay directly from your bank account. You can also make debit or credit card payments through an approved payment processor. Simply download IRS2Go from Google Play, the Apple App Store, or the Amazon Appstore, and make your payments anytime, anywhere.

What if I can't pay now? Click on the "Pay Your Tax Bill" icon on IRS.gov for more information about these additional options.

- Apply for an *online payment agreement* to meet your tax obligation in monthly installments if you cannot pay your taxes in full today. Once you complete the online process, you will receive immediate notification of whether your agreement has been approved.
- An offer in compromise allows you to settle your tax debt for less than the full amount you owe. Use the *Offer in Compromise Pre-Qualifier* to confirm your eligibility.

Checking the status of an amended return. Go to IRS.gov and click on the Tools tab and then *Where's My Amended Return?*

Understanding an IRS notice or letter. Enter "Understanding your notice" in the search box on IRS.gov to find additional information about your IRS notice or letter.

Visiting the IRS. Locate the nearest Taxpayer Assistance Center using the Office Locator tool on IRS.gov. Enter "office locator" in the search box. Or choose the "Contact Us" option on the IRS2Go app and search Local Offices. Before you visit, use the Locator tool to check hours and services available.

Watching IRS videos. The IRS Video portal *www.irsvideos.gov* contains video and audio presentations for individuals, small businesses, and tax professionals. You'll find video clips of tax topics, archived versions of panel discussions and Webinars, and audio archives of tax practitioner phone forums.

Getting tax information in other languages. For taxpayers whose native language is not English, we have the following resources available.

1. Taxpayers can find information on IRS.gov in the following languages.

   a. *Spanish*.

   b. *Chinese*.

   c. *Vietnamese*.

   d. *Korean*.

   e. *Russian*.

2. The IRS Taxpayer Assistance Centers provide over-the-phone interpreter service in over 170 languages, and the service is available free to taxpayers.

The Taxpayer Advocate Service Is Here To Help You
What is the Taxpayer Advocate Service?

The Taxpayer Advocate Service (TAS) is an *independent* organization within the Internal Revenue Service that helps taxpayers and protects taxpayer rights. Our job is to ensure that every taxpayer is treated fairly and that you know and understand your rights under the *Taxpayer Bill of Rights*.

What Can the Taxpayer Advocate Service Do For You?

We can help you resolve problems that you can't resolve with the IRS. And our service is free. If you qualify for our assistance, you will be assigned to one advocate who will work with you throughout the process and will do everything possible to resolve your issue. TAS can help you if:

- Your problem is causing financial difficulty for you, your family, or your business,
- You face (or your business is facing) an immediate threat of adverse action, or
- You've tried repeatedly to contact the IRS but no one has responded, or the IRS hasn't responded by the date promised.

How Can You Reach Us?

We have offices *in every state, the District of Columbia, and Puerto Rico*. Your local advocate's number is in your local directory and at *www.taxpayeradvocate.irs.gov*. You can also call us at 1-877-777-4778.

How Can You Learn About Your Taxpayer Rights?

The Taxpayer Bill of Rights describes ten basic rights that all taxpayers have when dealing with the IRS. Our Tax Toolkit at *www.taxpayeradvocate.irs.gov* can help you understand *what these rights mean to you* and how they apply. These are *your* rights. Know them. Use them.

How Else Does the Taxpayer Advocate Service Help Taxpayers?

TAS works to resolve large-scale problems that affect many taxpayers. If you know of one of these broad issues, please report it to us at *www.irs.gov/sams*.

Low Income Taxpayer Clinics

Low Income Taxpayer Clinics (LITCs) serve individuals whose income is below a certain level and need to resolve tax problems such as audits, appeals, and tax collection disputes. Some clinics can provide information about taxpayer rights and responsibilities in different languages for individuals who speak English as a second language. To find a clinic near you, visit *www.irs.gov/litc* or see IRS Publication 4134, *Low Income Taxpayer Clinic List*.

Index

To help us develop a more useful index, please let us know if you have ideas for index entries. See "Comments and Suggestions" in the "Introduction" for the ways you can reach us.

Page A-60

NOTE: IRS updates this publication periodically, most current version is at http//irs.gov

Department
of the
Treasury

**Internal
Revenue
Service**

Publication 561
(Rev. April 2007)
Cat. No. 15109Q

Determining the Value of Donated Property

**Get forms and other information
faster and easier by:**

Internet • www.irs.gov

Contents

Introduction

This publication is designed to help donors and appraisers determine the value of property (other than cash) that is given to qualified organizations. It also explains what kind of information you must have to support the charitable contribution deduction you claim on your return.

This publication does not discuss how to figure the amount of your deduction for charitable contributions or written records and substantiation required. See Publication 526, Charitable Contributions, for this information.

Comments and suggestions. We welcome your comments about this publication and your suggestions for future editions.

You can write to us at the following address:

Internal Revenue Service
Individual Forms and Publications Branch
SE:W:CAR:MP:T:I
1111 Constitution Ave. NW, IR-6406
Washington, DC 20224

We respond to many letters by telephone. Therefore, it would be helpful if you would include your daytime phone number, including the area code, in your correspondence.

You can email us at *taxforms@irs.gov. (The asterisk must be included in the address.) Please put "Publications Comment" on the subject line. Although we cannot respond individually to each email, we do appreciate your feedback and will consider your comments as we revise our tax products.

Ordering forms and publications. Visit *www.irs.gov/formspubs* to download forms and publications, call 1-800-829-3676, or write to the address below and receive a response within 10 business days after your request is received.

National Distribution Center
P.O. Box 8903
Bloomington, IL 61702–8903

Tax questions. If you have a tax question, visit *www.irs.gov* or call 1-800-829-1040. We cannot answer tax questions sent to either of the above addresses.

Useful Items

You may want to see:

Publication

❏ **526** Charitable Contributions

Form (and Instructions)

❏ **8282** Donee Information Return

❏ **8283** Noncash Charitable Contributions

❏ **8283-V** Payment Voucher for Filing Fee Under Section 170(f)(13)

See *How To Get Tax Help,* near the end of this publication, for information about getting these publications and forms.

What Is Fair Market Value (FMV)?

To figure how much you may deduct for property that you contribute, you must first determine its fair market value on the date of the contribution.

Fair market value. Fair market value (FMV) is the price that property would sell for on the open market. It is the price that would be agreed on between a willing buyer and a willing seller, with neither being required to act, and both having reasonable knowledge of the relevant facts. If you put a restriction on the use of property you donate, the FMV must reflect that restriction.

Example 1. If you give used clothing to the Salvation Army, the FMV would be the price that typical buyers actually pay for clothing of this age, condition, style, and use. Usually, such items are worth far less than what you paid for them.

Example 2. If you donate land and restrict its use to agricultural purposes, you must value the land at its value for agricultural purposes, even though it would have a higher FMV if it were not restricted.

Factors. In making and supporting the valuation of property, all factors affecting value are relevant and must be considered. These include:

- The cost or selling price of the item,
- Sales of comparable properties,
- Replacement cost, and
- Opinions of experts.

These factors are discussed later. Also, see *Table 1* for a summary of questions to ask as you consider each factor.

Date of contribution. Ordinarily, the date of a contribution is the date that the transfer of the property takes place.

Stock. If you deliver, without any conditions, a properly endorsed stock certificate to a qualified organization or to an agent of the organization, the date of the contribution is the date of delivery. If the certificate is mailed and received through the regular mail, it is the date of mailing. If you deliver the certificate to a bank or broker acting as your agent or to the issuing corporation or its agent, for transfer into the name of the organization, the date of the contribution is the date the stock is transferred on the books of the corporation.

Options. If you grant an option to a qualified organization to buy real property, you have not made a charitable contribution until the organization exercises the option. The amount of the contribution is the FMV of the property on the date the option is exercised minus the exercise price.

Example. You grant an option to a local university, which is a qualified organization, to buy real property. Under the option, the university could buy the property at any time during a 2-year period for $40,000. The FMV of the property on the date the option is granted is $50,000.

In the following tax year, the university exercises the option. The FMV of the property on the date the option is exercised is $55,000. Therefore, you have made a charitable contribution of $15,000 ($55,000, the FMV, minus $40,000, the exercise price) in the tax year the option is exercised.

Determining Fair Market Value

Determining the value of donated property would be a simple matter if you could rely only on fixed formulas, rules, or methods. Usually it is not that simple. Using such formulas, etc., seldom results in an acceptable determination of FMV. There is no single formula that always applies when determining the value of property.

This is not to say that a valuation is only guesswork. You must consider all the facts and circumstances connected with the property, such as its desirability, use, and scarcity.

For example, donated furniture should not be evaluated at some fixed rate such as 15% of the cost of new replacement furniture. When the furniture is contributed, it may be out of style or in poor condition, therefore having little or no market value. On the other hand, it may be an antique, the value of which could not be determined by using any formula.

Cost or Selling Price of the Donated Property

The cost of the property to you or the actual selling price received by the qualified organization may be the best indication of its FMV. However, because conditions in the market change, the cost or selling price of property may have less weight if the property was not bought or sold reasonably close to the date of contribution.

The cost or selling price is a good indication of the property's value if:

- The purchase or sale took place close to the valuation date in an open market,
- The purchase or sale was at "arm's-length,"
- The buyer and seller knew all relevant facts,
- The buyer and seller did not have to act, and
- The market did not change between the date of purchase or sale and the valuation date.

Example. Tom Morgan, who is not a dealer in gems, bought an assortment of gems for $5,000 from a promoter. The promoter claimed that the price was "wholesale" even though he and other dealers made similar sales at similar prices to other persons who were not dealers. The promoter said that if Tom kept the gems for more than 1 year and then gave them to charity, Tom could claim a charitable deduction of $15,000, which, according to the promoter, would be the value of the gems at the time of contribution. Tom gave the gems to a qualified charity 13 months after buying them.

The selling price for these gems had not changed from the date of purchase to the date he donated them to charity. The best evidence of FMV depends on actual transactions and not on some artificial estimate. The $5,000 charged Tom and others is, therefore, the best evidence of the maximum FMV of the gems.

Terms of the purchase or sale. The terms of the purchase or sale should be considered in determining FMV if they influenced the price. These terms include any restrictions, understandings, or covenants limiting the use or disposition of the property.

Rate of increase or decrease in value. Unless you can show that there were unusual circumstances, it is assumed that the increase or decrease in the value of your donated property from your cost has been at a reasonable rate. For time adjustments, an appraiser may consider published price indexes for information on general price trends, building costs, commodity costs, securities, and works of art sold at auction in arm's-length sales.

Example. Bill Brown bought a painting for $10,000. Thirteen months later he gave it to an art museum, claiming a charitable deduction of $15,000 on his tax return. The appraisal of the painting should include information showing that there were unusual circumstances that justify a 50% increase in value for the 13 months Bill held the property.

Table 1. **Factors That Affect FMV**

IF the factor you are considering is...	THEN you should ask these questions...
cost or selling price	Was the purchase or sale of the property reasonably close to the date of contribution? Was any increase or decrease in value, as compared to your cost, at a reasonable rate? Do the terms of purchase or sale limit what can be done with the property? Was there an arm's-length offer to buy the property close to the valuation date?
sales of comparable properties	How similar is the property sold to the property donated? How close is the date of sale to the valuation date? Was the sale at arm's-length? What was the condition of the market at the time of sale?
replacement cost	What would it cost to replace the donated property? Is there a reasonable relationship between replacement cost and FMV? Is the supply of the donated property more or less than the demand for it?
opinions of experts	Is the expert knowledgeable and competent? Is the opinion thorough and supported by facts and experience?

Arm's-length offer. An arm's-length offer to buy the property close to the valuation date may help to prove its value if the person making the offer was willing and able to complete the transaction. To rely on an offer, you should be able to show proof of the offer and the specific amount to be paid. Offers to buy property other than the donated item will help to determine value if the other property is reasonably similar to the donated property.

Sales of Comparable Properties

The sales prices of properties similar to the donated property are often important in determining the FMV. The weight to be given to each sale depends on the following.

- The degree of similarity between the property sold and the donated property.

- The time of the sale—whether it was close to the valuation date.

- The circumstances of the sale—whether it was at arm's-length with a knowledgeable buyer and seller, with neither having to act.

- The conditions of the market in which the sale was made—whether unusually inflated or deflated.

The comparable sales method of valuing real estate is explained later under *Valuation of Various Kinds of Property.*

Example 1. Mary Black, who is not a book dealer, paid a promoter $10,000 for 500 copies of a single edition of a modern translation of the Bible. The promoter had claimed that the price was considerably less than the "retail" price, and gave her a statement that the books had a total retail value of $30,000. The promoter advised

her that if she kept the Bibles for more than 1 year and then gave them to a qualified organization, she could claim a charitable deduction for the "retail" price of $30,000. Thirteen months later she gave all the Bibles to a church that she selected from a list provided by the promoter. At the time of her donation, wholesale dealers were selling similar quantities of Bibles to the general public for $10,000.

The FMV of the Bibles is $10,000, the price at which similar quantities of Bibles were being sold to others at the time of the contribution.

Example 2. The facts are the same as in Example 1, except that the promoter gave Mary Black a second option. The promoter said that if Mary wanted a charitable deduction within 1 year of the purchase, she could buy the 500 Bibles at the "retail" price of $30,000, paying only $10,000 in cash and giving a promissory note for the remaining $20,000. The principal and interest on the note would not be due for 12 years. According to the promoter, Mary could then, within 1 year of the purchase, give the Bibles to a qualified organization and claim the full $30,000 retail price as a charitable contribution. She purchased the Bibles under the second option and, 3 months later, gave them to a church, which will use the books for church purposes.

At the time of the gift, the promoter was selling similar lots of Bibles for either $10,000 or $30,000. The difference between the two prices was solely at the discretion of the buyer. The promoter was a willing seller for $10,000. Therefore, the value of Mary's contribution of the Bibles is $10,000, the amount at which similar lots of Bibles could be purchased from the promoter by members of the general public.

Replacement Cost

The cost of buying, building, or manufacturing property similar to the donated item should be considered in determining FMV. However, there must be a reasonable relationship between the replacement cost and the FMV.

The replacement cost is the amount it would cost to replace the donated item on the valuation date. Often there is no relationship between the replacement cost and the FMV. If the supply of the donated property is more or less than the demand for it, the replacement cost becomes less important.

To determine the replacement cost of the donated property, find the "estimated replacement cost new." Then subtract from this figure an amount for depreciation due to the physical condition and obsolescence of the donated property. You should be able to show the relationship between the depreciated replacement cost and the FMV, as well as how you arrived at the "estimated replacement cost new."

Opinions of Experts

Generally, the weight given to an expert's opinion on matters such as the authenticity of a coin or a work of art, or the most profitable and best use of a piece of real estate, depends on the knowledge and competence of the expert and the thoroughness with which the opinion is supported by experience and facts. For an expert's opinion to deserve much weight, the facts must support the opinion. For additional information, see *Appraisals,* later.

Problems in Determining Fair Market Value

There are a number of problems in determining the FMV of donated property.

Unusual Market Conditions

The sale price of the property itself in an arm's-length transaction in an open market is often the best evidence of its value. When you rely on sales of comparable property, the sales must have been made in an open market. If those sales were made in a market that was artificially supported or stimulated so as not to be truly representative, the prices at which the sales were made will not indicate the FMV.

For example, liquidation sale prices usually do not indicate the FMV. Also, sales of stock under unusual circumstances, such as sales of small lots, forced sales, and sales in a restricted market, may not represent the FMV.

Selection of Comparable Sales

Using sales of comparable property is an important method for determining the FMV of donated property. However, the amount of weight given to a sale depends on the degree of similarity between the comparable and the donated properties. The degree of similarity must be close enough so that this selling price would have been given consideration by reasonably well-informed buyers or sellers of the property.

Example. You give a rare, old book to your former college. The book is a third edition and is in poor condition because of a missing back cover. You discover that there was a sale for $300, near the valuation date, of a first edition of the book that was in good condition. Although the contents are the same, the books are not at all similar because of the different editions and their physical condition. Little consideration would be given to the selling price of the $300 property by knowledgeable buyers or sellers.

Future Events

You may not consider unexpected events happening after your donation of property in making the valuation. You may consider only the facts known at the time of the gift, and those that could be reasonably expected at the time of the gift.

Example. You give farmland to a qualified charity. The transfer provides that your mother will have the right to all income and full use of the property for her life. Even though your mother dies 1 week after the transfer, the value of the property on the date it is given is its present value, subject to the life interest as estimated from actuarial tables. You may not take a higher deduction because the charity received full use and possession of the land only 1 week after the transfer.

Using Past Events to Predict the Future

A common error is to rely too much on past events that do not fairly reflect the probable future earnings and FMV.

Example. You give all your rights in a successful patent to your favorite charity. Your records show that before the valuation date there were three stages in the patent's history of earnings. First, there was rapid growth in earnings when the invention was introduced. Then, there was a period of high earnings when the invention was being exploited. Finally, there was a decline in earnings when competing inventions were introduced. The entire history of earnings may be relevant in estimating the future earnings. However, the appraiser must not rely too much on the stage of rapid growth in earnings, or of high earnings. The market conditions at those times do not represent the condition of the market at the valuation date. What is most significant is the trend of decline in earnings up to the valuation date. For more information about donations of patents, see *Patents,* later.

Valuation of Various Kinds of Property

This section contains information on determining the FMV of ordinary kinds of donated property. For information on appraisals, see *Appraisals,* later.

Household Goods

The FMV of used household goods, such as furniture, appliances, and linens, is usually much lower than the price paid when new. Such used property may have little or no market value because of its worn condition. It may be out of style or no longer useful.

You cannot take a deduction for household goods donated after August 17, 2006, unless they are in good used condition or better. A household good that is not in good used condition or better for which you take a deduction of more than $500 requires a qualified appraisal. See *Deduction over $500 for certain clothing or household items*, later.

If the property is valuable because it is old or unique, see the discussion under *Paintings, Antiques, and Other Objects of Art.*

Used Clothing

Used clothing and other personal items are usually worth far less than the price you paid for them. Valuation of items of clothing does not lend itself to fixed formulas or methods.

The price that buyers of used items actually pay in used clothing stores, such as consignment or thrift shops, is an indication of the value.

You cannot take a deduction for clothing donated after August 17, 2006, unless it is in good used condition or better. An item of clothing that is not in good used condition or better for which you take a deduction of more than $500 requires a qualified appraisal. See *Deduction over $500 for certain clothing or household items*, later.

For valuable furs or very expensive gowns, a Form 8283 may have to be sent with your tax return.

Jewelry and Gems

Jewelry and gems are of such a specialized nature that it is almost always necessary to get an appraisal by a specialized jewelry appraiser. The appraisal should describe, among other things, the style of the jewelry, the cut and setting of the gem, and whether it is now in fashion. If not in fashion, the possibility of having the property redesigned, recut, or reset should be reported in the appraisal. The stone's coloring, weight, cut, brilliance, and flaws should be reported and analyzed. Sentimental personal value has no effect on FMV. But if the jewelry was owned by a famous person, its value might increase.

Paintings, Antiques, and Other Objects of Art

Your deduction for contributions of paintings, antiques, and other objects of art, should be supported by a written appraisal from a qualified and reputable source, unless the deduction is $5,000 or less. Examples of information that should be included in appraisals of art objects— paintings in particular—are found later under *Qualified Appraisal.*

Art valued at $20,000 or more. If you claim a deduction of $20,000 or more for donations of art, you must attach a complete copy of the signed appraisal to your return. For individual objects valued at $20,000 or more, a photograph of a size and quality fully showing the object, preferably an 8 x 10 inch color photograph or a color transparency no smaller than 4 x 5 inches, must be provided upon request.

Art valued at $50,000 or more. If you donate an item of art that has been appraised at $50,000 or more, you can request a Statement of Value for that item from the IRS. You must request the statement before filing the tax return that reports the donation. Your request must include the following.

- A copy of a qualified appraisal of the item. See *Qualified Appraisal,* later.

- A $2,500 check or money order payable to the Internal Revenue Service for the user fee that applies to your request regarding one, two, or three items of art. Add $250 for each item in excess of three.

- A completed Form 8283, Section B.

- The location of the IRS territory that has examination responsibility for your return.

If your request lacks essential information, you will be notified and given 30 days to provide the missing information.

Send your request to:

Internal Revenue Service
Attention: Art Appraisal (C:AP:ART)
P.O. Box 27720
McPherson Station
Washington, DC 20038

Refunds. You can withdraw your request for a Statement of Value at any time before it is issued. However, the IRS will not refund the user fee if you do.

If the IRS declines to issue a Statement of Value in the interest of efficient tax administration, the IRS will refund the user fee.

Authenticity. The authenticity of the donated art must be determined by the appraiser.

Physical condition. Important items in the valuation of antiques and art are physical condition and extent of restoration. These have a significant effect on the value and must be fully reported in an appraisal. An antique in damaged condition, or lacking the "original brasses," may be worth much less than a similar piece in excellent condition.

Art appraisers. More weight will usually be given to an appraisal prepared by an individual specializing in the kind and price range of the art being appraised. Certain art dealers or appraisers specialize, for example, in old masters, modern art, bronze sculpture, etc. Their opinions on the authenticity and desirability of such art would usually be given more weight than the opinions of more generalized art dealers or appraisers. They can report more recent comparable sales to support their opinion.

To identify and locate experts on unique, specialized items or collections, you may wish to use the current Official Museum Directory of the American Association of Museums. It lists museums both by state and by category.

To help you locate a qualified appraiser for your donation, you may wish to ask an art historian at a nearby college or the director or curator of a local museum. The Yellow Pages often list specialized art and antique dealers, auctioneers, and art appraisers. You may be able to find a qualified appraiser on the Internet. You may also contact associations of dealers for guidance.

Collections

Since many kinds of hobby collections may be the subject of a charitable donation, it is not possible to discuss all of the possible collectibles in this publication. Most common are rare books, autographs, sports memorabilia, dolls, manuscripts, stamps, coins, guns, phonograph records, and natural history items. Many of the elements of valuation that apply to paintings and other objects of art, discussed earlier, also apply to miscellaneous collections.

Reference material. Publications available to help you determine the value of many kinds of collections include catalogs, dealers' price lists, and specialized hobby periodicals. When using one of these price guides, you must use the current edition at the date of contribution. However, these sources are not always reliable indicators of FMV and should be supported by other evidence.

For example, a dealer may sell an item for much less than is shown on a price list, particularly after the item has remained unsold for a long time. The price an item sold for in an auction may have been the result of a rigged sale or a mere bidding duel. The appraiser must analyze the reference material, and recognize and make adjustments for misleading entries. If you are donating a valuable collection, you should get an appraisal. If your donation appears to be of little value, you may be able to make a satisfactory valuation using reference materials available at a state, city, college, or museum library.

Stamp collections. Most libraries have catalogs or other books that report the publisher's estimate of values. Generally, two price levels are shown for each stamp: the price postmarked and the price not postmarked. Stamp dealers generally know the value of their merchandise and are able to prepare satisfactory appraisals of valuable collections.

Coin collections. Many catalogs and other reference materials show the writer's or publisher's opinion of the value of coins on or near the date of the publication. Like many other collectors' items, the value of a coin depends on the demand for it, its age, and its rarity. Another important factor is the coin's condition. For example, there is a great difference in the value of a coin that is in mint condition and a similar coin that is only in good condition.

Catalogs usually establish a category for coins, based on their physical condition—mint or uncirculated, extremely fine, very fine, fine, very good, good, fair, or poor—with a different valuation for each category.

Books. The value of books is usually determined by selecting comparable sales and adjusting the prices according to the differences between the comparable sales and the item being evaluated. This is difficult to do and, except for a collection of little value, should be done by a specialized appraiser. Within the general category of literary property, there are dealers who specialize in certain areas, such as Americana, foreign imports, Bibles, and scientific books.

Modest value of collection. If the collection you are donating is of modest value, not requiring a written appraisal, the following information may help you in determining the FMV.

A book that is very old, or very rare, is not necessarily valuable. There are many books that are very old or rare, but that have little or no market value.

Condition of book. The condition of a book may have a great influence on its value. Collectors are interested in items that are in fine, or at least good, condition. When a book has a missing page, a loose binding, tears, stains, or is otherwise in poor condition, its value is greatly lowered.

Other factors. Some other factors in the valuation of a book are the kind of binding (leather, cloth, paper), page edges, and illustrations (drawings and photographs). Collectors usually want first editions of books. However, because of changes or additions, other editions are sometimes worth as much as, or more than, the first edition.

Manuscripts, autographs, diaries, and similar items. When these items are handwritten, or at least signed by famous people, they are often in demand and are valuable. The writings of unknowns also may be of value if they are of unusual historical or literary importance. Determining the value of such material is difficult. For example, there may be a great difference in value between two diaries that were kept by a famous person—one kept during childhood and the other during a later period in his or her life. The appraiser determines a value in these cases by applying knowledge and judgment to such factors as comparable sales and conditions.

Signatures. Signatures, or sets of signatures, that were cut from letters or other papers usually have little or no value. But complete sets of the signatures of U.S. presidents are in demand.

Cars, Boats, and Aircraft

If you donate a car, a boat, or an aircraft to a charitable organization, its FMV must be determined.

Certain commercial firms and trade organizations publish monthly or seasonal guides for different regions of the country, containing complete dealer sale prices or dealer average prices for recent model years. Prices are reported for each make, model, and year. These guides also provide estimates for adjusting for unusual equipment, unusual mileage, and physical condition. The prices are not "official," and these publications are not considered an appraisal of any specific donated property. But they do provide clues for making an appraisal and suggest relative prices for comparison with current sales and offerings in your area.

These publications are sometimes available from public libraries or at a bank, credit union, or finance company. You can also find pricing information about used cars on the Internet.

An acceptable measure of the FMV of a donated car, boat, or airplane is an amount not in excess of the price listed in a used vehicle pricing guide for a private party sale, not the dealer retail value, of a similar vehicle. However, the FMV may be less than that amount if the vehicle has engine trouble, body damage, high mileage, or any type of excessive wear. The FMV of a donated vehicle is the same as the price listed in a used vehicle pricing guide for a private party sale only if the guide lists a sales price for a vehicle that is the same make, model, and year, sold in the same area, in the same condition, with the same or similar options or accessories, and with the same or similar warranties as the donated vehicle.

Example. You donate a used car in poor condition to a local high school for use by students studying car repair. A used car guide shows the dealer retail value for this type of car in poor condition is $1,600. However, the guide shows the price for a private party sale of the car is only $750. The FMV of the car is considered to be no more than $750.

Boats. Except for inexpensive small boats, the valuation of boats should be based on an appraisal by a marine surveyor because the physical condition is so critical to the value.

More information. Your deduction for a donated car, boat, or airplane generally is limited to the gross proceeds from its sale by the qualified organization. This rule applies if the claimed value of the donated vehicle is more than $500. In certain cases, you can deduct the vehicle's FMV. For details, see Publication 526.

Inventory

If you donate any inventory item to a charitable organization, the amount of your deductible contribution generally is the FMV of the item, minus any gain you would have realized if you had sold the item at its FMV on the date of the gift. For more information, see Publication 526.

Patents

To determine the FMV of a patent, you must take into account, among other factors:

- Whether the patented technology has been made obsolete by other technology;

- Any restrictions on the donee's use of, or ability to transfer, the patented technology; and

- The length of time remaining before the patent expires.

However, your deduction for a donation of a patent or other intellectual property is its FMV, minus any gain you would have realized if you had sold the property at its FMV on the date of the gift. Generally, this means your deduction is the lesser of the property's FMV or its basis. For details, see Publication 526.

Stocks and Bonds

The value of stocks and bonds is the FMV of a share or bond on the valuation date. See *Date of contribution,* earlier, under *What Is Fair Market Value (FMV).*

Selling prices on valuation date. If there is an active market for the contributed stocks or bonds on a stock exchange, in an over-the-counter market, or elsewhere, the FMV of each share or bond is the average price between the highest and lowest quoted selling prices on the valuation date. For example, if the highest selling price for a share was $11, and the lowest $9, the average price is $10. You get the average price by adding $11 and $9 and dividing the sum by 2.

No sales on valuation date. If there were no sales on the valuation date, but there were sales within a reasonable period before and after the valuation date, you determine FMV by taking the average price between the highest and lowest sales prices on the nearest date before and on the nearest date after the valuation date. Then you weight these averages in inverse order by the respective number of trading days between the selling dates and the valuation date.

Example. On the day you gave stock to a qualified organization, there were no sales of the stock. Sales of the stock nearest the valuation date took place two trading days before the valuation date at an average selling price of $10 and three trading days after the valuation date at an average selling price of $15. The FMV on the valuation date was $12, figured as follows:

$$[(3 \times \$10) \quad + \quad (2 \times \$15)] \quad \div \quad 5 \quad = \quad \$12$$

Listings on more than one stock exchange. Stocks or bonds listed on more than one stock exchange are valued based on the prices of the exchange on which they are principally dealt. This applies if these prices are published in a generally available listing or publication of general circulation. If this is not applicable, and the stocks or bonds are reported on a composite listing of combined exchanges in a publication of general circulation, use the composite list. See also *Unavailable prices or closely held corporation,* later.

Bid and asked prices on valuation date. If there were no sales within a reasonable period before and after the valuation date, the FMV is the average price between the bona fide bid and asked prices on the valuation date.

Example. Although there were no sales of Blue Corporation stock on the valuation date, bona fide bid and asked prices were available on that date of $14 and $16, respectively. The FMV is $15, the average price between the bid and asked prices.

No prices on valuation date. If there were no prices available on the valuation date, you determine FMV by taking the average prices between the bona fide bid and asked prices on the closest trading date before and after the valuation date. Both dates must be within a reasonable period. Then you weight these averages in inverse order by the respective number of trading days between the bid and asked dates and the valuation date.

Example. On the day you gave stock to a qualified organization, no prices were available. Bona fide bid and asked prices 3 days before the valuation date were $10 and 2 days after the valuation date were $15. The FMV on the valuation date is $13, figured as follows:

$$[(2 \times \$10) \quad + \quad (3 \times \$15)] \quad \div \quad 5 \quad = \quad \$13$$

Prices only before or after valuation date, but not both. If no selling prices or bona fide bid and asked prices are available on a date within a reasonable period before the valuation date, but are available on a date within a reasonable period after the valuation date, or vice versa, then the average price between the highest and lowest of such available prices may be treated as the value.

Large blocks of stock. When a large block of stock is put on the market, it may lower the selling price of the stock if the supply is greater than the demand. On the other hand, market forces may exist that will afford higher prices for large blocks of stock. Because of the many factors to be considered, determining the value of large blocks of stock usually requires the help of experts specializing in underwriting large quantities of securities, or in trading in the securities of the industry of which the particular company is a part.

Unavailable prices or closely held corporation. If selling prices or bid and asked prices are not available, or if securities of a closely held corporation are involved, determine the FMV by considering the following factors.

- For bonds, the soundness of the security, the interest yield, the date of maturity, and other relevant factors.

- For shares of stock, the company's net worth, prospective earning power and dividend-paying capacity, and other relevant factors.

Other factors. Other relevant factors include:

- The nature and history of the business, especially its recent history,

- The goodwill of the business,

- The economic outlook in the particular industry,

- The company's position in the industry, its competitors, and its management, and

- The value of securities of corporations engaged in the same or similar business.

For preferred stock, the most important factors are its yield, dividend coverage, and protection of its liquidation preference.

You should keep complete financial and other information on which the valuation is based. This includes copies of reports of examinations of the company made by accountants, engineers, or any technical experts on or close to the valuation date.

Restricted securities. Some classes of stock cannot be traded publicly because of restrictions imposed by the Securities and Exchange Commission, or by the corporate charter or a trust agreement. These restricted securities usually trade at a discount in relation to freely traded securities.

To arrive at the FMV of restricted securities, factors that you must consider include the resale provisions found in the restriction agreements, the relative negotiating strengths of the buyer and seller, and the market experience of freely traded securities of the same class as the restricted securities.

Real Estate

Because each piece of real estate is unique and its valuation is complicated, a detailed appraisal by a professional appraiser is necessary.

The appraiser must be thoroughly trained in the application of appraisal principles and theory. In some instances the opinions of equally qualified appraisers may carry unequal weight, such as when one appraiser has a better knowledge of local conditions.

The appraisal report must contain a complete description of the property, such as street address, legal description, and lot and block number, as well as physical features, condition, and dimensions. The use to which the property is put, zoning and permitted uses, and its potential use for other higher and better uses are also relevant.

In general, there are three main approaches to the valuation of real estate. An appraisal may require the combined use of two or three methods rather than one method only.

1. Comparable Sales

The comparable sales method compares the donated property with several similar properties that have been sold. The selling prices, after adjustments for differences in date of sale, size, condition, and location, would then indicate the estimated FMV of the donated property.

If the comparable sales method is used to determine the value of unimproved real property (land without significant buildings, structures, or any other improvements that add to its value), the appraiser should consider the following factors when comparing the potential comparable property and the donated property:

- Location, size, and zoning or use restrictions,

- Accessibility and road frontage, and available utilities and water rights,

- Riparian rights (right of access to and use of the water by owners of land on the bank of a river) and existing easements, rights-of-way, leases, etc.,

- Soil characteristics, vegetative cover, and status of mineral rights, and

- Other factors affecting value.

For each comparable sale, the appraisal must include the names of the buyer and seller, the deed book and page number, the date of sale and selling price, a property description, the amount and terms of mortgages, property surveys, the assessed value, the tax rate, and the assessor's appraised FMV.

The comparable selling prices must be adjusted to account for differences between the sale property and the donated property. Because differences of opinion may arise between appraisers as to the degree of comparability and the amount of the adjustment considered necessary for comparison purposes, an appraiser should document each item of adjustment.

Only comparable sales having the least adjustments in terms of items and/or total dollar adjustments should be considered as comparable to the donated property.

2. Capitalization of Income

This method capitalizes the net income from the property at a rate that represents a fair return on the particular investment at the particular time, considering the risks involved. The key elements are the determination of the income to be capitalized and the rate of capitalization.

3. Replacement Cost New or Reproduction Cost Minus Observed Depreciation

This method, used alone, usually does not result in a determination of FMV. Instead, it generally tends to set the upper limit of value, particularly in periods of rising costs, because it is reasonable to assume that an informed buyer will not pay more for the real estate than it would cost to reproduce a similar property. Of course, this reasoning does not apply if a similar property cannot be created because of location, unusual construction, or some other reason. Generally, this method serves to support the value determined from other methods. When the replacement cost method is applied to improved realty, the land and improvements are valued separately.

The replacement cost of a building is figured by considering the materials, the quality of workmanship, and the number of square feet or cubic feet in the building. This cost represents the total cost of labor and material, overhead, and profit. After the replacement cost has been figured, consideration must be given to the following factors:

- Physical deterioration—the wear and tear on the building itself,

- Functional obsolescence—usually in older buildings with, for example, inadequate lighting, plumbing, or heating, small rooms, or a poor floor plan, and

- Economic obsolescence—outside forces causing the whole area to become less desirable.

Interest in a Business

The FMV of any interest in a business, whether a sole proprietorship or a partnership, is the amount that a willing buyer would pay for the interest to a willing seller after consideration of all relevant factors. The relevant factors to be considered in valuing the business are:

- The FMV of the assets of the business,

- The demonstrated earnings capacity of the business, based on a review of past and current earnings, and

- The other factors used in evaluating corporate stock, if they apply.

The value of the goodwill of the business should also be taken into consideration. You should keep complete financial and other information on which you base the valuation. This includes copies of reports of examinations of the business made by accountants, engineers, or any technical experts on or close to the valuation date.

Annuities, Interests for Life or Terms of Years, Remainders, and Reversions

The value of these kinds of property is their present value, except in the case of annuities under contracts issued by companies regularly engaged in their sale. The valuation of these commercial annuity contracts and of insurance policies is discussed later under *Certain Life Insurance and Annuity Contracts*.

To determine present value, you must know the applicable interest rate and use actuarial tables.

Interest rate. The applicable interest rate varies. It is announced monthly in a news release and published in the Internal Revenue Bulletin as a Revenue Ruling. The interest rate to use is under the heading "Rate Under Section 7520" for a given month and year. You can call the IRS office at 1-800-829-1040 to obtain this rate.

Actuarial tables. You need to refer to actuarial tables to determine a qualified interest in the form of an annuity, any interest for life or a term of years, or any remainder interest to a charitable organization.

Use the valuation tables set forth in IRS Publications 1457, Actuarial Values (Book Aleph), and 1458, Actuarial Values (Book Beth). Both of these publications provide tables containing actuarial factors to be used in determining the present value of an annuity, an interest for life or for a term of years, or a remainder or reversionary interest. For qualified charitable transfers, you can use the factor for the month in which you made the contribution or for either of the 2 months preceding that month. Publication 1457 also contains actuarial factors for computing the value of a remainder interest in a charitable remainder annuity trust and a pooled income fund. Publication 1458 contains the factors for valuing the remainder interest in a charitable remainder unitrust. You can download Publications 1457 and 1458 from *www.irs.gov*. In addition, they are available for purchase via the website of the U. S. Government Printing Office, by phone at (202) 512-1800, or by mail from the:

Superintendent of Documents
P.O. Box 371954
Pittsburgh, PA 15250-7954

Tables containing actuarial factors for transfers to pooled income funds may also be found in Income Tax Regulation 1.642(c)-6(e)(6), transfers to charitable remainder unitrusts in Regulation 1.664-4(e), and other transfers in Regulation 20.2031-7(d)(6).

Special factors. If you need a special factor for an actual transaction, you can request a letter ruling. Be sure to include the date of birth of each person the duration of whose life may affect the value of the interest. Also include copies of the relevant instruments. IRS charges a user fee for providing special factors.

For more information about requesting a ruling, see Revenue Procedure 2006-1 (or annual update), 2006-1 I.R.B. 1. Revenue Procedure 2006-1 is available at *www.irs.gov/irb/2006-01_IRB/ar06.html*.

For information on the circumstances under which a charitable deduction may be allowed for the donation of a partial interest in property not in trust, see *Partial Interest in Property Not in Trust,* later.

Certain Life Insurance and Annuity Contracts

The value of an annuity contract or a life insurance policy issued by a company regularly engaged in the sale of such contracts or policies is the amount that company would charge for a comparable contract.

But if the donee of a life insurance policy may reasonably be expected to cash the policy rather than hold it as an investment, then the FMV is the cash surrender value rather than the replacement cost.

If an annuity is payable under a combination annuity contract and life insurance policy (for example, a retirement income policy with a death benefit) and there was no insurance element when it was transferred to the charity, the policy is treated as an annuity contract.

Partial Interest in Property Not in Trust

Generally, no deduction is allowed for a charitable contribution, not made in trust, of less than your entire interest in property. However, this does not apply to a transfer of less than your entire interest if it is a transfer of:

- A remainder interest in your personal residence or farm,

- An undivided part of your entire interest in property, or

- A qualified conservation contribution.

Remainder Interest in Real Property

The amount of the deduction for a donation of a remainder interest in real property is the FMV of the remainder interest at the time of the contribution. To determine this value, you must know the FMV of the property on the date of the contribution. Multiply this value by the appropriate factor. Publications 1457 and 1458 contain these factors.

You must make an adjustment for depreciation or depletion using the factors shown in Publication 1459, Actuarial Values (Book Gimel). You can use the factors for the month in which you made the contribution or for either of the two months preceding that month. See the earlier discussion on *Annuities, Interests for Life or Terms of Years, Remainders, and Reversions*. You can download Publication 1459 from *www.irs.gov*.

For this purpose, the term "depreciable property" means any property subject to wear and tear or obsolescence, even if not used in a trade or business or for the production of income.

If the remainder interest includes both depreciable and nondepreciable property, for example a house and land, the FMV must be allocated between each kind of property at the time of the contribution. This rule also applies to a gift of a remainder interest that includes property that is part depletable and part not depletable. Take into account depreciation or depletion only for the property that is subject to depreciation or depletion.

For more information, see section 1.170A-12 of the Income Tax Regulations.

Undivided Part of Your Entire Interest

A contribution of an undivided part of your entire interest in property must consist of a part of each and every substantial interest or right you own in the property. It must extend over the entire term of your interest in the property. For example, you are entitled to the income from certain property for your life (life estate) and you contribute 20% of that life estate to a qualified organization. You can claim a deduction for the contribution if you do not have any other interest in the property. To figure the value of a contribution involving a partial interest, see Publication 1457.

If the only interest you own in real property is a remainder interest and you transfer part of that interest to a qualified organization, see the previous discussion on valuation of a remainder interest in real property.

Qualified Conservation Contribution

A qualified conservation contribution is a contribution of a qualified real property interest to a qualified organization to be used only for conservation purposes.

Qualified organization. For purposes of a qualified conservation contribution, a qualified organization is:

- A governmental unit,
- A publicly supported charitable, religious, scientific, literary, educational, etc., organization, or
- An organization that is controlled by, and operated for the exclusive benefit of, a governmental unit or a publicly supported charity.

The organization also must have a commitment to protect the conservation purposes of the donation and must have the resources to enforce the restrictions.

Conservation purposes. Your contribution must be made only for one of the following conservation purposes.

- Preserving land areas for outdoor recreation by, or for the education of, the general public.
- Protecting a relatively natural habitat of fish, wildlife, or plants, or a similar ecosystem.
- Preserving open space, including farmland and forest land, if it yields a significant public benefit. It must be either for the scenic enjoyment of the general public or under a clearly defined federal, state, or local governmental conservation policy.
- Preserving a historically important land area or a certified historic structure. There

must be some visual public access to the property. Factors used in determining the type and amount of public access required include the historical significance of the property, the remoteness or accessibility of the site, and the extent to which intrusions on the privacy of individuals living on the property would be unreasonable.

Building in registered historic district. A contribution after July 25, 2006, of a qualified real property interest that is an easement or other restriction on the exterior of a building in a registered historic district is deductible only if it meets all of the following three conditions.

1. The restriction must preserve the entire exterior of the building and must prohibit any change to the exterior of the building that is inconsistent with its historical character.

2. You and the organization receiving the contribution must enter into a written agreement certifying, that the organization is a qualified organization and that it has the resources and commitment to maintain the property as donated.

3. If you make the contribution in a tax year beginning after August 17, 2006, you must include with your return:

   a. A qualified appraisal,

   b. Photographs of the building's entire exterior, and

   c. A description of all restrictions on development of the building, such as zoning laws and restrictive covenants.

If you make this type of contribution after February 12, 2007, and claim a deduction of more than $10,000, your deduction will not be allowed unless you pay a $500 filing fee. See Form 8283-V, Payment Voucher for Filing Fee Under Section 170(f)(13), and its instructions.

Qualified real property interest. This is any of the following interests in real property.

1. Your entire interest in real estate other than a mineral interest (subsurface oil, gas, or other minerals, and the right of access to these minerals).

2. A remainder interest.

3. A restriction (granted in perpetuity) on the use that may be made of the real property.

Valuation. A qualified real property interest described in (1) should be valued in a manner that is consistent with the type of interest transferred. If you transferred all the interest in the property, the FMV of the property is the amount of the contribution. If you do not transfer the mineral interest, the FMV of the surface rights in the property is the amount of the contribution.

If you owned only a remainder interest or an income interest (life estate), see *Undivided Part of Your Entire Interest,* earlier. If you owned the entire property but transferred only a remainder interest (item (2)), see *Remainder Interest in Real Property,* earlier.

In determining the value of restrictions, you should take into account the selling price in arm's-length transactions of other properties

that have comparable restrictions. If there are no comparable sales, the restrictions are valued indirectly as the difference between the FMVs of the property involved before and after the grant of the restriction.

The FMV of the property before contribution of the restriction should take into account not only current use but the likelihood that the property, without the restriction, would be developed. You should also consider any zoning, conservation, or historical preservation laws that would restrict development. Granting an easement may increase, rather than reduce, the value of property, and in such a situation no deduction would be allowed.

Example. You own 10 acres of farmland. Similar land in the area has an FMV of $2,000 an acre. However, land in the general area that is restricted solely to farm use has an FMV of $1,500 an acre. Your county wants to preserve open space and prevent further development in your area.

You grant to the county an enforceable open space easement in perpetuity on 8 of the 10 acres, restricting its use to farmland. The value of this easement is $4,000, determined as follows:

```
FMV of the property before
granting easement:
  $2,000 × 10 acres . . . . . . . . . . . .  $20,000
FMV of the property after
granting easement:
  $1,500 × 8 acres . . . . . .  $12,000
  $2,000 × 2 acres . . . . . .    4,000   16,000
Value of easement . . . . . .            $4,000
```

If you later transfer in fee your remaining interest in the 8 acres to another qualified organization, the FMV of your remaining interest is the FMV of the 8 acres reduced by the FMV of the easement granted to the first organization.

More information. For more information about qualified conservation contributions, see Publication 526.

Appraisals

Appraisals are not necessary for items of property for which you claim a deduction of $5,000 or less. (There is one exception, described next, for certain clothing and household items.) However, you generally will need an appraisal for donated property for which you claim a deduction of more than $5,000. There are exceptions. See *Deductions of More Than $5,000,* later.

The weight given an appraisal depends on the completeness of the report, the qualifications of the appraiser, and the appraiser's demonstrated knowledge of the donated property. An appraisal must give all the facts on which to base an intelligent judgment of the value of the property.

The appraisal will not be given much weight if:

- All the factors that apply are not considered,
- The opinion is not supported with facts, such as purchase price and comparable sales, or

- The opinion is not consistent with known facts.

The appraiser's opinion is never more valid than the facts on which it is based; without these facts it is simply a guess.

The opinion of a person claiming to be an expert is not binding on the Internal Revenue Service. All facts associated with the donation must be considered.

Deduction over $500 for certain clothing or household items. You must include with your return a qualified appraisal of any single item of clothing or any household item that is not in good used condition or better, that you donated after August 17, 2006, and for which you deduct more than $500. See *Household Goods* and *Used Clothing*, earlier.

Cost of appraisals. You may not take a charitable contribution deduction for fees you pay for appraisals of your donated property. However, these fees may qualify as a miscellaneous deduction, subject to the 2% limit, on Schedule A (Form 1040) if paid to determine the amount allowable as a charitable contribution.

Deductions of More Than $5,000

Generally, if the claimed deduction for an item or group of similar items of donated property is more than $5,000, you must get a qualified appraisal made by a qualified appraiser, and you must attach Section B of Form 8283 to your tax return. There are exceptions, discussed later. You should keep the appraiser's report with your written records. Records are discussed in Publication 526.

The phrase "similar items" means property of the same generic category or type (whether or not donated to the same donee), such as stamp collections, coin collections, lithographs, paintings, photographs, books, nonpublicly traded stock, nonpublicly traded securities other than nonpublicly traded stock, land, buildings, clothing, jewelry, furniture, electronic equipment, household appliances, toys, everyday kitchenware, china, crystal, or silver. For example, if you give books to three schools and you deduct $2,000, $2,500, and $900, respectively, your claimed deduction is more than $5,000 for these books. You must get a qualified appraisal of the books and for each school you must attach a fully completed Form 8283, Section B, to your tax return.

Exceptions. You do not need an appraisal if the property is:

- Nonpublicly traded stock of $10,000 or less,

- A vehicle (including a car, boat, or airplane) for which your deduction is limited to the gross proceeds from its sale,

- Qualified intellectual property, such as a patent,

- Certain publicly traded securities described next,

- Inventory and other property donated by a corporation that are "qualified contributions" for the care of the ill, the needy, or infants, within the meaning of section

170(e)(3)(A) of the Internal Revenue Code, or

- Stock in trade, inventory, or property held primarily for sale to customers in the ordinary course of your trade or business.

Although an appraisal is not required for the types of property just listed, you must provide certain information about a donation of any of these types of property on Form 8283.

Publicly traded securities. Even if your claimed deduction is more than $5,000, neither a qualified appraisal nor Section B of Form 8283 is required for publicly traded securities that are:

- Listed on a stock exchange in which quotations are published on a daily basis,

- Regularly traded in a national or regional over-the-counter market for which published quotations are available, or

- Shares of an open-end investment company (mutual fund) for which quotations are published on a daily basis in a newspaper of general circulation throughout the United States.

Publicly traded securities that meet these requirements must be reported on Form 8283, Section A.

A qualified appraisal is not required, but Form 8283, Section B, Parts I and IV, must be completed, for an issue of a security that does not meet the requirements just listed but does meet these requirements:

1. The issue is regularly traded during the computation period (defined later) in a market for which there is an "interdealer quotation system" (defined later),

2. The issuer or agent computes the "average trading price" (defined later) for the same issue for the computation period,

3. The average trading price and total volume of the issue during the computation period are published in a newspaper of general circulation throughout the United States, not later than the last day of the month following the end of the calendar quarter in which the computation period ends,

4. The issuer or agent keeps books and records that list for each transaction during the computation period the date of settlement of the transaction, the name and address of the broker or dealer making the market in which the transaction occurred, and the trading price and volume, and

5. The issuer or agent permits the Internal Revenue Service to review the books and records described in item (4) with respect to transactions during the computation period upon receiving reasonable notice.

An interdealer quotation system is any system of general circulation to brokers and dealers that regularly disseminates quotations of obligations by two or more identified brokers or dealers who are not related to either the issuer or agent who computes the average trading price of the security. A quotation sheet prepared and distributed by a broker or dealer in the regular course of business and containing only quotations of

that broker or dealer is not an interdealer quotation system.

The average trading price is the average price of all transactions (weighted by volume), other than original issue or redemption transactions, conducted through a United States office of a broker or dealer who maintains a market in the issue of the security during the computation period. Bid and asked quotations are not taken into account.

The computation period is weekly during October through December and monthly during January through September. The weekly computation periods during October through December begin with the first Monday in October and end with the first Sunday following the last Monday in December.

Nonpublicly traded stock. If you contribute nonpublicly traded stock, for which you claim a deduction of $10,000 or less, a qualified appraisal is not required. However, you must attach Form 8283 to your tax return, with Section B, Parts I and IV, completed.

Deductions of More Than $500,000

If you claim a deduction of more than $500,000 for a donation of property, you must attach a qualified appraisal of the property to your return. This does not apply to contributions of cash, inventory, publicly traded stock, or intellectual property.

If you do not attach the appraisal, you cannot deduct your contribution, unless your failure to attach the appraisal is due to reasonable cause and not to willful neglect.

Qualified Appraisal

Generally, if the claimed deduction for an item or group of similar items of donated property is more than $5,000, you must get a qualified appraisal made by a qualified appraiser. You must also complete Form 8283, Section B, and attach it to your tax return. See *Deductions of More Than $5,000*, earlier.

A qualified appraisal is an appraisal document that:

- Is made, signed, and dated by a qualified appraiser (defined later) in accordance with generally accepted appraisal standards,

- Meets the relevant requirements of Regulations section 1.170A-13(c)(3) and Notice 2006-96, 2006-46 I.R.B. 902 (available at *www.irs.gov/irb/2006-46_IRB/ar13.html*),

- Relates to an appraisal made not earlier than 60 days before the date of contribution of the appraised property,

- Does not involve a prohibited appraisal fee, and

- Includes certain information (covered later).

You must receive the qualified appraisal before the due date, including extensions, of the return on which a charitable contribution deduction is first claimed for the donated property. If the deduction is first claimed on an amended return, the qualified appraisal must be received before the date on which the amended return is filed.

Form 8283, Section B, must be attached to your tax return. Generally, you do not need to attach the qualified appraisal itself, but you should keep a copy as long as it may be relevant under the tax law. There are four exceptions.

- If you claim a deduction of $20,000 or more for donations of art, you must attach a complete copy of the appraisal. See *Paintings, Antiques, and Other Objects of Art,* earlier.

- If you claim a deduction of more than $500,000 for a donation of property, you must attach the appraisal. See *Deductions of More Than $500,000,* earlier.

- If you claim a deduction of more than $500 for an article of clothing, or a household item, that is not in good used condition or better, that you donated after August 17, 2006, you must attach the appraisal. See *Deduction over $500 for certain clothing or household items*, earlier.

- If you claim a deduction in a tax year beginning after August 17, 2006, for an easement or other restriction on the exterior of a building in a historic district, you must attach the appraisal. See *Building in registered historic district*, earlier.

Prohibited appraisal fee. Generally, no part of the fee arrangement for a qualified appraisal can be based on a percentage of the appraised value of the property. If a fee arrangement is based on what is allowed as a deduction, after Internal Revenue Service examination or otherwise, it is treated as a fee based on a percentage of appraised value. However, appraisals are not disqualified when an otherwise prohibited fee is paid to a generally recognized association that regulates appraisers if:

- The association is not organized for profit and no part of its net earnings benefits any private shareholder or individual,

- The appraiser does not receive any compensation from the association or any other persons for making the appraisal, and

- The fee arrangement is not based in whole or in part on the amount of the appraised value that is allowed as a deduction after an Internal Revenue Service examination or otherwise.

Information included in qualified appraisal. A qualified appraisal must include the following information:

1. A description of the property in sufficient detail for a person who is not generally familiar with the type of property to determine that the property appraised is the property that was (or will be) contributed,

2. The physical condition of any tangible property,

3. The date (or expected date) of contribution,

4. The terms of any agreement or understanding entered into (or expected to be entered into) by or on behalf of the donor that relates to the use, sale, or other disposition of the donated property, including, for example, the terms of any agreement or understanding that:

    a. Temporarily or permanently restricts a donee's right to use or dispose of the donated property,

    b. Earmarks donated property for a particular use, or

    c. Reserves to, or confers upon, anyone (other than a donee organization or an organization participating with a donee organization in cooperative fundraising) any right to the income from the donated property or to the possession of the property, including the right to vote donated securities, to acquire the property by purchase or otherwise, or to designate the person having the income, possession, or right to acquire the property,

5. The name, address, and taxpayer identification number of the qualified appraiser and, if the appraiser is a partner, an employee, or an independent contractor engaged by a person other than the donor, the name, address, and taxpayer identification number of the partnership or the person who employs or engages the appraiser,

6. The qualifications of the qualified appraiser who signs the appraisal, including the appraiser's background, experience, education, and any membership in professional appraisal associations,

7. A statement that the appraisal was prepared for income tax purposes,

8. The date (or dates) on which the property was valued,

9. The appraised FMV on the date (or expected date) of contribution,

10. The method of valuation used to determine FMV, such as the income approach, the comparable sales or market data approach, or the replacement cost less depreciation approach, and

11. The specific basis for the valuation, such as any specific comparable sales transaction.

Art objects. The following are examples of information that should be included in a description of donated property. These examples are for art objects. A similar detailed breakdown should be given for other property. Appraisals of art objects—paintings in particular—should include all of the following.

1. A complete description of the object, indicating the:

    a. Size,

    b. Subject matter,

    c. Medium,

    d. Name of the artist (or culture), and

    e. Approximate date created.

2. The cost, date, and manner of acquisition.

3. A history of the item, including proof of authenticity.

4. A professional quality image of the object.

5. The facts on which the appraisal was based, such as:

    a. Sales or analyses of similar works by the artist, particularly on or around the valuation date.

    b. Quoted prices in dealer's catalogs of the artist's works or works of other artists of comparable stature.

    c. A record of any exhibitions at which the specific art object had been displayed.

    d. The economic state of the art market at the time of valuation, particularly with respect to the specific property.

    e. The standing of the artist in his profession and in the particular school or time period.

Number of qualified appraisals. A separate qualified appraisal is required for each item of property that is not included in a group of similar items of property. You need only one qualified appraisal for a group of similar items of property contributed in the same tax year, but you may get separate appraisals for each item. A qualified appraisal for a group of similar items must provide all of the required information for each item of similar property. The appraiser, however, may provide a group description for selected items the total value of which is not more than $100.

Qualified appraiser. A qualified appraiser is an individual who meets all the following requirements.

1. The individual either:

    a. Has earned an appraisal designation from a recognized professional appraiser organization for demonstrated competency in valuing the type of property being appraised, or

    b. Has met certain minimum education and experience requirements. For real property, the appraiser must be licensed or certified for the type of property being appraised in the state in which the property is located. For property other than real property, the appraiser must have successfully completed college or professional-level coursework relevant to the property being valued, must have at least 2 years of experience in the trade or business of buying, selling, or valuing the type of property being valued, and must fully describe in the appraisal his or her qualifying education and experience.

2. The individual regularly prepares appraisals for which he or she is paid.

3. The individual demonstrates verifiable education and experience in valuing the type of property being appraised. To do this, the appraiser can make a declaration in the

appraisal that, because of his or her background, experience, education, and membership in professional associations, he or she is qualified to make appraisals of the type of property being valued.

4. The individual has not been prohibited from practicing before the IRS under section 330(c) of title 31 of the United States Code at any time during the 3-year period ending on the date of the appraisal.

5. The individual is not an excluded individual.

In addition, the appraiser must complete Form 8283, Section B, Part III. More than one appraiser may appraise the property, provided that each complies with the requirements, including signing the qualified appraisal and Form 8283, Section B, Part III.

Excluded individuals. The following persons cannot be qualified appraisers with respect to particular property.

1. The donor of the property, or the taxpayer who claims the deduction.

2. The donee of the property.

3. A party to the transaction in which the donor acquired the property being appraised, unless the property is donated within 2 months of the date of acquisition and its appraised value is not more than its acquisition price. This applies to the person who sold, exchanged, or gave the property to the donor, or any person who acted as an agent for the transferor or donor in the transaction.

4. Any person employed by any of the above persons. For example, if the donor acquired a painting from an art dealer, neither the dealer nor persons employed by the dealer can be qualified appraisers for that painting.

5. Any person related under section 267(b) of the Internal Revenue Code to any of the above persons or married to a person related under section 267(b) to any of the above persons.

6. An appraiser who appraises regularly for a person in (1), (2), or (3), and who does not perform a majority of his or her appraisals made during his or her tax year for other persons.

In addition, a person is not a qualified appraiser for a particular donation if the donor had knowledge of facts that would cause a reasonable person to expect the appraiser to falsely overstate the value of the donated property. For example, if the donor and the appraiser make an agreement concerning the amount at which the property will be valued, and the donor knows that amount is more than the FMV of the property, the appraiser is not a qualified appraiser for the donation.

Appraiser penalties. An appraiser who prepares an incorrect appraisal may have to pay a penalty if:

1. The appraiser knows or should have known the appraisal would be used in connection with a return or claim for refund, and

2. The appraisal results in the 20% or 40% penalty for a valuation misstatement described later under *Penalty.*

The penalty imposed on the appraiser is the smaller of:

1. The greater of:

   a. 10% of the underpayment due to the misstatement, or

   b. $1,000, or

2. 125% of the gross income received for the appraisal.

In addition, any appraiser who falsely or fraudulently overstates the value of property described in a qualified appraisal of a Form 8283 that the appraiser has signed may be subject to a civil penalty for aiding and abetting as understatement of tax liability, and may have his or her appraisal disregarded.

Form 8283

Generally, if the claimed deduction for an item of donated property is more than $5,000, you must attach Form 8283 to your tax return and complete Section B.

If you do not attach Form 8283 to your return and complete Section B, the deduction will not be allowed unless your failure was due to reasonable cause, and not willful neglect, or was due to a good faith omission. If the IRS requests that you submit the form because you did not attach it to your return, you must comply within 90 days of the request or the deduction will be disallowed.

You must attach a separate Form 8283 for each item of contributed property that is not part of a group of similar items. If you contribute similar items of property to the same donee organization, you need attach only one Form 8283 for those items. If you contribute similar items of property to more than one donee organization, you must attach a separate form for each donee.

Internal Revenue Service Review of Appraisals

In reviewing an income tax return, the Service may accept the claimed value of the donated property, based on information or appraisals sent with the return, or may make its own determination of FMV. In either case, the Service may:

- Contact the taxpayer to get more information,

- Refer the valuation problem to a Service appraiser or valuation specialist,

- Refer the issue to the Commissioner's Art Advisory Panel (a group of dealers and museum directors who review and recommend acceptance or adjustment of taxpayers' claimed values for major paintings, sculptures, decorative arts, and antiques), or

- Contract with an independent dealer, scholar, or appraiser to appraise the property when the objects require appraisers of highly specialized experience and knowledge.

Responsibility of the Service. The Service is responsible for reviewing appraisals, but it is not responsible for making them. Supporting the FMV listed on your return is your responsibility.

The Service does not accept appraisals without question. Nor does the Service recognize any particular appraiser or organization of appraisers.

Timing of Service action. The Service generally does not approve valuations or appraisals before the actual filing of the tax return to which the appraisal applies. In addition, the Service generally does not issue advance rulings approving or disapproving such appraisals.

Exception. For a request submitted as described earlier under *Art valued at $50,000 or more,* the Service will issue a Statement of Value that can be relied on by the donor of the item of art.

Penalty

You may be liable for a penalty if you overstate the value or adjusted basis of donated property.

20% penalty. The penalty is 20% of the underpayment of tax related to the overstatement if:

- The value or adjusted basis claimed on the return is 200% (150% for returns filed after August 17, 2006) or more of the correct amount, and

- You underpaid your tax by more than $5,000 because of the overstatement.

40% penalty. The penalty is 40%, rather than 20%, if:

- The value or adjusted basis claimed on the return is 400% (200% for returns filed after August 17, 2006) or more of the correct amount, and

- You underpaid your tax by more than $5,000 because of the overstatement.

How To Get Tax Help

You can get help with unresolved tax issues, order free publications and forms, ask tax questions, and get information from the IRS in several ways. By selecting the method that is best for you, you will have quick and easy access to tax help.

Contacting your Taxpayer Advocate. The Taxpayer Advocate Service is an independent organization within the IRS whose employees assist taxpayers who are experiencing economic harm, who are seeking help in resolving tax problems that have not been resolved through normal channels, or who believe that an IRS system or procedure is not working as it should.

You can contact the Taxpayer Advocate Service by calling toll-free 1-877-777-4778 or TTY/TDD 1-800-829-4059 to see if you are eligible for assistance. You can also call or write to your local taxpayer advocate, whose phone number and address are listed in your local telephone directory and in Publication 1546, The Taxpayer Advocate Service of the IRS - How To Get Help With Unresolved Tax Problems. You can file Form 911, Application for Taxpayer Assistance Order, or ask an IRS employee to complete it on your behalf. For more information, go to *www.irs.gov/advocate*.

Low income tax clinics (LITCs). LITCs are independent organizations that provide low income taxpayers with representation in federal tax controversies with the IRS for free or for a nominal charge. The clinics also provide tax education and outreach for taxpayers with limited English proficiency or who speak English as a second language. Publication 4134, Low Income Taxpayer Clinic List, provides information on clinics in your area. It is available at *www.irs.gov* or at your local IRS office.

Free tax services. To find out what services are available, get Publication 910, IRS Guide to Free Tax Services. It contains a list of free tax publications and describes other free tax information services, including tax education and assistance programs and a list of TeleTax topics.

 Internet. You can access the IRS website at *www.irs.gov* 24 hours a day, 7 days a week to:

- *E-file* your return. Find out about commercial tax preparation and *e-file* services available free to eligible taxpayers.
- Check the status of your 2006 refund. Click on *Where's My Refund*. Wait at least 6 weeks from the date you filed your return (3 weeks if you filed electronically). Have your 2006 tax return available because you will need to know your social security number, your filing status, and the exact whole dollar amount of your refund.
- Download forms, instructions, and publications.
- Order IRS products online.
- Research your tax questions online.
- Search publications online by topic or keyword.

- View Internal Revenue Bulletins (IRBs) published in the last few years.
- Figure your withholding allowances using our withholding calculator.
- Sign up to receive local and national tax news by email.
- Get information on starting and operating a small business.

 Phone. Many services are available by phone.

- *Ordering forms, instructions, and publications.* Call 1-800-829-3676 to order current-year forms, instructions, and publications, and prior-year forms and instructions. You should receive your order within 10 days.
- *Asking tax questions.* Call the IRS with your tax questions at 1-800-829-1040.
- *Solving problems.* You can get face-to-face help solving tax problems every business day in IRS Taxpayer Assistance Centers. An employee can explain IRS letters, request adjustments to your account, or help you set up a payment plan. Call your local Taxpayer Assistance Center for an appointment. To find the number, go to *www.irs.gov/localcontacts* or look in the phone book under *United States Government, Internal Revenue Service*.
- *TTY/TDD equipment.* If you have access to TTY/TDD equipment, call 1-800-829-4059 to ask tax questions or to order forms and publications.
- *TeleTax topics.* Call 1-800-829-4477 to listen to pre-recorded messages covering various tax topics.
- *Refund information.* To check the status of your 2006 refund, call 1-800-829-4477 and press 1 for automated refund information or call 1-800-829-1954. Be sure to wait at least 6 weeks from the date you filed your return (3 weeks if you filed electronically). Have your 2006 tax return available because you will need to know your social security number, your filing status, and the exact whole dollar amount of your refund.

Evaluating the quality of our telephone services. To ensure IRS representatives give accurate, courteous, and professional answers, we use several methods to evaluate the quality of our telephone services. One method is for a second IRS representative to listen in on or record random telephone calls. Another is to ask some callers to complete a short survey at the end of the call.

 Walk-in. Many products and services are available on a walk-in basis.

- *Products.* You can walk in to many post offices, libraries, and IRS offices to pick up certain forms, instructions, and publications. Some IRS offices, libraries, grocery

stores, copy centers, city and county government offices, credit unions, and office supply stores have a collection of products available to print from a CD or photocopy from reproducible proofs. Also, some IRS offices and libraries have the Internal Revenue Code, regulations, Internal Revenue Bulletins, and Cumulative Bulletins available for research purposes.

- *Services.* You can walk in to your local Taxpayer Assistance Center every business day for personal, face-to-face tax help. An employee can explain IRS letters, request adjustments to your tax account, or help you set up a payment plan. If you need to resolve a tax problem, have questions about how the tax law applies to your individual tax return, or you're more comfortable talking with someone in person, visit your local Taxpayer Assistance Center where you can spread out your records and talk with an IRS representative face-to-face. No appointment is necessary, but if you prefer, you can call your local Center and leave a message requesting an appointment to resolve a tax account issue. A representative will call you back within 2 business days to schedule an in-person appointment at your convenience. To find the number, go to *www.irs.gov/localcontacts* or look in the phone book under *United States Government, Internal Revenue Service*.

 Mail. You can send your order for forms, instructions, and publications to the address below. You should receive a response within 10 business days after your request is received.

National Distribution Center
P.O. Box 8903
Bloomington, IL 61702-8903

 CD for tax products. You can order Publication 1796, IRS Tax Products CD, and obtain:

- A CD that is released twice so you have the latest products. The first release ships in January and the final release ships in March.
- Current-year forms, instructions, and publications.
- Prior-year forms, instructions, and publications.
- Bonus: Historical Tax Products DVD - Ships with the final release.
- Tax Map: an electronic research tool and finding aid.
- Tax law frequently asked questions.
- Tax Topics from the IRS telephone response system.
- Fill-in, print, and save features for most tax forms.
- Internal Revenue Bulletins.
- Toll-free and email technical support.

Buy the CD from National Technical Information Service (NTIS) at *www.irs.gov/cdorders* for

$25 (no handling fee) or call 1-877-CDFORMS (1-877-233-6767) toll free to buy the CD for $25 (plus a $5 handling fee). Price is subject to change.

 CD for small businesses. Publication 3207, The Small Business Resource Guide CD for 2006, is a must for every small business owner or any taxpayer about to start a business. This year's CD includes:

- Helpful information, such as how to prepare a business plan, find financing for your business, and much more.

- All the business tax forms, instructions, and publications needed to successfully manage a business.

- Tax law changes for 2006.

- Tax Map: an electronic research tool and finding aid.

- Web links to various government agencies, business associations, and IRS organizations.

- "Rate the Product" survey—your opportunity to suggest changes for future editions.

- A site map of the CD to help you navigate the pages of the CD with ease.

- An interactive "Teens in Biz" module that gives practical tips for teens about starting their own business, creating a business plan, and filing taxes.

An updated version of this CD is available each year in early April. You can get a free copy by calling 1-800-829-3676 or by visiting *www.irs.gov/smallbiz.*

Index To help us develop a more useful index, please let us know if you have ideas for index entries. See "Comments and Suggestions" in the "Introduction" for the ways you can reach us.

Tax Publications for Individual Taxpayers

See *How To Get Tax Help* for a variety of ways to get publications, including by computer, phone, and mail.

General Guides

- 1 Your Rights as a Taxpayer
- 17 Your Federal Income Tax (For Individuals)
- 334 Tax Guide for Small Business (For Individuals Who Use Schedule C or C-EZ)
- 509 Tax Calendars for 2007
- 553 Highlights of 2006 Tax Changes
- 910 IRS Guide to Free Tax Services

Specialized Publications

- 3 Armed Forces' Tax Guide
- 54 Tax Guide for U.S. Citizens and Resident Aliens Abroad
- 225 Farmer's Tax Guide
- 463 Travel, Entertainment, Gift, and Car Expenses
- 501 Exemptions, Standard Deduction, and Filing Information
- 502 Medical and Dental Expenses (Including the Health Coverage Tax Credit)
- 503 Child and Dependent Care Expenses
- 504 Divorced or Separated Individuals
- 505 Tax Withholding and Estimated Tax
- 514 Foreign Tax Credit for Individuals
- 516 U.S. Government Civilian Employees Stationed Abroad
- 517 Social Security and Other Information for Members of the Clergy and Religious Workers
- 519 U.S. Tax Guide for Aliens
- 521 Moving Expenses
- 523 Selling Your Home
- 524 Credit for the Elderly or the Disabled
- 525 Taxable and Nontaxable Income
- 526 Charitable Contributions
- 527 Residential Rental Property
- 529 Miscellaneous Deductions
- 530 Tax Information for First-Time Homeowners

- 531 Reporting Tip Income
- 536 Net Operating Losses (NOLs) for Individuals, Estates, and Trusts
- 537 Installment Sales
- 541 Partnerships
- 544 Sales and Other Dispositions of Assets
- 547 Casualties, Disasters, and Thefts
- 550 Investment Income and Expenses
- 551 Basis of Assets
- 552 Recordkeeping for Individuals
- 554 Older Americans' Tax Guide
- 555 Community Property
- 556 Examination of Returns, Appeal Rights, and Claims for Refund
- 559 Survivors, Executors, and Administrators
- 561 Determining the Value of Donated Property
- 564 Mutual Fund Distributions
- 570 Tax Guide for Individuals With Income From U.S. Possessions
- 571 Tax-Sheltered Annuity Plans (403(b) Plans)
- 575 Pension and Annuity Income
- 584 Casualty, Disaster, and Theft Loss Workbook (Personal-Use Property)
- 587 Business Use of Your Home (Including Use by Daycare Providers)
- 590 Individual Retirement Arrangements (IRAs)
- 593 Tax Highlights for U.S. Citizens and Residents Going Abroad
- 594 What You Should Know About the IRS Collection Process
- 596 Earned Income Credit (EIC)
- 721 Tax Guide to U.S. Civil Service Retirement Benefits
- 901 U.S. Tax Treaties
- 907 Tax Highlights for Persons with Disabilities

- 908 Bankruptcy Tax Guide
- 915 Social Security and Equivalent Railroad Retirement Benefits
- 919 How Do I Adjust My Tax Withholding?
- 925 Passive Activity and At-Risk Rules
- 926 Household Employer's Tax Guide
- 929 Tax Rules for Children and Dependents
- 936 Home Mortgage Interest Deduction
- 946 How To Depreciate Property
- 947 Practice Before the IRS and Power of Attorney
- 950 Introduction to Estate and Gift Taxes
- 967 The IRS Will Figure Your Tax
- 969 Health Savings Accounts and Other Tax-Favored Health Plans
- 970 Tax Benefits for Education
- 971 Innocent Spouse Relief
- 972 Child Tax Credit
- 1542 Per Diem Rates
- 1544 Reporting Cash Payments of Over $10,000 (Received in a Trade or Business)
- 1546 The Taxpayer Advocate Service of the IRS – How to Get Help With Unresolved Tax Problems

Spanish Language Publications

- 1SP Derechos del Contribuyente
- 579SP Cómo Preparar la Declaración de Impuesto Federal
- 594SP Que es lo que Debemos Saber sobre el Proceso de Cobro del IRS
- 596SP Crédito por Ingreso del Trabajo
- 850 English-Spanish Glossary of Words and Phrases Used in Publications Issued by the Internal Revenue Service
- 1544SP Informe de Pagos en Efectivo en Exceso de $10,000 (Recibidos en una Ocupación o Negocio)

Commonly Used Tax Forms

See *How To Get Tax Help* for a variety of ways to get forms, including by computer, phone, and mail.

Form Number and Title

- 1040 U.S. Individual Income Tax Return
  - Sch A&B Itemized Deductions & Interest and Ordinary Dividends
  - Sch C Profit or Loss From Business
  - Sch C-EZ Net Profit From Business
  - Sch D Capital Gains and Losses
  - Sch D-1 Continuation Sheet for Schedule D
  - Sch E Supplemental Income and Loss
  - Sch EIC Earned Income Credit
  - Sch F Profit or Loss From Farming
  - Sch H Household Employment Taxes
  - Sch J Income Averaging for Farmers and Fishermen
  - Sch R Credit for the Elderly or the Disabled
  - Sch SE Self-Employment Tax
- 1040A U.S. Individual Income Tax Return
  - Sch 1 Interest and Ordinary Dividends for Form 1040A Filers
  - Sch 2 Child and Dependent Care Expenses for Form 1040A Filers
  - Sch 3 Credit for the Elderly or the Disabled for Form 1040A Filers
- 1040EZ Income Tax Return for Single and Joint Filers With No Dependents
- 1040-ES Estimated Tax for Individuals
- 1040X Amended U.S. Individual Income Tax Return

Form Number and Title

- 2106 Employee Business Expenses
- 2106-EZ Unreimbursed Employee Business Expenses
- 2210 Underpayment of Estimated Tax by Individuals, Estates, and Trusts
- 2441 Child and Dependent Care Expenses
- 2848 Power of Attorney and Declaration of Representative
- 3903 Moving Expenses
- 4562 Depreciation and Amortization
- 4868 Application for Automatic Extension of Time To File U.S. Individual Income Tax Return
- 4952 Investment Interest Expense Deduction
- 5329 Additional Taxes on Qualified Plans (Including IRAs) and Other Tax-Favored Accounts
- 6251 Alternative Minimum Tax—Individuals
- 8283 Noncash Charitable Contributions
- 8582 Passive Activity Loss Limitations
- 8606 Nondeductible IRAs
- 8812 Additional Child Tax Credit
- 8822 Change of Address
- 8829 Expenses for Business Use of Your Home
- 8863 Education Credits
- 9465 Installment Agreement Request

Exhibit I - Resources

Planned Giving in a Nutshell

Resources

WEB RESOURCES

Partnership for Philanthropic Planning – http://pppnet.org

Valuation Standards for Charitable Planned Gifts
https://pppnet.org/valuationstandards

Charitable Life Insurance Evaluation Guidelines
https://pppnet.org/charitablelifeinsurance

Guidelines for Counting and Reporting Charitable Gifts
https://pppnet.org/guidelinesforreporting

American Council of Gift Annuities – http://acga-web.org

Suggested Gift Annuity Rates
http://www.acga-web.org/resources-top/gift-annuity-rates

State Regulations
http://www.acga-web.org/state-regulations

Internal Revenue Service – http://irs.gov

Charitable Contributions, IRS Publication 526
http://www.irs.gov/pub/irs-pdf/p526.pdf

Determining the Value of Donated Property, IRS Publication 561
http://www.irs.gov/pub/irs-pdf/p561.pdf

Exhibit I - Resources

EDUCATIONAL RESOURCES

Planned Giving Today Newsletter
140 Huguenot Street, 3rd Floor
New Rochelle, NY 10801-5215
800 654-3237
http://pgtoday.com

The Journal of Gift Planning
Partnership for Philanthropic Planning
233 McCrea, Suite 400
Indianapolis, MN 46225
317 269-6274
http://pppnet.org

Taxwise Giving Newsletter
PO Box 299
Old Greenwich, CT 06870
800 243-9122
http://taxwisegiving.com

The Art of Planned Giving
Douglas White
John Wiley & Sons, Inc
605 Third Avenue, New York, NY
800 879-4539
http://wiley.com

The Complete Guide to Planned Giving
Debra Ashton
24 Robertson Street
Quincy MA 02169
617 472-9316
http://debraashton.com

The Planned Giving Idea Book
Robert F. Sharpe
6410 Poplar Avenue, Seventh Floor
Memphis, TN 38119
901 680-5300
http://sharpenet.com

MARKETING AND SOFTWARE RESOURCES

Crescendo Interactive (Comdel, Inc.)
110 Camino Ruiz
Camarillo, CA 93012
800 858-9154
http://crescendointeractive.com

Pentera
8650 Commerce Park Place, Suite G
Indianapolis, Indiana 46268
317 875-0910
http://pentera.com

PG Calc
129 Mt. Auburn Street
Cambridge, MA02138
888 497-4970
http://pgcalc.com

R & R Newkirk
8695 South Archer, Suite #10
Willow Springs, Illinois 60480
800 342-2375
http://rrnewkirk.com

Robert F. Sharpe & Company
6410 Poplar Avenue, Suite 700
Memphis, TN 38119
800 238-3253
http://sharpenet.com

The Stelter Company
10435 New York Avenue
Des Moines, IA
866 783-5837
http://stelter.com

Virtual Giving
1288 Valley Forge Road, Building 82
Phoenixville, PA 19460
800 490-7090
http://virtualgiving.com

Made in the USA
Lexington, KY
20 January 2018